INVESTIGATING INFANT DEATHS

INVESTIGATING INFANT DEATHS

BOBBI JO O'NEAL

CRC Press
Taylor & Francis Group
Boca Raton London New York

CRC Press is an imprint of the
Taylor & Francis Group, an informa business

First published in paperback 2024

First Published 2007
by CRC Press
2385 NW Executive Center Drive, Suite 320, Boca Raton FL 33431

and by CRC Press
4 Park Square, Milton Park, Abingdon, Oxon, OX14 4RN

CRC Press is an imprint of Taylor & Francis Group, LLC

Publisher's Note
The publisher has gone to great lengths to ensure the quality of this reprint but points out that some imperfections in the original copies may be apparent.

Library of Congress Cataloging-in-Publication Data

O'Neal, Bobbi Jo.
Investigating infant deaths / Bobbi Jo O'Neal.
p. cm.
Includes bibliographical references and index.
ISBN 978-0-8493-8204-8 (alk. paper)
1. Infants--Death. 2. Medicolegal investigators. 3. Death--Proof and certification. I. Title.

RJ59.O64 2007
614'.1--dc22 2006039231

ISBN: 978-1-032-92514-1 (pbk)

ISBN: 978-0-849-38204-8 (hbk)

ISBN: 978-0-429-24534-3 (ebk)

DOI: 10.1201/9781420008067

Visit the Taylor & Francis Web site at
http://www.taylorandfrancis.com

and the CRC Press Web site at
http://www.crcpress.com

Dedication

To mommies and daddies who have suffered the tragic death of an infant. It is my hope and prayer that medicolegal death investigators across the country will investigate all infant deaths thoroughly, completely, and empathetically; and that their comprehensive investigations will lead to prevention and research initiatives that will prevent other families from experiencing every parent's nightmare: the death of their precious child.

With much gratitude, I dedicate this book to Arnold, my spouse and best friend, and to my sweet spirited son, Taylor. Thank you for your support, encouragement, and prayers. Without the two of you, my life would be nothing. I love you both.

Table of Contents

Foreword

This protocol integrates materials that were previously separated into criminal forensics, pediatrics, social services, and public health. The author draws from her experience as a health professional and experience as a medicolegal death investigator to address investigation of sudden unexpected infant death (SUID). She brings us a welcome resource joining a spectrum of materials into a single document. The logic is simple. For living children, we seek child and family evaluation with pediatric and social service expertise. For suspicious deaths, we seek forensic experts and family investigation. Management of infant death requires all of these.

The first year of life is the most common age for a child to die. Infant deaths occur most commonly in the first minutes, days, weeks, and months of life. Most infant deaths are natural with premature birth and congenital defects being the most common causes. Natural infant deaths are managed in pediatric medical systems with sophisticated medical tools and a health history from caretakers. Most infant deaths are not sudden and unexpected and are not cases for a medical examiner (ME) or coroner. However, infant deaths may be ME-coroner cases if the death is unexpected or explained. On occasion, if a pregnant woman is assaulted, even fetal deaths may become ME-coroner cases.

The ME or coroner is responsible for determining the cause and manner of some natural deaths and all deaths designated as homicide, suicide, accidental (also known as nonintentional) and deaths that are from undetermined causes. The manner of death may be listed as undetermined if the cause or circumstances of the death are not clear even after autopsy. These cases provide management problems that may include trying to separate natural sudden infant death syndrome (SIDS) deaths from intentional or unintentional suffocation or other mechanisms of death with no visible injury. Deaths attributed to SIDS have decreased as prevention programs have addressed sleep positioning. Attention to the nuances of infant death investigation may have resulted in the increase in the rate of the infant deaths designated as undetermined.

Statistically, infants seldom die from injury; however, infancy is the most common age for homicide by caretaker. Historically, child homicide has dual peaks in regard to age; infants and those 17 years of age, with older teen homicide rates surpassing infants. Drops in the rate of teen homicide matched with a rather steady rate for infant and toddler homicide have caused a change in that pattern from 1993 to 2003 with infant homicide roughly matching or surpassing the homicide rate for 17-year-olds. The relative difficulty of designating infant homicide may cause a false low in the rate of infant homicide data.

Older child victims are more apt to have injuries that make the investigation easier; in contrast, infant homicide may occur from suffocation with no visible injury even on autopsy. Medical examiners may conduct special studies during infant autopsies to include a skeletal x-ray survey, toxicology, and microscopic examination of sections of the brain and retina. These studies are not so commonly required with older child deaths and may extend the time to final examination by months. This unique delay in sending infant records to the state may cause that case to be lost from the official final count as state and federal statistics "close their books" on that year. These lost cases added to the cases lost from the unique problems with infant homicide data may result in a false low count for infant homicide.

MEs or coroners use *homicide* to designate death from injury that was intentional. Criminal justice systems use *homicide* with similar but separate definitions. Social service records use *fatal child abuse/neglect*. This separation of records that different agencies have on the same case creates problems with case management. Matching and reconciling these separate infant records provides a simple tool that can improve case and system management.

This protocol integrates different resources and adds other concerns with perinatal records, issues of child development, and a concern for family grief after the death of a child. Most of the tasks are simple and reachable. The world of child death investigation is changing, and this text is part of that change.

The tasks outlined reflect real experience with infant death investigation. The Charleston County Coroner's Office in South Carolina created a system with an all-female investigative staff, made up mostly of nurses. All are diplomats or fellows of the American Board of Medical Death Investigators. Staff include Rae Wooten, registered nurse (R.N.); coroner and deputy coroners Judy Koelpin, Dottie Lindsay; and Bobbi Jo O'Neal, R.N., the author of this text. All of whom were mentored by retired coroner, Susan Chewning, R.N.

Gender is not necessary for a quality investigation of infant death; however, females do provide most parenting for infants and play a major role in providing formation and support of a child death review. Charleston County infant death investigations include females and males from multiple professions and agencies working together. Cases are usually reviewed by the Charleston County team within a week, and the line staff from multiple agencies share records and personal experiences. Two deputy coroners are used to cover the hospital and the death scene and coordinate their findings using cell phones. The process puts resources in the front end of the process to capture evidence and prevent the need for additional resources later.

We may be approaching 1000 child death review teams internationally in 2006. The quality and focus of these teams vary. Some teams become dormant after the loss of major resources, but most of these teams are activated again. Multiagency child death review provides a more vigorous process than single agencies in isolation. We are learning and the mixture of professions with male and female members is improving our vision.

No single profession can do this work in isolation. Criminal justice systems may miss human service records, particularly records from well baby care or prenatal health care. Human service professionals lack experience with violent death and resist the value of sanctions. Team members, with time, learn to appreciate and respect the work of others.

Sophisticated data systems measure child victims and their families; there are few ways to measure the quality of professionals who intervene. We are also part of the problem. Infanticide is ancient. Our ability to acknowledge infanticide is new. This protocol is a reflection of new technology and a reflection of changing cultural attitudes and beliefs. As a technical movement, we are moving slowly, but as a cultural movement, we are moving rapidly. Technical and cultural changes are interconnected and changes in one affect the other.

The literature on infant deaths is growing along with the literature on child abuse. The French physician, Ambrose Tardieu, described fatal child abuse in the 1860s. He received little recognition for his work and is generally unknown today. *Child abuse* was indexed in *Index Medicus* in 1965. Little was written about the topic for the next few years. *Infanticide* was not indexed until 1970, and many of our programs that address infanticide did not begin until the 1990s, a century after Dr. Tardieu.

The decade 2000 to 2010 has and will continue to include an explosion of literature on the dangers of shaking babies, potential dangers of cosleeping with infants, and the development of programs in which mothers may safely surrender babies rather then abandon them to die. Technology has brought us new tools; the major change, however, may be our attitude toward information that was available centuries ago. Gathering in peer groups that mix professions and genders seems to be part of our increased tolerance of information that can be painful to accept when we are isolated.

Laws also reflect our beliefs and potential conflicts about the death of infants. The British Infanticide Act of 1938 stated that a mother could be convicted of manslaughter but not murder in the first years of a child's life because of a belief in her limited ability to "think clearly." A fetus may not be subject of child abuse laws because the fetus is not legally a child; however, an assault of a pregnant woman that results in the death of a fetus may be treated as a homicide in the criminal justice system. The issues are complex and our attempts to resolve them require new concepts.

SUID is not new. Our ability to think clearly about our role with these deaths may be our major change. This work can be personally and professionally difficult. Application of these guidelines will improve our ability to address these deaths.

I have worked for more than 30 years to promote competence and accountability for the investigation of the deaths of children. This protocol is a major new resource in that process. I am honored to write this foreword.

Michael Durfee, M.D.
Founder and Chief Consultant
International Association of Forensic Nurses (IAFN),
National Center for Child Fatality Review
Los Angeles, California

Preface

Sensational true crimes abound in the media as the lay public has become fascinated with forensic science. The more spectacular, bizarre, and remarkable the case, the more likely it will be featured in newspaper headlines, reenacted during investigative news segments or be fictionalized on a prime time television show. This media attention has glamorized the criminal justice profession and those individuals who investigate deaths. This publicity has resulted in an increased number of individuals who want to pursue this profession and have dreams and aspirations of investigating spectacular newsworthy cases.

What the lay public does not realize is that often the most complicated and challenging cases to investigate are those in which the individual's death was sudden, unexpected, and unexplained. Very few deaths occur in which the decedent has no significant medical history, no trauma, no significant autopsy findings, and very little social history to investigate. The majority of infant deaths, however, fit this category. When I entered the forensic field, I too had "delusions of grandeur." Although some of those sensational cases have come my way, I have come to realize that the most complicated and challenging deaths to investigate are those of infants.

Infants have vulnerabilities that place them at greater risk of falling victim to health or medical problems, environmental hazards, as well as lifestyle and child care decisions made by the individuals responsible for their care and safety. As a result of their vulnerabilities and inabilities to fend for themselves, they are at risk of injury or death due to unintentional accidents, neglect, and intentional acts of violence.

This book was conceived years ago when I was fortunate to be mentored by professionals who recognized the complicated nature of infant death investigations, sought to make system and investigational changes, and then shared their insight, expertise, and wisdom with me. As an investigative team, we continued to seek ways to improve our skills and educate other professionals about infant and child death investigation. We also developed and implemented prevention and education programs for the residents of our community to attempt to save lives and decrease the number of infant deaths that needed investigating. Discussions in this office often centered on the idea of putting our thoughts and ideas regarding infant death investigation into a book; however, it was something we would get to "one day."

Our office organized and implemented an extensive Back-to-Sleep campaign to educate professionals and the lay public regarding risks associated with unsafe sleep positions and environments. Educational programs were directed toward hospitals, pediatricians, child care providers, public health representatives, retail establishments that sold baby supplies, and the media. After implementing this extensive and successful prevention and educational campaign, I was honored to be asked to join the board of directors for the SIDS Alliance of the Carolinas. The experience was extremely rewarding; however, it was during that time that it became apparent that to prevent infant death, we must first ensure that each infant death is thoroughly and completely investigated.

After learning of our unique approach to infant death investigation, I was honored again to be asked by Dr. Kay Tomashek and her peers at the Centers for Disease Control and Prevention (CDC) to be a part of the Sudden Unexpected Infant Death Investigation National Training and Dissemination Core Team, a group of infant death investigation experts, brought together to assist in the development of the Sudden Unexplained Infant Death Investigation training text. It was a great experience being able to share experiences and investigational ideas with other professionals and use our collective expertise to develop a guide that will be widely disseminated.

The goal of this project, which in no way takes the place of the comprehensive training guide that was developed with the CDC team, is to provide information about additional techniques and approaches that may be used to thoroughly investigate infant deaths, in particular those infant deaths that occur in an emergency room setting. All of the techniques presented are used during all infant death investigations in Charleston County, South Carolina. Our approach to infant death investigation may seem to some to be "ideal" but not "practical." It is, however, a workable approach that may require investigators and agencies to evaluate their investigational approach and determine what changes may be made to improve the effectiveness of infant death investigation. It is only through continued improvement that we will be able to ensure that all infant deaths are investigated thoroughly and completely. Information obtained from those investigations may then be used to prevent future premature infant deaths from occurring.

Acknowledgments

This project would not have been possible had it not been for mentors who took me under their wing and taught me how to be the best medicolegal death investigator I could be. It is through their guidance, encouragement, and support that I learned about the unique qualities of infant death investigation as well as unique and effective ways in which these deaths can best be investigated. I owe much to retired Charleston County Coroner Susan Chewning, R.N., and the current Charleston County Coroner Rae Wooten, R.N.

Rae Wooten provided insight, suggestions, and encouragement. I appreciate her use of the red pen.

I would also like to acknowledge Deputy Coroners Judy Koelpin and Dottie Lindsay; I could not have asked for better peers to work with.

I thank Kim Collins, M.D., Erin Presnell, M.D., and the Medical University of South Carolina Forensic Pathology Department for all that they taught me over the years and for their contributions to this project.

Dr. Michael Durfee truly deserves the title, "Father of Child Death Review." I appreciate his years of dedication and utmost support.

I am truly grateful to those who offered their time, support, encouragement, and prayers during the preparation of this project: Kerry Haupert, Karen Hobcroft, Dana Hiller, Margaret Maynard, Amy Desjardins, June Resnick, Christi Bolchoz, Danielle Cluver, Wayne Nelson, Margaret Winter, Margaret Mosley, and Berri Feller.

Finally, I thank Becky McEldowney Masterman and the entire staff at Taylor & Francis for providing me an opportunity to write about this important topic.

Author

Bobbi Jo O'Neal, a registered nurse and board certified medicolegal death investigator with the American Board of Medicolegal Death Investigators, is a deputy coroner for the Charleston County Coroner's Office in Charleston, South Carolina. An experienced emergency room nurse who received her B.S. in nursing from Belmont University in Nashville, Tennessee, she became actively involved in the specialty of forensic nursing first in the area of sexual assault then as a death investigator.

She is a 2007–2008 Director-at-Large for the International Association of Forensic Nurses (IAFN), is a past cochair for the IAFN Death Investigation Council (2002 to 2006), and a member of the National Association of Medical Examiners. A past board president for the SIDS Alliance of the Carolinas, she has been active in educating and training others how to investigate infant deaths and in the development and implementation of infant death prevention initiatives. She developed and coordinated, "Introduction to Death Investigation: A Nursing Internship," the only hands-on death investigation educational program for nurses in the country and has been an active member of the Centers for Disease Control and Prevention's National Training and Dissemination Core Team for Sudden Unexpected Infant Death.

1 Investigating Infant Deaths: Why Is It Important?

1.1 INTRODUCTION

Healthy People 2010 is a national agenda established by the U.S. Department of Health and Human Services to improve the health of all citizens. Increasing the quality and years of healthy life is one of the many goals of this program. Infant health is an area of focus as the agenda seeks to improve the health and well-being of women, infants, children, and families.

The United States and other countries gauge the health of their nations on many statistical factors. One of those is the infant mortality rate, which is defined as the number of infant deaths, under 1 year of age, per 1000 live births. Nations with high infant mortality rates are considered to be less healthy than those with low infant mortality rates. The United States, even with all of its medical advances, has one of the highest infant mortality rates among industrialized nations; as a result, one of the *Healthy People 2010* national goals is to reduce the number of infant deaths.[1]

Before the United States will be able to reach the *Healthy People 2010* goal, the nation must first accurately identify what is causing or contributing to infant deaths in this country. Once the statistics are accurate, then prevention programs can be developed, implemented, and promoted to at-risk and vulnerable populations. Accurate statistics regarding the cause and manner of infant deaths is only possible if there is consistent certification and classification of those deaths on death certificates. It is not possible, however, to have consistent reporting on death certificates if infant death investigations at the local level are not thorough and complete.

1.2 THE PROCESS

A death certificate is a legal document that must be completed by an authorized individual, usually a physician, medical examiner (ME), or coroner. This certification provides demographic information regarding the deceased as well as the cause and manner of the individual's death. The certificate is filed with the vital statistics office in the state in which the death occurred and the information is then forwarded from each state to the National Center for Health Statistics (NCHS), a division of the Centers for Disease Control and Prevention (CDC). The NCHS compiles the data received and reports statistical information for the country; this information guides public policy and funding to improve the health of the American people.[2]

The NCHS receives information from each state's vital record office. The state offices receive their information from the local jurisdictions in which the deaths occur. The investigation of a death provides the information needed to accurately certify the cause and manner of death. If deaths are not thoroughly and completely investigated, the cause and manner of death listed on the certificate may be inaccurate. These inaccuracies will then impact individuals, communities, and the nation as a whole.

1.3 THE IMPACT

The impact of a poor investigation and inaccurate classification of an infant's death is far reaching. At the center, a poor investigation is an injustice to the deceased infant, which may then impact the infant's family, the community in which the infant resided, and the nation as a whole. Poor investigations also affect the integrity of persons and agencies responsible for conducting these investigations. Investigators should understand the impact a poor investigation has and how it may affect each of these entities.

Following a death, it is the medicolegal death investigator's (MDI) responsibility to investigate and accurately document the circumstances surrounding that death. This investigation is crucial to the cause and manner of death determination. According to the National Association of Medical Examiners,[3] the cause of death (COD) is the disease or injury responsible for setting in motion a series of physiologic events culminating in death. The manner of death (MOD) is a system for classifying the circumstances surrounding a death to include natural, suicide, accident, homicide, and undetermined. If either of these determinations is incorrect, a snowball effect may occur.

1.3.1 The Infant

The MDI represents the decedent and a specific jurisdiction, usually a county or municipality, ensuring that both the decedent and the state's interests are represented. Poor investigations are an injustice to both parties as justice cannot occur if the state is not able to prosecute persons who may have caused the infant's death. Law enforcement officials and prosecutors may press criminal charges against innocent persons if an infant death is classified incorrectly, and a poor investigation may result in a natural death classification when the death was the result of an accident or homicide.

1.3.2 The Family and Caregivers

Surviving family members and caregivers are impacted by poor infant death investigations if they are given inaccurate information or no information regarding the cause of the infant's death. It may be devastating to a family to receive wrong or no information and the error may have lasting consequences. Either scenario may impact the family's ability to heal, their ability to make health care decisions, to change unsafe sleep environments, and address environment hazards. A lack of information may impact the safety of surviving family members who may be at risk for injury or death if changes are not made.

Families who receive little or no information following the death of a child may have feelings of fear and anger while trying to cope with unanswered questions and their questions about the death may linger for years. It is common for family members to search for answers following an infant death. Lack of information can have lifelong effects on individuals, impacting their interpersonal relationships with significant others, surviving children, extended family, friends, and coworkers. Additional frustration may occur if they believe that the death of their child was poorly investigated leaving them with questions that may have been answered had the death been investigated thoroughly and completely.

Inaccurate information regarding the infant's COD impacts the family's ability to make health care decisions that may reduce the risk of injury or death for other children. Families who are made aware of previously unknown medical conditions can take steps to have other children evaluated and treated. These families may benefit from receiving information about genetic counseling, smoking cessation programs, the effects of drugs and alcohol, vaccination information, and other important medical and health care information.

Unsafe sleep environments that may have placed the infant at increased risk for injury or death should be discussed with caregivers. Families who are made aware of unsafe practices can make educated decisions regarding them and whether to change or not. Many families are unaware of the national recommendations for safe sleep environments, such as the risks associated with bed sharing or cosleeping, the risks of soft bedding and pillows in an infant's sleep environment, and the potential risk associated with items that are not safe for infants, such as antique and vintage cribs.

Environmental hazards such as lead paint, carbon monoxide, and other hazards may be overlooked if an infant death investigation is not conducted thoroughly. Safety issues associated with domestic violence and drug abuse, for example, may also be missed if a complete investigation does not occur. Family members may then remain in an unsafe environment and at risk themselves.

1.3.3 The Community

The community in which the infant death occurred may be affected by a poor investigation and inaccurate classification. Communities that have a vested interest in the care and safety of children will seek ways to ensure the safety of children in their community. Communities benefit when agencies within the jurisdiction work together. A team approach is vital if communities strive to effectively investigate infant deaths. All agencies benefit when each recognizes its role in the investigation and tries to work cooperatively with others to obtain necessary information. If one or more agencies refuse or are unable to participate effectively in the investigative process, the entire investigation may be in jeopardy. A poor working relationship can impact community resources and the individuals necessary for a complete investigation. Strained working relationships within the community may result if individuals see their roles, and the information they may be able to provide, as unnecessary or nonvital to the investigation.

Agencies in the community that assist families are at a disadvantage when accurate information is not available. Local social service agencies are unable to refer families appropriately, provide adequate counseling, or offer social service assistance effectively if the needs are not clearly identified. These social service agencies may question local authorities and their protocols for investigating child deaths, which may further strain interagency working relationships.

1.3.4 The Nation

The entire nation will be affected if national statistics are inaccurate due to poor infant death investigation. A snowball effect will occur if statistics are skewed, as public policy is guided by national statistics. Public agencies and private organizations develop and promote prevention and education programs and initiate research studies based on national statistics to address the types of deaths that are reported to be prevalent. Agencies and organizations may invest time and resources to develop unnecessary programs and fail to develop needed programs if statistics are not accurate. Educational programs may not offer appropriate information, and prevention programs may not address the real issues causing infant deaths. Statistics also help determine the type and amount of research funded by health organizations. Resources may be used to fund nonessential medical and health care topics if statistics are not accurate. Public agencies, and many private organizations, rely on tax dollars to fund their programs; as a result, tax payers are penalized if funds are not used in the needed areas.

1.3.5 Professional Impact

Poor infant death investigations are a reflection on the individual investigator, the agency and jurisdiction in which they practice, and the professional category in which they place themselves. The integrity of the investigator, the agency, and the jurisdiction may be evidenced by the way these and all deaths are, or are not, investigated. Erroneous statistics and the inconsistent classification of infant deaths is a reflection of how deaths were investigated. Investigators should be aware of the ways their practice impacts others. When those impacts are realized, changes can and should be made.

1.4 WHY ARE THEY DIFFICULT TO INVESTIGATE?

Many forensic pathologists and MDIs will agree that historically infant deaths have been poorly investigated. All too often, the pathologist will perform the autopsy without receiving adequate information about the infant or the circumstances surrounding the death, which makes it difficult for the pathologist to accurately determine the COD and MOD. The majority of infants and very young children who die suddenly and unexpectedly have no known medical conditions and the autopsy often reveals no significant findings. It is imperative that death investigators ensure that all information regarding the infant, the infant's family and home, the incident location, and the circumstances surrounding the death is obtained.

Infant deaths are complicated and present a unique challenge to investigators. Unlike adults, infants and young children usually have an abbreviated medical and social history. It is not until children reach school age that other records may be available. As a result, investigators must rely heavily on information provided by other individuals through interviews, recognizing that the process of verifying that information can be difficult if there are no records to substantiate their statements. Investigators must rely on their observations, their ability to interview, and their knowledge of infant growth and development in their search for answers.

1.4.1 Reasons for Poor Investigations

Before it is possible to change the way infant deaths are investigated, there must be an understanding of what hinders an investigator's ability to investigate these challenging and often complicated cases. Once the reasons for poor investigations are identified, then strategies can be developed to address each of those issues. Poor infant death investigation can be attributed to many things; what affects each individual and jurisdiction may vary. Some of the reasons that infant deaths are investigated poorly include lack of knowledge regarding infant growth and development; time delays in the investigation; inexperience interviewing grieving parents or caregivers; denial, bias, no or miscommunication; and a lack of guidelines and protocols.

1.4.1.1 Lack of Knowledge

An investigator's lack of knowledge about infant growth and development is one factor that may lead to a poor investigation. Investigators who are knowledgeable in this area understand how infants develop, the order in which development occurs, and in what age range each developmental milestone occurs. This knowledge can and will affect the investigator's ability to determine the reliability of information provided by the family and caregivers and whether their descriptions of the incident is possible or even probable.

Armed with information about normal growth and development, an investigator can have witnesses immediately clarify their statements if information provided by them is questionable. Investigators are also better equipped to recognize and identify growth and developmental delays when reviewing medical records that may substantiate or contradict information provided by caregivers. Knowledge of growth and development is needed when assessing the age appropriateness of activities and skills that a caregiver may describe an infant capable of. Likewise, the behaviors and childcare methods of caregivers may or may not be age appropriate for the infant's age and developmental level. Knowledgeable investigators will be more confident when interviewing caregivers, when conducting the initial postmortem external assessment, when communicating with the infant's primary medical provider, and when performing a doll reenactment. Additionally when inconsistencies occur between witness statements and normal growth and development, investigators with knowledge of growth and development are more prepared and confident if and when it is necessary to reinterview a witness.

1.4.1.2 Time Delays in the Investigation

Investigations are affected by time. The sooner an investigation begins after an infant's death, the better. One of the major problems associated with infant death investigation is the time delay from the time an infant is pronounced dead to when investigators are notified. Delays also occur when investigators fail to respond quickly to the scene or hospital, to immediately interview witnesses, to immediately conduct a scene investigation after the death, and to participate in a local investigative child death review. Possible results of time delays may include: lost evidence, witnesses may forget or be unable to recall important details, the incident location may be altered either intentionally or unintentionally, and communication gaps may occur between investigative agencies.

A majority of infant deaths occur in emergency rooms, and as a result, the incident location may not be secured, which may result in changes and loss of evidence. If investigators do not respond immediately to an infant death that occurs in an emergency room, it may be hours, sometimes days, before caregivers are interviewed and investigators complete a scene investigation. Time delays are critical and affect the quality of infant death investigations.

1.4.1.3 Inexperience Interviewing Grieving Parents/Caregivers

Strong interview skills are needed when investigating an infant's death and poor investigations may result if investigators lack skills needed to interview grieving caregivers. Law enforcement agencies have investigators who specialize in interviewing witnesses of a multitude of crimes; however, few agencies designate an investigator to handle cases in which the deceased victim is an infant. Very little has been written or taught in regard to techniques that are helpful when interviewing parents and primary caregivers of deceased infants and very young children. It may seem that investigators would interview them just as any other witness; however, that may not be the case. Adjusting the interview technique may enhance the investigation and the amount of information obtained from caregivers. Some investigators, due to inexperience and training, lack the confidence needed to interview grieving caregivers following the sudden and unexpected death of an infant.

The emotions of surviving family members, as well as the emotions of the investigator, can interfere with a thorough investigation resulting in one that is short and lacking in completeness. Infant and child deaths are often extremely emotional for all parties and the investigator may not feel comfortable interviewing a highly emotional parent or caregiver. Investigators who are not equipped to deal with an emotional investigation may rush the process and end the investigation prematurely. The investigator may decide that the family has gone through enough and that investigators should not add to their pain with an in-depth investigation. In order to give caregivers an opportunity to compose themselves, investigators may believe that interviewing witnesses and investigating the scene at a later time would be helpful to the family. The investigation will then be delayed, which compromises the investigation. Regardless of the emotional circumstances surrounding an investigation, the death should be investigated immediately. When investigators lack experience interviewing grieving parents or caregivers, the investigation as a whole may suffer; however, as skills and techniques are developed, investigators will become more effective when investigating emotional and challenging cases such as infant deaths.

1.4.1.4 Denial

It may be difficult for some investigators to believe that anyone, particularly a parent, could or would purposely harm a child. Some investigators believe that parents who unintentionally cause harm to their child (i.e., overlying), have suffered enough and should not be burdened with an intensive investigation, and as a result, the investigation may be abbreviated, rushed, and left incomplete. These investigators ask few questions, rush to a conclusion, and may not request or authorize necessary tests including an autopsy. The death may then be certified inaccurately even if not all of the criteria for that classification have been met.

Some investigators do not want parents to feel guilty. Some investigators may try to make parents feel they are not at fault if the death is believed to be the result of an accident. They attempt to accomplish this by closing the investigation quickly and may attribute the death to sudden infant death syndrome (SIDS) or another generic nonclassified cause. Investigators who feel they are protecting the family may minimize the investigation, attribute the death to natural causes, and fail to provide needed education, referral, and support to the family.

1.4.1.5 Bias

Bias can lead to a poor investigation. Investigators may not recognize biases that could affect their investigation, and these biases can be detrimental. Biases can result from negative or positive opinions regarding persons of different races and socioeconomic status. Investigators who fail to completely investigate an infant death because a family is of a certain race, lives in a certain neighborhood, or is known to be a "good family" may reach inaccurate conclusions that will impact many.

A person's past interactions with the criminal justice system is a bias that may impact infant death investigations. This information, acquired too soon in the investigation, may bias investigators in a number of ways. In some jurisdictions, police dispatchers immediately look up all past emergency calls for the incident location and provide that information to the lead investigator prior to their arrival on scene or at the hospital. Investigators who learn that no prior emergency calls have come from the incident location may be inadvertently biased toward a natural death. Investigators, who learn that prior domestic violence calls have come from the incident location, may be biased that the death is from unnatural causes. Armed with either set of facts, bias may affect the investigation before it gets started. Biases may occur in all types of investigations; however, when a bias occurs in conjunction with an investigator's lack of knowledge of infant growth and development and an emotional scene, disaster may result.

1.4.1.6 No Communication or Miscommunication

Incomplete investigations can result from poor communication between investigative agencies. Gaps in communication between law enforcement officers, the MDI, the forensic pathologist, social service personnel, and prosecutors can have a damaging effect to the investigation. All investigative agencies should be aware of the roles and responsibilities of the other professionals involved in the investigation of the infant's death and each must engage in open communication with the other to ensure that all pertinent information is shared with the appropriate agencies.

Death investigators in some jurisdictions do not communicate their investigative findings to the forensic pathologist. This lack of communication greatly affects the pathologist's ability to identify the COD. Law enforcement officials who fail to notify the social service agency in their jurisdiction that is charged with the responsibility of protecting children, that the death of a child has occurred, may not learn of prior abuse allegations that may have been reported to that social service agency. MDIs and law enforcement officials who fail to communicate with one another may each miss important information. For example, the MDI may review the decedent's medical record, while law enforcement personnel review witness criminal records. These investigators must share the findings of their independent investigations with one other to ensure that both have a complete picture of the death. A lack of communication between multiple agencies can be eliminated by conducting a local investigative child death review, which will be discussed in Chapter 11.

1.4.1.7 Lack of Guidelines and Policies

Infant deaths may be poorly investigated if there are no guidelines, polices, or protocols established by investigative agencies. Some states have developed guidelines, investigative forms, and policies to help investigators; however, investigators in local jurisdictions must be aware they exist and follow them. Agencies may have their own method for investigating infant deaths. They should, however, ensure that their investigators successfully acquire the information needed with those methods and techniques. Agencies that are not cognizant of the unique qualities of infant death investigation will miss important information if investigational policies are not developed to address these complicated cases.

1.5 WHAT IS BEING DONE ABOUT IT?

In 1992, the U.S. Senate and the U.S. House of Representatives recommended that a standard death scene investigation protocol be developed for sudden unexplained infant deaths (SUIDs). These protocols were to be developed by the U.S. Department of Health and Human Services Interagency Panel of Sudden Infant Death Syndrome. The CDC along with the National Institute of Health (NIH) convened a multidisciplinary team that developed guidelines for the investigation of sudden, unexplained infant deaths, along with the Sudden Unexplained Infant Death Scene Investigation Report Form (SUIDIRF).[4] The form was released in 1996 and was intended to be used by investigators who were investigating a SUID. The form was not nationally mandated and was therefore used on a volunteer basis by some investigative agencies.

Research studies revealed that the quality of data collected during infant death investigations was inconsistent, and that there was inconsistency in the manner by which infant deaths were being certified on death certificates. These inconsistencies made it difficult to identify and monitor trends, evaluate prevention programs, and conduct research. During this time, researchers noticed a decrease in the number of infant deaths due to SIDS, yet observed an increase in the number of infant deaths due to unknown or unspecified causes. National prevention programs such as the Back-to-Sleep campaign may have contributed to some of the decrease in the SIDS rate; however, how infant deaths were investigated and then classified on death certificates may also have contributed to the decline in the SIDS rate.[5,6]

In 2004, the CDC convened another national work group to revise the 1996 SUIDIRF after it was determined that the form was not widely used and was not considered to be user friendly. This national work group, made up of MEs, coroners, MDIs, law enforcement officials, researchers, and representatives from SIDS organizations, worked to improve the form. In 2006, a revised edition was released.

Realizing that the 1996 SUIDIRF may not have been used due to a lack of investigator training, the CDC in collaboration with Occupational Research and Assessment, Inc. and a national group of infant death investigation experts developed training material to instruct investigators how to use the SUIDIRF and conduct an infant death investigation. Training academies were conducted to train selected professionals from each state. Those individuals returned to their states prepared to train additional personnel involved in the investigation of infant deaths.

1.6 CURRENT STATISTICS

NCHS published *Death: Final Data for 2004*,[7] which is, as of this publication, the most current and complete statistical report on infant mortality. According to this data, the infant mortality rate was 6.79 in 2004, a slight decrease from 6.85 reported in 2003.[8] Infant deaths, those occurring under the age of 1 year, are broken down into two categories: neonatal and postneonatal. The neonatal mortality rate covers those deaths that occurred when the infant was under 28 days of age. The postneonatal period covers those deaths that occurred between 28 days and 11 months of age.

The leading causes of infant death remained relatively unchanged from 2003 to 2004 with the exception that deaths caused by accidents and those by the result of complications of placenta, cord, and membranes swapped positions with each other relative to their previous placement in 2003. The leading causes of infant deaths for 2004 are listed in Table 1.1. The types of deaths that should be of particular interest to MDIs are those deaths that are the result of nonnatural causes being either accidental unintentional injuries, which increased from 2003, or assaults (homicides) and those that are "not elsewhere classified." The number of deaths reported in 2003, that fit these categories are listed in Table 1.2. In 2003, there were a total of 28,025 infant deaths, of those 4,694 were either the result of unintentional accidents, intentional acts of violence or neglect, medical or surgical complications, or were not elsewhere classified. The statistics for 2004 were not available at the date of publication.

Infant deaths in which no obvious cause was apparent when the infant died are referred to as SUIDs.[4] Causes of death that fit under the larger umbrella of SUID include neglect, suffocation, poisoning, choking, and SIDS to name a few. In the later group, SIDS is the category in which a large percentage of deaths fall and is also the category by which certain criteria must be met to classify the death as such.

TABLE 1.1
Infant Deaths: Leading Causes in 2004

Infant Deaths: Leading Causes
1. Congenital malformations, deformities and chromosomal abnormalities
2. Disorders relating to short gestation and low birth weight
3. Sudden infant death syndrome (SIDS)
4. Newborn affected by maternal complications of pregnancy
5. Accidents — unintentional injuries
6. Newborn affected by complications of placenta, cord, and membranes
7. Respiratory distress of newborn
8. Bacterial sepsis of newborn
9. Neonatal hemorrhage
10. Disease of circulatory system (2003) or intrauterine hypoxia and birth asphyxia (2004)

Source: Miniño, A.M. et al., *Deaths: Final Data for 2004,* Health E-Stats. Released November 24, 2006.

TABLE 1.2
Nonnatural and Not Elsewhere Classified Causes of Death

Infant Deaths: Nonnatural and Not Elsewhere Classified Causes of Death	Number of Deaths in 2003
1. Symptoms, signs and abnormal clinical and lab findings not elsewhere classified:	3,318
A. SIDS	2,162
B. Others	1,156
2. External causes of mortality:	1,376
A. Accident (unintentional injuries) Such as motor vehicle accidents, falls, drowning, suffocation, strangulation, choking, fire related, poisoning, and other unspecified accidents	945
B. Assault (homicide) Such as neglect, hanging, strangulation, suffocation, firearms related, other unspecified means	341
C. Complication of medical and surgical care	15
D. Other external causes and their sequelae	75

Source: Hoyert, D.L. et al., *Deaths: Final Data for 2003,* National Vital Statistics Reports, Vol. 54, No. 13, National Center for Health Statistics, Hyattsville, MD, 2006.

SIDS is defined as the "death of an infant under 1 year of age that remains unexplained after a thorough case investigation, including performance of a complete autopsy, examination of the death scene, and a review of the clinical history."[9] SIDS is a diagnosis of exclusion and should only be used to classify a death when all of the criteria for doing so are met. According to Krous et al.,[10] the term *SIDS* "has been overused and applied to cases in which there have been obvious natural or unnatural causes of death; also the term has been underused in favor of imprecise terms such as undetermined and unascertained." In recent years, the number of SIDS deaths have declined; however, that is believed to be the result of a change in the way investigators are classifying infant deaths as the number of infant deaths has not declined significantly yet the number of undetermined or unclassified deaths has increased.[5,6]

The data suggest that the way infant deaths are investigated and classified impacts national statistics; therefore, thorough and complete infant death investigations at the local level are of utmost importance. To ensure that infant deaths are comprehensively investigated, MDIs should follow national guidelines, develop advanced investigation techniques, implement effective approaches to infant death investigations that may not be utilized in their jurisdiction, and effectively communicate with the other investigative agencies within their community.

1.7 GOAL AND TEXT ORGANIZATION

The infant deaths most difficult to investigate are those in which the infant died in a hospital emergency room after unsuccessful resuscitation and which no obvious cause is noted at the time of death (SUID). Kiernan and Beckerman[11] noted that infant death scene investigations are affected by the timing and circumstances surrounding the case. They noted that "infants who are found dead at home generally have a death scene investigation completed within hours of the death, usually with the infant body still in place and the scene relatively undisturbed." They also noted that death scene investigations following infant deaths that occur at a local hospital after unsuccessful resuscitation are not helpful as the delay in conducting the death scene investigation hampers the collection of critical data.

A large number of infant deaths occur in an emergency room setting. These infants are found unresponsive by a caregiver, a call is placed to 9-1-1 requesting the assistance of emergency personnel. Professional first responders arrive on scene and begin lifesaving techniques that are continued during transport to a local hospital where the infant is pronounced dead in an emergency room by a physician. It is at this point that law enforcement personnel and MDIs are notified of the death. The goal of this text is to provide information regarding investigative techniques and approaches that will assist investigators when investigating an infant's death that occurred in an emergency room. As noted by Kiernan and Beckerman, the above scenario depicts the circumstances of infant deaths that are most complicated and least effectively investigated. The techniques and approaches described in this text will decrease time delays, ensure critical data is recovered in a timely manner from the hospital and scene, ensure that interviews with primary witnesses at both locations occur, and provide detailed information regarding doll reenactments and child death reviews.

This text is organized in the same chronological order in which these difficult cases may present and therefore should be investigated. The legal guardian is often the individual who finds the infant, usually at the infant's primary residence. There are many other possible scenarios as infant deaths may occur in other locations, in the presence of other people, or under different circumstances. The incident location may be different from the primary residence, such as a day-care setting. The individual who finds the infant may be someone other than the legal guardian, such as a baby sitter. The infant may be transported to a local hospital in a private vehicle rather than in an ambulance. Some deaths are verified at the incident location, resulting in the infant's body remaining on the scene. These variations, as well additional areas of concern, will be discussed throughout this book.

1.7.1 Case Examples

Case examples will be presented to bring emphasis and clarification to the topic and technique discussed. One investigative agency, the Charleston County Coroner's Office in South Carolina, has implemented these investigative techniques and approaches. The case examples are included to demonstrate how the suggested techniques may be put into action so that readers will be able to visualize the process being explained and will then be able to put those suggestions into practice in their respective offices and specialties. The techniques and approaches suggested may initially appear to be ideal but not practical. The goal of the case examples is to show that the techniques and approaches are practical and are being used during every infant death investigation in some jurisdictions and that they will positively impact the investigation.

1.7.2 Terminology

The individual(s) who find an infant unresponsive may have a number of different titles. In this book, these individuals will be referred to as a *primary witness, witness, caregiver,* and, on occasion, *family member.* During actual investigations, these persons may have a number of different titles and describe their relationship to the infant in numerous ways. For simplicity's sake, they will be referred to as *family, witnesses,* or *caregivers* in this book.

Investigators who are responsible for the investigation of circumstances surrounding an infant's death may also have numerous titles. These individuals may represent local police agencies, sheriffs' departments, or coroners' or MEs' offices. The titles used vary from jurisdiction to jurisdiction and are not consistent even with the same type of agency. Investigators in a coroner's office, for example, may be referred to as deputy coroners, coroner assistants, forensic investigators, and death investigators among others. Regardless of the individual's actual title, the agency they represent, or their formal job description, these persons are investigators, who are investigating a death, in which medical and legal (medicolegal) knowledge is necessary. Therefore, this book refers to individuals who are responsible for investigating infant deaths as *medicolegal death investigators* (MDIs), *death investigators,* or simply *investigators.*

REFERENCES

1. U.S. Department of Health and Human Services, *Healthy People 2010,* Government Printing Office, Washington, D.C., 2000. Available at http://www.health.gov/healthypeople (accessed August 19, 2006).

2. National Center for Health Statistics, *Health, United States, 1999,* U.S. Department of Health and Human Services, Hyattsville, MD, 1999.
3. National Association of Medical Examiners, Forensic Autopsy Performance Standards, 2005, report, available at http://www.orainc.com/reports/NAMEForensicAutopsy-Standards.pdf (accessed August 19, 2006).
4. Centers for Disease Control and Prevention, Guidelines for death scene investigations of sudden, unexplained infant deaths: Recommendations of the Interagency Panel on Sudden Infant Death Syndrome, *Morbid. Mortal. Wkly. Rep.,* 45, RR-10, 1996.
5. Shapiro-Mendoza, C.K., Tomashek, K.M., Anderson, R.N., and Wingo, J. Recent national trends in sudden, unexpected infant death: More evidence supporting a change in classification or reporting, *Am. J. Epidemiol.,* 163 (8), 762–792, 2006.
6. Malloy, M.H. and MacDorman, M., Changes in the classification of sudden unexpected infant deaths: United States, 1992–2001, *Pediatrics,* 115 (5), 1247–1253, 2005.
7. Miniño, A.M., Heron, M.P., Smith, B.L., and Kochanek, K.D., *Deaths: Final Data for 2004.* Health E-Stats. Released November 24, 2006. Available at http://www.cdc.gov/nchs/products/pubs/pubd/hestats/finaldeaths04/finaldeaths04.htm.
8. Hoyert, D.L., Heron, M.P., Murphy, S.L., and Kung, H., *Deaths: Final Data for 2003,* National Vital Statistics Reports, Vol. 54, No. 13, National Center for Health Statistics, Hyattsville, MD, 2006.
9. Willinger, M., James, L.S., and Catz, C., Defining the sudden infant death syndrome (SIDS): Deliberations of an expert panel convened by the National Institute of Child Health and Human Development, *Pediatr. Pathol.,* 11 (5), 677–684, 1991.
10. Krous, H.F., Beckwith, J.B., Byard, R.W., Rognum, T.O., Bajanowski, T., Corey, T., Cutz, E.C., Hanzlick, R., Keens, T.G., and Mitchell, E.A., Sudden infant death syndrome and unclassified sudden infant deaths: A definitional and diagnostic approach, *Pediatrics,* 114 (1), 234–238, 2004.
11. Kiernan, M.P. and Beckerman, R.C., Is it sudden infant death syndrome or sudden unexpected infant death? *Pediatrics,* 116 (3), 800–801, 2005.

RESOURCES

Centers for Disease Control and Prevention, Sudden, Unexplained Infant Death Initiative (SUIDI): Overview, available at http://www.cdc.gov/SIDS/SUID.htm.

Corey, T.S., Hanzlick, R., Howard, J., Nelson, C., and Krous, H., A Functional Approach to Sudden Unexplained Infant Deaths. Prepared by the NAME Ad Hoc Committee on Sudden Unexplained Infant Death. Approved by the NAME Board of Directors on October 14, 2005. http://www.thename.org.

Healthy People 2010, available at http://www.health.gov/healthypeople.

Hymel, K.P., Distinguishing sudden infant death syndrome from child abuse fatalities, *Pediatrics*, 118 (1), 421–427, 2006.

Mathews, T.J. and MacDorman, M.F., *Infant Mortality Statistics from the 2003 Period Linked Birth/Infant Death Data Set*, National Vital Statistics Reports, Vol. 54, No. 16, National Center for Health Statistics, Hyattsville, MD, 2006.

Munson, M.L. and Sutton, P.D., *Births, Marriages, Divorces, and Deaths: Provisional Data for 2005*, National Vital Statistics Report, Vol. 54, No. 20, National Center for Health Statistics, Hyattsville, MD, 2006.

National Center for Health Statistics, http://www.cdc.gov/nchs/index.htm.

National SIDS/Infant Death Resource Center, http://www.sidscenter.org.

National Vital Statistics System, http://www.cdc.gov/nchs/nvss.htm.

Occupational Research and Assessment, Inc., http://www.orainc.com/suidi.

Overpeck, M.D., Brenner, R.A., Cosgrove, C., Trumble, A.C., Kochanek, K., and MacDorman, M., National underascertainment of sudden unexplained infant deaths associated with deaths of unknown cause, *Pediatrics,* 109 (2), 274–283, 2002.

Pickett, K.E., Luo, Y., and Lauderdale, D.S., Widening social inequalities in risk for sudden infant death syndrome, *Am. J. Public Health,* 95 (11), 1976–1981, 2005.

2 Maternal and Infant Health: What Investigators Should Know

2.1 INTRODUCTION

The National Association of Medical Examiners (NAME), Ad Hoc Committee on Sudden Unexplained Infant Death (SUID) recommends that "a medical history of the infant should be conducted to identify any birth related problems and to assess the infant's growth, development, immunization history, and medical history."[1] The committee recommends that the infant's medical record be used to verify the medical history that is provided by caregivers and family. Medicolegal death investigators (MDIs) who have the responsibility of investigating infant deaths must have knowledge of infant growth and development to be able to accurately assess all circumstances surrounding the infant's death.

To ensure the best possible investigation, investigators should go one step further. They should have basic knowledge of maternal and infant health as this information will be helpful when obtaining details from primary witnesses and medical records about the infant and its death. Investigators should have basic knowledge of medical terminology, pregnancy, prenatal care, delivery modes and potential complications, gestation, birth weight, physical assessment methods for infants, normal growth and development milestones, developmental assessment methods, and the recommended childhood immunization schedule. Investigators who are knowledgeable in these areas are better able to recognize when an infant's physical findings or statements from caregivers or witnesses are consistent or inconsistent with the predictable normal growth milestones for infants.

2.2 MATERNAL HEALTH

The health of the mother prior to and during pregnancy along with the mode of delivery may affect the health and physical appearance of the infant. Knowledge of maternal health issues is essential when investigating the death of an infant. During interviews, investigators should obtain information about the mother's health, the progression of the pregnancy, the prenatal care she received, and the type of delivery. The medical record should be reviewed to confirm the information obtained during interviews. Knowledge of pregnancy-related medical terminology will assist investigators during interviews with caregivers and when reviewing the medical record.

2.2.1 Medical Terminology

Prenatal and delivery records provide valuable information about the biological mother's health during pregnancy and any complications that occurred during pregnancy and delivery. During the review of these records, medical terminology and abbreviations will be present that may not be understood by investigators who do not have a medical background. The medical information is needed, however, to conduct a thorough and complete infant death investigation. This information can only be obtained, considered, and accurately evaluated if the investigator is familiar with the medical terminology that will be noted in the medical record. Additionally, medical information that should be obtained during interviews with the family or caregivers should be compared to that which is noted in the records reviewed. Common medical terminology encountered during an infant death investigation will be discussed extensively throughout this chapter.

2.2.2 Pregnancy History

The biological mother's pregnancy history will be documented in the medical record and may be important in some infant death investigations. Medical terminology used to describe a woman's pregnancy include:

- Gravidity — The total number of pregnancies that a woman has had including the current pregnancy. For example, a woman who has only been pregnant one time is considered to be gravida 1, and a woman who has been pregnant three times is a gravida 3. This may be documented in the medical record as G1 or G3, respectively.
- Parity — The number of pregnancies that have reached viability. Viability is the ability and capacity of a fetus to live outside the uterus and is considered to be approximately 24-weeks gestation or a fetal weight of more than 550 grams.
- Term — The number of live births that were born between 38- and 42-weeks gestation.
- Preterm — The number of live births that occurred between 24- and 37-weeks gestation.
- Postterm — A pregnancy that goes past 42-weeks gestation.

The pregnancy history may be recorded a number of different ways in the medical record. The two most common methods are a two digit system and a more detailed five-digit system. The first system uses two digits to represent the mother's pregnancy history. The first digit represents gravidity, the second digit represents parity. The pregnancy history may be documented in the medical record as G2 P2 or simply 2/2. The woman in this example has been pregnant two times and has carried each pregnancy to viability.

The five-digit system, which infant death investigators may find to be the most useful during an infant death investigation, is a much more detailed method of documenting a woman's pregnancy history. The five digits represent gravida (G), term (T), preterm (P), abortions (A), and living children (L). Along with the previously mentioned descriptions for gravidity, term, and parity, this system includes information regarding the number of elective or nonelective abortions (i.e., miscarriages) that a woman has had and the number of children that are currently living. The five-digit system may be documented in a number of ways. Two examples include G2 T1 P0 A1 L1 or simply 2-1-0-1-1.

Case Example 2.1 The prenatal medical record states that the biological mother is a 2-1-0-0-1 (which may also be documented as G2 T1 L1). This woman has had two pregnancies including the current pregnancy, delivered one full-term live infant, had no preterm live births, no abortions or miscarriages, and has one living child. The mother has previously delivered one child and that child is currently living. Following delivery of another full-term infant, her pregnancy history would be documented as 2-2-0-0-2.

Case Example 2.2 While interviewing the mother of a 4-week-old infant who died, the mother reports that she has had two pregnancies. During the medical records review it was noted that her pregnancy history was documented as 3-1-1-0-1 (G3 T1 P1 L1). In this example, the history indicates three pregnancies, one full-term live infant, one preterm live infant, no abortions or miscarriages, and one living child. This mother previously delivered two live infants yet only one of those infants is currently living. Following delivery of another full-term live infant (the infant whose death is under current investigation) her pregnancy history should be 3-2-1-0-2. During the interview with the mother, information regarding the first infant who died will be important. The investigator will need to investigate further if the mother did not reveal information about the prior infant death during the initial interview. The death of the first infant should be reviewed to determine if there are any similarities between the cases.

2.2.3 Prenatal History

The mother's prenatal history may provide valuable information to MDIs following the death of an infant. The prenatal history will provide information regarding the mother's health, before and during pregnancy, and the progress of the pregnancy. Additionally, it will provide information regarding the well-being of the fetus to include lifestyle of the mother and medical complications that may have placed the infant at risk. The prenatal history may also provide psychosocial information regarding the parents' desire to have this child, which may be valuable information during some complicated cases.

The prenatal record will provide information regarding the past medical history of the mother including medical diagnoses, medications, and lifestyle choices to include smoking, alcohol consumption, and drug history. Of particular interest to MDIs will be the mother's use of tobacco, alcohol, prescription and nonprescription medications, herbal remedies, and illegal drugs. Information regarding the mother's use of the above substances, either during or before the pregnancy, may raise questions about substances that may have been used by the mother after the birth, given to the infant, or been within a child's reach resulting in accidental ingestion. The use of these substances can place the infant at a higher risk for low birth weight and prematurity and, therefore, at an increased risk for death.

The medical record that documents the mother's first prenatal visit may reveal psychosocial information. Some records may reveal that the mother or parents scheduled a prenatal visit immediately after suspecting the pregnancy and the health care provider's progress notes may reveal that the parents were excited about the pregnancy. A review of a prenatal record in another case, however, may reveal that the mother did not seek prenatal care until the second trimester, was distraught about the pregnancy, and concerned about her ability to care for the newborn.

2.2.4 Delivery Modes and Potential Complications

The birth process can occur one of two ways: vaginal delivery, either assisted or unassisted, and cesarean section (C-section). During infant death investigations, and particularly those of neonates (i.e., infants under the age of 1 month), investigators should obtain delivery information from the medical records or medical providers regarding the mode by which the infant was born. There are risks associated with each mode of delivery that can cause injury to the infant and each mode may leave different markings and bruises on the newborn. Injuries or marks noted on the infant that are initially thought to have occurred during delivery should be compared to the delivery record for corroboration.

2.2.4.1 Vaginal Delivery

Vaginal deliveries may occur with or without the assistance of medical intervention. Unassisted vaginal deliveries are those in which no medical intervention is needed to assist the infant out of the vaginal canal. Assisted vaginal deliveries are those in which medical intervention is needed to assist the infant out of the vaginal canal. All infants born vaginally may have molding of the head. *Molding* is a term used to describe how the shape of the head changes as the baby is moved through the vaginal canal. The bones that make up the skull have not yet grown together, which allows the skull to be slightly flexible, thus allowing the infant to be delivered through the vaginal canal. The fontanels (soft spots) are the soft places on the infant's head where the skull has not yet fused together. Infants' heads may appear cone-shaped due to molding and this may occur with all vaginal deliveries.

Two methods for assisting the delivery of an infant born vaginally are forceps and vacuum extraction. *Forceps* are slightly curved spoon-shaped surgical tongs that are applied to the sides of the infant's head while in the vaginal canal. During contractions, the infant is gently pulled down and out of the vaginal canal. The infant may have bruising or abrasions at the site where the forceps came in contact with the infant's head. Occasionally, a scalp blister or subdural hematoma will form where the forceps gripped the infant's head. These injuries may heal in as little as a few days and up to a few weeks.

During vacuum-assisted deliveries, also known as *vacuum extraction,* the medical practitioner applies a flexible, rounded cup to the infant's head while in the vaginal canal. The cup is connected to an electric suction pump or a small handheld pump to create a vacuum pressure that holds the cup securely to the infant's head. While the mother pushes during contractions, the medical provider gently pulls on a handle attached to the cup, helping move the infant down and out of the vaginal canal. Injuries associated with vacuum extraction usually heal within a few weeks and may include a scalp laceration, subdural hematoma, or cephalhematoma.[2,3] A *subdural hematoma* is a collection of blood on the surface of the brain that is located beneath the dura (outer covering) of the brain and the brain's surface. A *cephalhematoma* is a raised bruise on the top of the head, which is the result of a collection of blood between the skull bone and the periosteum, the lining that covers the skull. Retinal hemorrhages, which may result from ruptured capillaries caused by increased pressure during birth, may also be a risk of vacuum-assisted delivery, although are most often associated with the duration of labor.

2.2.4.2 C-Section Delivery

A *C-section* is an operation, by which an obstetrician or surgeon surgically removes the infant from the uterus. This medical procedure may be done as a scheduled elective surgery. An emergency C-section may be required, however, if the mother's labor is not progressing or if the fetus or mother's health is potentially compromised. Infants born via C-section often appear to have rounder heads as they have not had to pass through the vaginal canal.

2.3 INFANT HEALTH

The health of the infant, including the gestational age and birth weight, is an indicator of the infant's risk for morbidity and mortality. Both indicators are pieces of information that investigators should acquire and consider when investigating an infant's death. MDIs should also be aware of physical assessment methods that may be used to assess the infant immediately after birth and to assess the infant's growth and development.

2.3.1 Gestation

Gestation, the length of time from conception to birth, is 280 days or 40 weeks. Infants born after 37 weeks are considered to be *full-term*. Infants born before 37 weeks, yet past the age of viability, are considered to be *premature* or *preterm*. As MDIs interview caregivers, assess the body of the decedent, and review medical records, it will be important that the investigator determine the gestational age of the infant when born. Normal variations in growth and development may occur based on the infant's gestation at delivery.

Two infants born on the same day could be very different in regard to what they are able to do. For example, the first infant, born at 32-weeks gestation, will not be at the same developmental level as another infant who was born on the same day but at 40-weeks gestation. Even though both infants may be the same age, their abilities and rate at which they reach the growth and developmental milestones may be different.

2.3.2 Birth Weight

The birth weight of an infant is an important piece of information that may help evaluate an infant's morbidity and mortality risk. A normal range of birth weights has been determined based on gestational age. Birth weights are classified as:

- Large for gestational age (LGA) — The infant's weight is above the 90th percentile for the gestational age, which means the infant weighs more than 90% of other infants at the same gestational age.
- Appropriate for gestational age (AGA) — The infant's weight is between the 10th and 90th percentile for the infant's gestational age.
- Small for gestational age (SGA) — The infant's weight is below the 10th percentile for the gestational age.
- Low birth weight (LBW) — Infants who weigh 2500 grams or less at birth.
- Very low birth weight (VLBW) — Infants who weigh 1500 grams or less at birth.

2.3.3 Physical Assessment Methods

Infants grow at an amazing rate the first year of life as their bodies are developing and changing. As MDIs review medical records and gather information from family and caregivers regarding the infant, investigators will best be able to recognize potential inconsistencies if they are familiar with infant growth and developmental milestones. Familiarity with some of the assessment methods used by medical personnel to evaluate how an infant is thriving, including physical assessments, developmental assessments, and comparative growth charts will also be helpful.

2.3.4 Apgar Scores

Immediately following a birth, an initial physical assessment is completed by medical personnel known as the *Apgar score*. This quick assessment of the newborn's skin color, respiratory rate, heart rate, muscle tone, and reflex activity is completed twice: 1 minute after birth and then 5 minutes after birth. The five items being assessed may each be given 1 or 2 points, for a total possible score of 10 points. Ten points indicates that the infant is healthy and responded well to labor, delivery, and the new environment. A score below 5 points indicates that the newborn needed immediate medical assistance and did not adapt well to the new environment.

Apgar scores are documented in the infant's birth record and investigators should have an understanding of what the scores mean and the potential importance to the investigation. Scores of 8 or above are considered normal, while scores less than 8 indicate the newborn needed medical assistance. These scores, however, do not predict the infant's future well-being as there is no research to suggest that infants with a low 1-minute score that normalizes at the 5-minute assessment will have any long-term effects, including an increased risk of unexpected infant death. There has been some suggestion, however, that the degree of risk for neonatal morbidity and mortality may correlate with a low 5-minute Apgar score.[4,5]

2.3.5 Gestational Age Assessment

An assessment of the gestational age of the child may be completed between 2 and 12 hours after birth. The results of this assessment may be important as infant morbidity and mortality may be related to gestational age and birth weight. The most common method for assessing gestational age is the *New Ballard Scale*, which can be used on newborns as young as 20 weeks of gestation. The results of the gestational assessment may be found in the infant's medical record. This result may be valuable to investigators because the infant's age at which growth and development milestones may be reached is based on the gestational age when born. Investigators need to be aware of the infant's gestational age when comparing the level of growth and development of the infant to the descriptions of the family or caregivers.

2.4 INFANT GROWTH AND DEVELOPMENT

Knowledge of infant growth and development, which includes the rate at which infants grow and the approximate age by which specific developmental milestones occur, may prove to be valuable during an infant death investigation. As infants develop and get older, they are able to do more complex tasks. Investigators need to be aware of the ages at which certain tasks may be reached by an infant to be able to compare that information to the reported incident and circumstances of the infant's death.

The growth of an infant and the development of an infant are not the same thing. Growth refers to the size of the infant and whether the infant is getting larger. Development refers to the infant's ability to be able to reach milestones, which are age-specific tasks that most children are able to do at a certain age. A developmental delay may be occurring if a child does not reach milestones at the same time as other children the same age and these delays sometimes require further evaluation by medical personnel.

Growth and developmental patterns are orderly and predictable. These patterns are continuous, and the infant will progress from simple to more complex tasks and from one developmental milestone to the next. Infants do not skip developmental milestones as they must be able to do an easier task before moving to a more difficult one. For example, infants learn to stand before they walk and walk before they run. The pattern and sequence are predictable although each infant may progress at a different rate.

2.4.1 Growth Patterns

Infants grow at an amazing rate during the first year of life. The amount that an infant has or has not grown may be an important indicator of medical or environmental problems that may have contributed to a death. As a result, infant death investigators should have basic knowledge regarding normal growth patterns of healthy newborns.

During the first week of life, it is not unusual for infants to lose up to 10% of their birth weight. Usually by the second week however, they will regain any weight that was lost. By 5 to 6 months of age, infants double their birth weight, and by 12 months of age, their weight triples. Growth and development proceeds in a head-to-toe direction (cephalocaudal) and an inward-to-outward progression (proximodistal). The amount and rate of an infant's growth is often tracked on growth charts during health care visits.

2.4.2 Growth Charts

Growth charts are assessment and documentation tools that will be included in infants' and children's medical records. As a routine part of medical checkups, pediatricians, as well as other physicians, track the growth of infants and children. Over time and after documenting multiple measurements, a pattern of growth is noted. This pattern of growth provides information regarding how the child is growing as compared to other children of the same age and sex. If the pattern indicates that the child is not growing appropriately, the physician will try to determine why the child is falling behind.

The charts used by most physicians are standard growth charts that were developed by the Centers for Disease Control and Prevention (CDC) based on measurement data that was collected by the National Center for Health Statistics (NCHS). The standard growth charts (Figure 2.1 through Figure 2.4) are broken down by age, birth to 36 months and 2 to 20 years, and sex of the child. The measurements that are vital and plotted on the appropriate growth chart include head circumference, weight, and length. The location of the plotted measurement will indicate which percentile the child is in: 5th, 10th, 25th, 50th, 75th, 90th, or 95th.[6] For example, a child noted to be in the 75th percentile for weight indicates that the child's weight is greater than 75% of children in that age and sex category, or that 25% of children that age and sex weigh more than the child measured.

Even though infants grow rapidly the first year of life, it is common for them to have brief periods when they do not gain weight and may even lose weight. Weight loss or lack of weight gain for 3 consecutive months during the first year of their life, triggers health care providers to further evaluate and determine the reason for the lack of growth. Infants who continue to not meet expected standards of growth may be diagnosed as *failure to thrive,* a general diagnosis with many potential causes.

Failure to thrive may have one of two causes: organic and nonorganic. *Organic causes* are those that result from an underlying medical condition, which may be a chronic illness, such as a metabolic and malabsorption disorder, gastrointestinal problem, or infection. *Nonorganic causes* are those that are environmental in natural or may be the result of actions by the caregivers or parents including neglect or poverty, which results in the child not getting enough caloric intake. Once health care personnel recognize that an infant is failing to thrive, they work with the family and perform medical tests and screenings to try to determine the reason for the lack of growth.

MDIs should have a general understanding of growth charts, how and why they are used, and be able to identify what information may be gained from them. If there are no growth charts in the medical record, MDIs may find it helpful to plot the infant's weight and length based on documented information in the medical record and compare it with the infant's measurements at death. This may raise the possibility of failure to thrive, which may not have been noted prior to death by the health care provider.

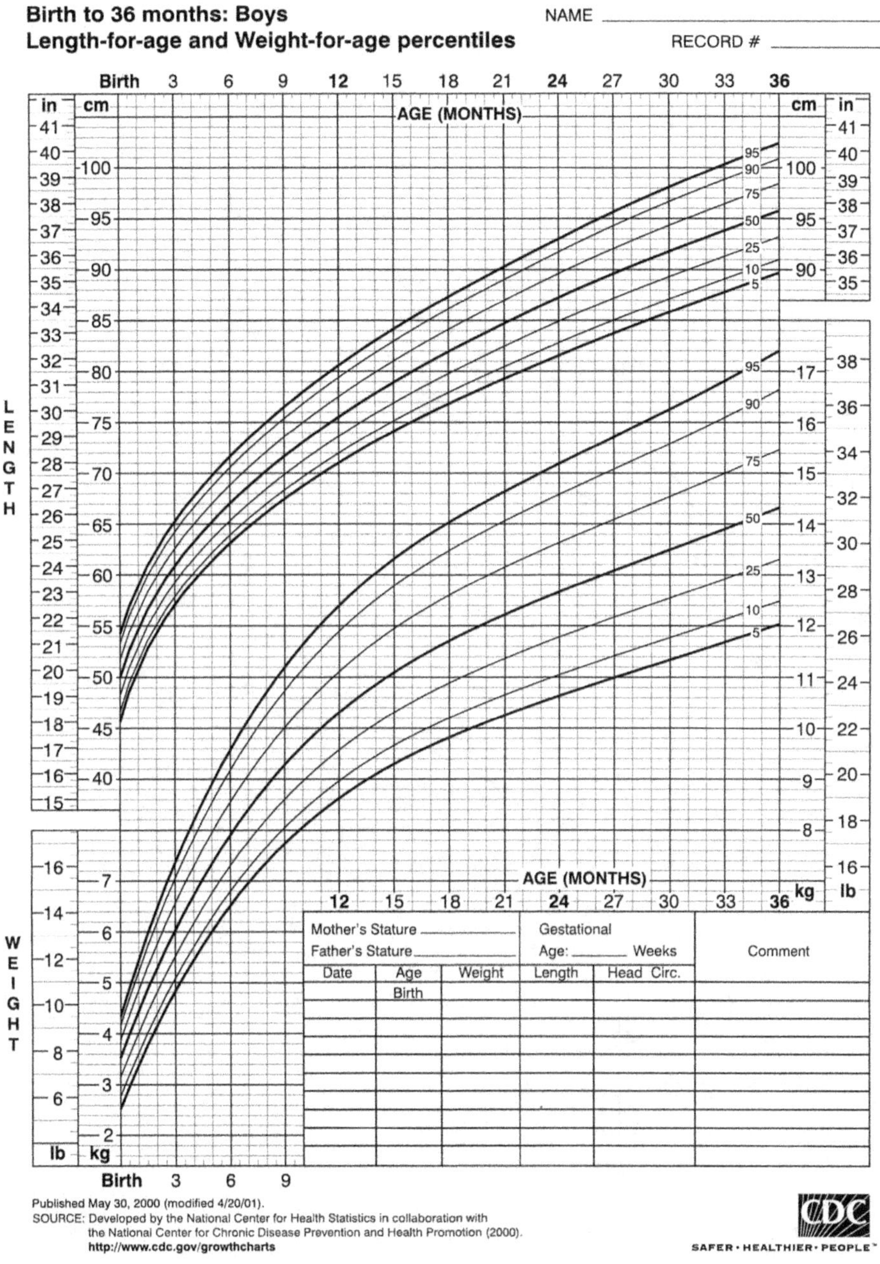
Birth to 36 months: Boys
Length-for-age and Weight-for-age percentiles
NAME
RECORD #
Birth 3 6 9 12 15 18 21 24 27 30 33 36
AGE (MONTHS)
in
cm
LENGTH
WEIGHT
kg
lb
95
90
75
50
25
10
5
Mother's Stature
Father's Stature
Gestational Age: Weeks
Comment
Date
Age
Weight
Length
Head Circ.
Birth
Published May 30, 2000 (modified 4/20/01).
SOURCE: Developed by the National Center for Health Statistics in collaboration with the National Center for Chronic Disease Prevention and Health Promotion (2000).
http://www.cdc.gov/growthcharts
CDC
SAFER · HEALTHIER · PEOPLE

FIGURE 2.1

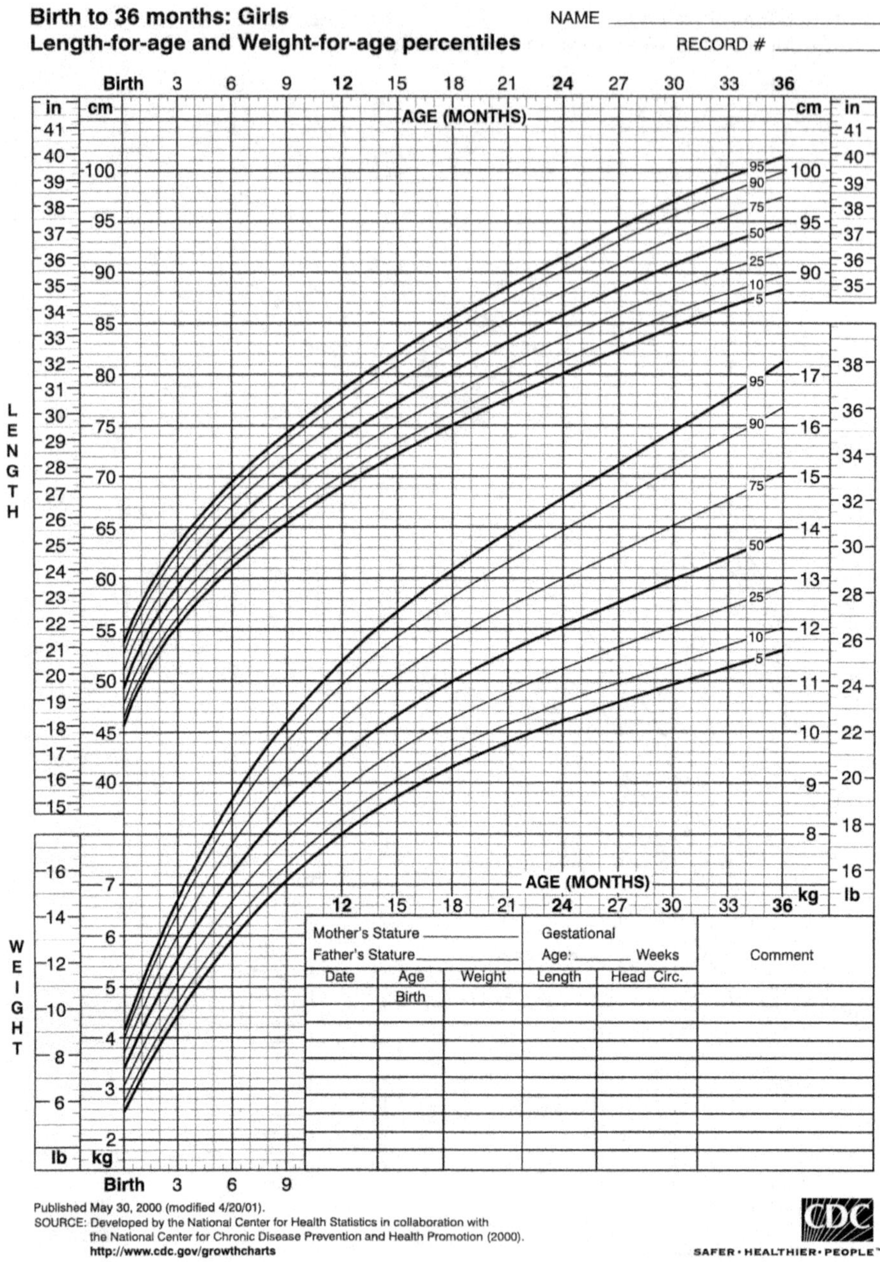

Birth to 36 months: Girls
Length-for-age and Weight-for-age percentiles
NAME
RECORD #
AGE (MONTHS)
LENGTH
WEIGHT
Mother's Stature
Father's Stature
Gestational Age: Weeks
Comment
Date
Age
Birth
Weight
Length
Head Circ.
Published May 30, 2000 (modified 4/20/01).
SOURCE: Developed by the National Center for Health Statistics in collaboration with the National Center for Chronic Disease Prevention and Health Promotion (2000).
http://www.cdc.gov/growthcharts
CDC
SAFER · HEALTHIER · PEOPLE

FIGURE 2.2

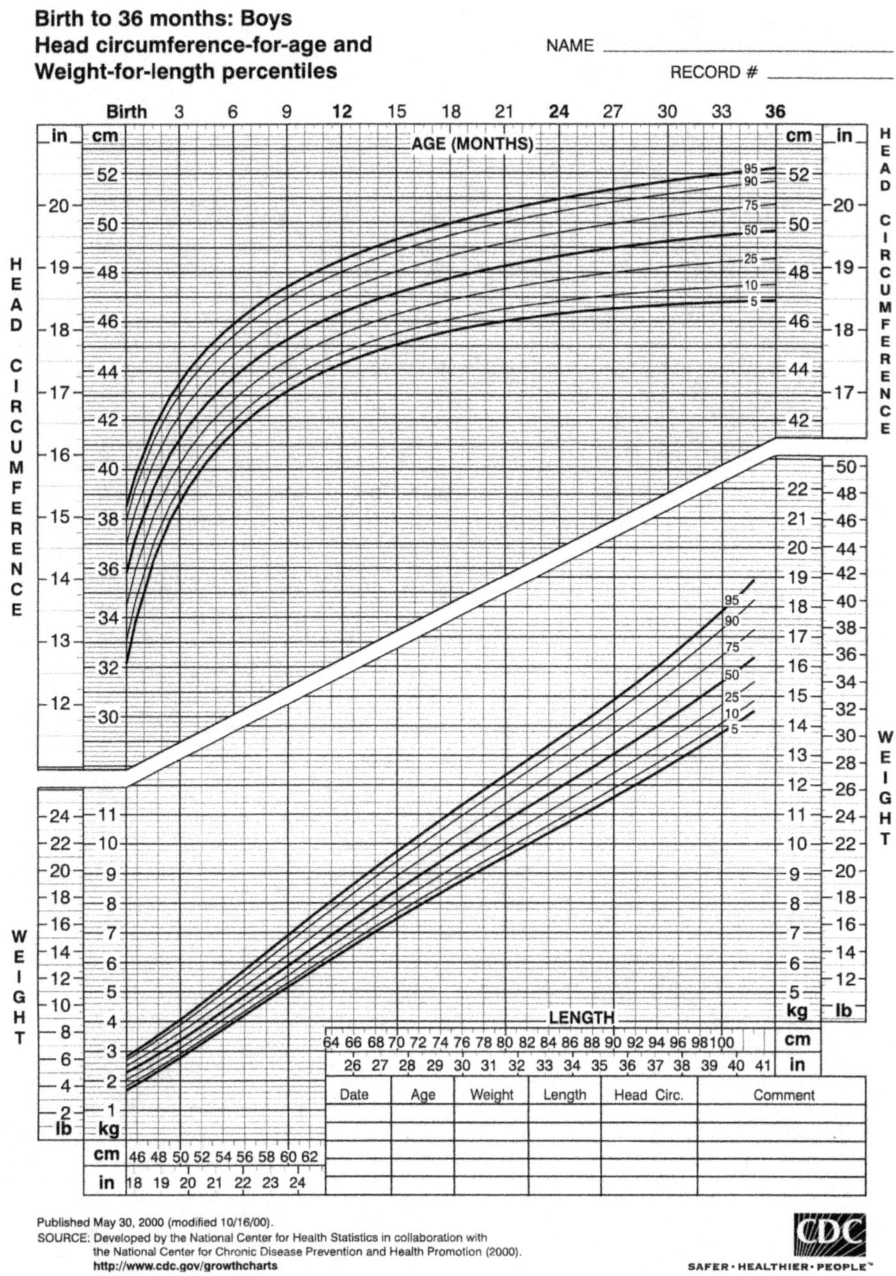
Birth to 36 months: Boys
Head circumference-for-age and
Weight-for-length percentiles
NAME
RECORD #
Birth 3 6 9 12 15 18 21 24 27 30 33 36
AGE (MONTHS)
in cm
HEAD CIRCUMFERENCE
WEIGHT
95 90 75 50 25 10 5
LENGTH
cm 46 48 50 52 54 56 58 60 62 64 66 68 70 72 74 76 78 80 82 84 86 88 90 92 94 96 98 100
in 18 19 20 21 22 23 24 25 26 27 28 29 30 31 32 33 34 35 36 37 38 39 40 41
kg lb
Date
Age
Weight
Length
Head Circ.
Comment
Published May 30, 2000 (modified 10/16/00).
SOURCE: Developed by the National Center for Health Statistics in collaboration with
the National Center for Chronic Disease Prevention and Health Promotion (2000).
http://www.cdc.gov/growthcharts
CDC
SAFER · HEALTHIER · PEOPLE™

FIGURE 2.3

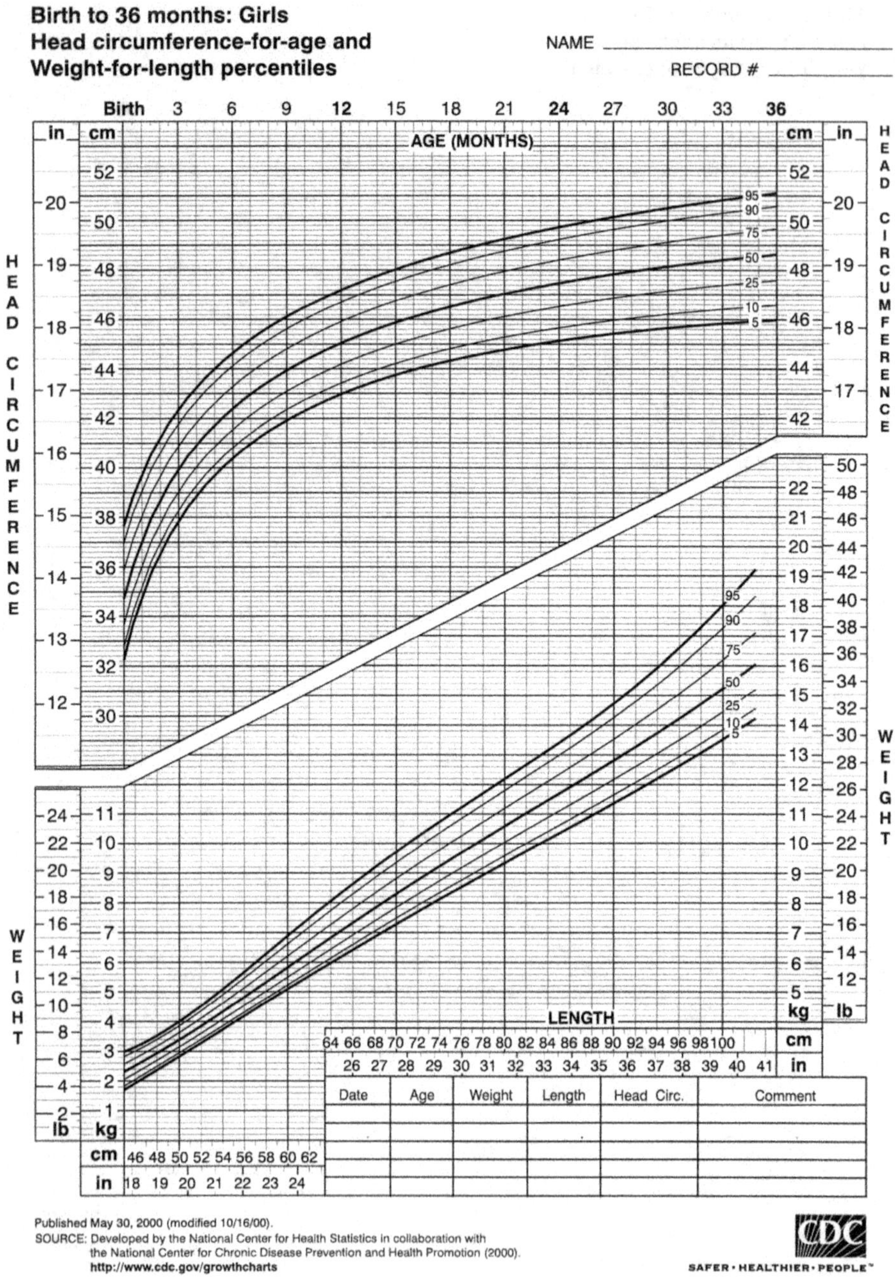
Birth to 36 months: Girls
Head circumference-for-age and
Weight-for-length percentiles
NAME
RECORD #
Birth 3 6 9 12 15 18 21 24 27 30 33 36
AGE (MONTHS)
HEAD CIRCUMFERENCE
in
cm
95
90
75
50
25
10
5
WEIGHT
LENGTH
cm 46 48 50 52 54 56 58 60 62
in 18 19 20 21 22 23 24
64 66 68 70 72 74 76 78 80 82 84 86 88 90 92 94 96 98 100 cm
26 27 28 29 30 31 32 33 34 35 36 37 38 39 40 41 in
kg
lb
Date
Age
Weight
Length
Head Circ.
Comment
Published May 30, 2000 (modified 10/16/00).
SOURCE: Developed by the National Center for Health Statistics in collaboration with
the National Center for Chronic Disease Prevention and Health Promotion (2000).
http://www.cdc.gov/growthcharts
CDC
SAFER · HEALTHIER · PEOPLE™

FIGURE 2.4

2.4.3 Developmental Milestones

Developmental milestones are specific tasks that children should be able to do by certain ages. Knowledge of these milestones and the approximate age at which infants typically are able to do them may be crucial in an infant death investigation. Investigators should take into account, however, that infants develop at their own pace and that the age at which an infant is expected to reach certain milestones is based on the infant's gestational age not their birth date. However, most infants will reach milestones at similar ages.

There are five areas of development in which milestones are reached. The five areas include gross motor skills, fine motor skills, language skills, cognitive skills, and social skills:

- *Gross motor skills* are skills or tasks associated with the ability to control large muscles, such as the arms, legs, and torso, to be able to perform bigger movements, such as crawling or walking.
- *Fine motor skills* are skills or tasks associated with the ability to control small muscles, such as the hands and fingers, to perform smaller more precise movements, such as grasping an object or picking up a small object with the thumb and first finger.
- *Language skills* are skills or tasks associated with the ability to communicate through speaking and the ability to understand others who are speaking.
- *Cognitive skills* are skills or tasks associated with the ability to think, reason, remember, and problem solve.
- *Social skills* are those skills or tasks associated with interacting with others and with the environment, such as the ability to smile and laugh.

Although a general understanding of all developmental areas is helpful to an infant death investigation, two areas, gross and fine motor skill development, may be critical. The investigator should determine what the infant was physically able to do. Knowing if the infant was able to lift its head, roll over, crawl, or walk as well as if the infant was able to grab and pick up small items may be extremely important to the case. This knowledge allows the MDI to identify safety issues in the infant's environment that may have contributed to the death as well as the credibility or reliability of information provided by caregivers and witnesses.

Case Example 2.3 A mother reported she placed her 2-month-old infant on his back to sleep. She reported that she found the infant deceased a few hours later and that the infant was found lying on his stomach. Investigators knowledgeable about gross motor skills of 2-month-old infants will recognize that an infant that age is not able to roll over from its back to its stomach. The investigator must clarify the mother's statement, try to determine if another caregiver may have turned the infant over, or verify from other sources that the infant was advanced in his development and able to roll over.

2.4.4 Age-Specific Milestones

As children get older, language, social, and cognitive developmental milestones will be more important; however, for children under the age of 1 year, the physical milestones are the skills and tasks that MDIs should be most familiar with. Developmental milestones usually occur within an age range. A task that is listed for a 6-month old may be reached by some 5-month olds and others may not reach the same milestone until they are 7 months old. A more detailed list of developmental milestones and the age range in which they are usually reached can be found on the Denver II. The Denver II was formally known as the DDST (Denver Developmental Screening Test) and is referred to by some health professionals as the DDST-II. The Denver II is a chart on which evaluators track developmental milestones to identify developmental delays.[7] This chart may be located in an infant's medical record. In some cases, investigators may want to fill out the chart after the death of an infant to determine if the infant may have had any developmental delays that were not picked up by health care personnel or in cases where the infant did not receive medical follow-up after birth. Investigators should have a general understanding of developmental milestones, screening methods, and where to seek additional resources if there are concerns during an investigation.

A month-by-month list of age-specific gross and fine motor skill developmental milestones are listed in Table 2.1 for infants 1 to 12 months of age. Investigators should have a general understanding of the age ranges by which milestones may be reached; however, all infants are different and some will be more advanced than others. During an investigation, investigators should be aware of developmental milestones and when milestones are reached. If inconsistency or concerns arise, the investigator should follow up on those concerns, clarify information received, and try to validate information obtained with other witnesses, the infant's health care providers, and the infant's medical record. Children's risk for injuries and accidents increases as does their ability to become more mobile; however, their risk of accidental deaths, due to overlying or suffocation, may be greater when they are less mobile.

2.4.5 Immunizations and Vaccines

During infant death investigations, a review of the infant's medical record would not be complete without reviewing the infant's immunization and vaccine record. Parents or caregivers should be asked to provide information regarding the infant's immunization history during interviews and the investigator should obtain a copy of the immunization record for review and comparison. As mentioned earlier, NAME recommends that the immunization record be gathered for the investigation to be complete. Depending on the jurisdiction, a copy of the immunization record should either be provided to the forensic pathologist or the MDI should relay information about the record to the pathologist. For the latter to be accurate, MDIs must have knowledge regarding the immunizations that should be given to infants and the recommended time frame in which they should be given. It is not enough for investigators to ask caregivers, "Are the infant's immunizations up to date?" Investigators must take the next step and obtain the immunization record to verify whether immunizations are, or are not, up to date based on recommended guidelines.

Guidelines for childhood immunizations are developed and published by the CDC National Immunization Program. Recommendations regarding immunizations are

TABLE 2.1
Gross and Fine Motor Developmental Milestones: 1 to 12 Months of Age

Infant's Age (months)	Gross and Fine Motor Skills Developmental Milestones
1	Startles at loud noises
	Keeps hands in a tight fist
	Able to bring hands up to face (scratches)
	Lifts head slightly when lying on stomach
2	Able to move head from side to side while on stomach
	When pulled to a sitting position has head lag, unable to keep head completely straight
	Unable to keep head steady when held upright
3	Able to open and shut hands
	Able to grasp an object placed in their hand, however, will not spontaneously reach for it (i.e., rattle)
	Able to lift head and chest when lying on stomach
	Maintains good head control when help upright
	Wiggles and kicks legs
4	Plays with hands
	Lifts head 90 degrees when on stomach
	Demonstrates very little head lag when pulled to a sitting position
	When propped up or supported from the back may be able to maintain a sitting position
	May be able to roll from their stomach to their back
5	Extends arms and legs
	Reaches for objects
	Able to fully lift head and shoulders off the ground when lying on stomach
	Able to sit in a tripod position
	Bears some weight on legs when held in a standing position
6	Picks up objects
	Brings objects to their mouth at will
	Holds head up and looks around
	Able to roll from their back to their stomach
7	Reaches for objects using a raking motion with one hand
	Able to transfer an object from one hand to the other
	May be able to sit alone
	Supports all of their weight when held upright
8	Beginning to use pincer grasp (thumb-finger grasp)
	Sits steadily
	May begin to crawl or scoot
	May be able to stand while holding on to something
9	Able to hold a cup with two hands, does not have the fine motor skills to easily drink its contents
	Crawling or scooting forward established
	Begins to pull self up to a standing position
	May walk or "cruise" while holding on to furniture

continued

TABLE 2.1 (continued)
Gross and Fine Motor Developmental Milestones: 1 to 12 Months of Age

Infant's Age (months)	Gross and Fine Motor Skills Developmental Milestones
10	Established pincer grasp
	Able to stand while holding on to furniture
	May stand alone for a few seconds
11	May begin to use spoon
	Stands alone
12	Able to stoop while standing and grasping an item
	Cruises easily around holding on to furniture
	Takes beginning steps toward walking alone

made and then approved by the Advisory Committee on Immunization Practices, the American Academy of Pediatrics, and the American Academy of Family Physicians. The recommendations are updated yearly and can be viewed and downloaded from the National Immunization Program Web site at http://www.cdc.gov/nip.[8,9] MDIs should become familiar with recommended guidelines to be able to determine if the infant received immunizations during the suggested time frame. If the infant has not received the recommended immunizations, the investigator should determine why the immunizations were not given. There are many reasons why immunizations may not have been given during the recommended time frame: the infant may have a chronic medical condition which affects their immune system; the infant was noted to be sick at the doctor's appointment when the immunization was scheduled to be given and as a result the immunization was postponed; the caregiver missed scheduled appointments for immunizations; or the caregiver may have refused to allow the child to receive the immunizations. Regardless of the reason for the delay, investigators may need to determine if the delay or the reason for the delay contributed to the infant's death.

Immunizations that were administered shortly prior to an infant's death are important to investigators and the forensic pathologist. Documentation regarding the immunization given, including the type, date, and time along with any significant side effects should be provided to the forensic pathologist and reported to the Vaccine Adverse Event Reporting System (VAERS). The Food and Drug Administration (FDA) and the CDC established VAERS to monitor the safety of vaccines.[10] The VAERS report form is available online at the VAERS Web site at http://vaers.hhs.gov.

The National Childhood Vaccine Injury Act of 1986 requires that health care providers report any adverse event after a vaccination that occurred within a specified period and is listed on the Reportable Events Table of VAERS. Adverse events are health-related side effects that occur after an immunization is administered that may or may not be related to the vaccine. MDIs should report infant deaths that occur within a few days of receiving vaccinations, even if they are unsure whether the vaccine contributed to the death.

After a death is reported to VAERS, a clinical research team follows up and requests a copy of medical records and the autopsy report. According to the CDC, the majority of deaths that occur following vaccination administration are classified as sudden infant death syndrome (SIDS) after autopsy and investigation. Their analysis determined that there is no relationship between SIDS and vaccines. This finding was partly because there was a decrease in deaths reported to VAERS that parallels the overall decrease in SIDS in the U.S. population. What may not have been considered in their analysis was the increased number of undetermined causes of infant deaths that occurred during that same time frame. According to Brotherton et al., numerous studies have concluded that there is no relationship between routine childhood vaccinations and SIDS.[11] The relationship to other SUIDs may be less known. As part of a complete and thorough investigation, however, MDIs should report infant deaths that occur within a few days of vaccine administration and provide that information to the forensic pathologist to ensure that all possible causes or contributors to the death are documented and analyzed.[12]

2.5 SUMMARY

MDIs with knowledge in maternal and infant health are better able to thoroughly and completely investigate an infant's death. This knowledge allows them to recognize normal and abnormal findings as they are reported by family members and witnesses, observed on the body and at the incident location, and documented in the medical record. Investigators are able to identify inconsistencies that may be present. Without this knowledge, the inconsistencies and possible abnormal findings may go unnoticed and undocumented resulting in a cause and manner of death determination that may be inaccurate.

REFERENCES

1. Corey, T.S., Hanzlick, R., Howard, J., Nelson, C., and Krous, H., A Functional Approach to Sudden Unexplained Infant Deaths. Prepared by the NAME Ad Hoc Committee on Sudden Unexplained Infant Death. Approved by the NAME Board of Directors on October 14, 2005. http://www.thename.org.
2. Lucas, M.J., The role of vacuum extraction in modern obstetrics, *Clin. Obstet. Gynecol.*, 37, 794–805, 1994.
3. Putta, L.V. and Spencer, J.P., Assisted vaginal delivery using the vacuum extractor, *Am. Fam. Physician*, 62, 1316–1320, 2000.
4. Thorngren-Jerneck, K. and Herbst, A., Low 5-minute Apgar score: A population based register study of 1 million term births, *Obstet. Gynecol.*, 98 (1), 65–70, 2001.
5. Wong, D., Perry, S., and Hockenberry, M., *Maternal Child Nursing Care*, 2nd ed., Mosby, St. Louis, 2002, chap. 25.
6. Centers for Disease Control and Prevention, National Center for Health Statistics, CDC growth charts: United States, available at http://www.cdc.gov/growthcharts/ (accessed May 30, 2000).
7. Denver Developmental Materials, Inc., www.denverii.com (accessed July 2, 2006).

8. National Immunization Program, 2006 Childhood immunization schedule, available at http://www.cdc.gov/nip (accessed July 2, 2006).
9. Centers for Disease Control and Prevention, Recommended childhood and adolescent immunization schedule—United States, 2006, *Morbid. Mortal. Wkly. Rep.*, 54, Q1–Q4, 2005.
10. Vaccine Adverse Events Reporting System, http://vaers.hhs.gov (accessed July 2, 2006).
11. Brotherton, J.M., Hull, B.P., Hayde, A., Giddin, H.F., and Burgess, M.A., Probability of coincident vaccination in the 24 or 48 hours preceding sudden infant death syndrome in Australia, *Pediatrics,* 115 (6), e643–e646, 2005.
12. Centers for Disease Control and Prevention, Surveillance for safety after immunization: Vaccine adverse event reporting system (VAERS)—United States, *Morbid. Mortal. Wkly. Rep.,* 52, SS-1, 2003.

3 The Investigation Begins: Timing Is Everything

3.1 INTRODUCTION

Time is of the essence. This could not be truer than when investigating the circumstances of an infant's death. The way in which the investigation begins can greatly impact the outcome. Time delays in notifying the appropriate personnel; lack of agency polices, protocols, and guidelines; and poor communication among agencies can hinder an investigation, even before it begins. Infant death investigations that are preplanned, coordinated, and organized lay the foundation for a thorough and complete investigation. This foundation positively affects the remainder of the investigation ensuring that all agencies work together to ensure that the cause and manner of the infant's death is accurately determined.

3.2 A COMMON BEGINNING

When an infant is found unresponsive, family or caregivers usually respond in one of two ways: they activate the emergency response system by calling 9-1-1; or they transport the infant, in a private vehicle, to an emergency room. If they call 9-1-1, emergency dispatchers will dispatch response personnel based on the information that they receive from the caller. In some situations, emergency dispatchers may only dispatch emergency medical services (EMS); in other situations, they may dispatch EMS, fire, and law enforcement personnel.

Upon EMS's arrival to the incident location and after assessing the infant, EMS will proceed in one of three ways: (1) If on arrival they determine that the infant is irreversibly dead, they will not initiate resuscitative efforts, will document that the infant is deceased, and leave the infant's body on scene with law enforcement personnel. (2) If upon their arrival, they believe that there is a chance that the infant might be resuscitated, they will initiate resuscitative efforts. (3) They may transport the infant to the nearest emergency room or, if directed by their medical director or another physician, may terminate resuscitative efforts while on scene. The third scenario is much less common. Hall et al.[1] determined that paramedics are relatively uncomfortable with the concept of terminating resuscitation efforts in children in the prehospital setting.

For cases in which the infant is pronounced dead on scene, law enforcement, or in some jurisdictions EMS, will notify either the medical examiner's (ME) or coroner's office of the death. A medicolegal death investigator (MDI) will either respond to the incident location or authorize the body to be removed from the scene by a transportation service and taken either to an autopsy facility or to a funeral home.

For cases in which the infant is pronounced dead in an emergency room, hospital personnel will notify either the ME's or coroner's office of the death and a MDI will either respond to the hospital, respond to the incident location, or decide not to respond to either location, opting to have the infant's body either placed in the hospital morgue, transported to an autopsy facility, or to a funeral home.

The time delay from the moment an infant is pronounced dead to the moment the MDI is notified of the death may be as short as a few minutes or as long as a few hours. Once notified, another time delay occurs as the MDI determines a course of action, whether to respond to the hospital, the incident location, or neither. Regardless of the decision, there is another time delay as the MDI travels to that location. If the MDI responds immediately to the hospital, the incident location or scene is at risk of being altered if it is not secured by law enforcement. If the MDI decides to immediately respond to the scene, evidence on the infant may be lost and interviews with caregivers who responded to the hospital will be delayed. In cases in which the MDI opts not to respond immediately to either location, evidence from the scene and from the infant may be altered or lost forever.

The timeliness with which MDIs are notified of an infant's death, where they respond once notified, and the time that has lapsed between the notification and their arrival to that location can and will affect the investigation making it more difficult to determine the cause of death (COD) and manner of death (MOD). Recognizing that these time delays may negatively impact the investigation, investigative agencies should open the lines of communication within their jurisdiction to ensure prompt notification. Additionally, agencies should develop and implement polices and practices to decrease the likelihood that evidence may be altered or lost. They must think outside the box to initiate investigative techniques and approaches that may ensure that these delays do not occur and do not impact or impede the infant death investigations.

3.3 THINK OUTSIDE THE BOX

MDIs are stuck inside an investigative box as all deaths are typically investigated the same general way regardless of the decedent's age or the circumstances of the death. There are times, however, when investigators should consider implementing new approaches and protocols for deaths that are often complicated to investigate: infant deaths are one such category.

There are a number of ways infant death investigations differ from others, and those differences may greatly affect the outcome. When and by whom MDIs are notified, whether MDIs respond to the hospital or incident location, and their roles once they arrive are important considerations during infant death investigations that may impact the outcome. The organization of the initial interview with caregivers, the inclusion of a doll reenactment, and the addition of an investigative child death review are all approaches that should be considered that will also impact the outcome. Many times, new techniques are not utilized because "that's the way they have always been investigated" or "we don't do it that way." Infant deaths can and should be thoroughly and completely investigated in all jurisdictions if agencies will think

BOX 3.1
An Exercise in Thought

We have all heard the phrase, think outside the box, but what does it actually mean? This exercise is a simple way to understand just what it means to think outside the box. When MDIs think outside the box, the box goes away. Draw the box of nine dots depicted below on a scrap of paper. The goal is to connect all of the dots using four straight lines.

- Position a pencil on one of the dots, and do not allow the pencil to come off the paper. Do not pick up the pencil and start from another place in the box. It must be a continuous flow of writing.
- Think outside the box.
- The answer is located at the end of the chapter.

outside their investigative boxes. Some of these approaches will be discussed in this chapter, while others will be found elsewhere throughout the book. A visual concept was developed to help others think outside the box. The exercise, located in Box 3.1, may assist investigators in understanding what it means to think outside the box. The answer is located at the end of the chapter in Box 3.2.

3.4 ADVANCED NOTIFICATION

As previously discussed, the timeliness with which MDIs are notified of an infant's death can affect the investigation. Recognizing the effect of delayed notification, some local and county jurisdictions have developed close working relationships between EMS communications departments and investigators from the ME's or coroner's office. These jurisdictions developed and implemented a communications protocol in which dispatchers notify the on-call MDI of emergency 9-1-1 calls involving children with life-threatening injuries. Infants who are found unresponsive, apneic, or pulseless are included in that category.

Infant death investigations in these jurisdictions begin the moment the investigator is notified by dispatchers of an emergency. This courtesy call or page may be sent while EMS personnel are en route to the incident location or once they have left the scene and are en route to a hospital. This early notification allows the MDI to prepare and respond quickly should death be confirmed on the scene or at an emergency room. Many emergency rooms are extremely busy and hospital personnel may be delayed in notifying the appropriate agency when a death has occurred. If the death investigator has been given a courtesy call or page by EMS dispatch personnel, this time delay can often be reduced, and many times eliminated, allowing the investigation to proceed sooner.

Prior to initiating any new technique or protocol, investigators should be able to explain and justify the change. Changes in protocol and policy should only be made when there is evidence to support the change. It is also easier to change policies and practices and gain the support of other agencies if the reasons for the changes can be justified. Concerning early notification, research suggests that the survival rates of children who experience an out-of-hospital cardiac or respiratory arrest are extremely poor.[2–8] In a study out of California, Young et al. found that only 8.6% of children who suffered an out-of-hospital cardiac arrest survived and were discharged from the hospital.[2] Another study completed in Singapore reported that only 4.6% of children survived and were discharged from a hospital following an out-of-hospital cardiac arrest.[3] A third study found that only 33 out of 300 children (11%) who suffered an out-of-hospital cardiac arrest had a return of spontaneous circulation after resuscitative efforts were initiated. Of those, however, only six children survived to be discharged from the hospital (2%), and that five of the six children had significant neurological problems.[4]

It is evident that the survival rate is dismally low for infants and children who suffer some type of life-threatening trauma or injury including cardiac or respiratory arrest or in which the infant or child is found unresponsive requiring emergency resuscitative efforts. With that knowledge, investigators can decrease time delays that occur in infant death investigations by working with communications personnel to provide advanced notification of potential infant and child deaths. The time that lapses between the time the 9-1-1 call is placed, the length of time it takes EMS to arrive on scene, assess and initiate emergency resuscitative efforts, and transport the infant to an emergency room is tremendously variable. Additionally, the amount of time hospital personnel continue emergency treatment prior to pronouncing the death, plus the time lapse before the MDI is notified of the death may be as short as a few minutes or as long as a few hours. The time delay can be greatly reduced if investigators receive one courtesy call and then act on that call. During the time lapse, investigators can be in transit to the scene or hospital, further reducing time delays. Investigators should not consider it a nuisance to be paged or called prior to a death being pronounced, instead they should view it as an opportunity to more thoroughly, completely, and quickly investigate the death. The number of infant deaths that occur each year is relatively low compared to the total number of deaths that investigators respond to each year. Therefore, the number of infant deaths that occur in each jurisdiction is also relatively low. Notifying investigators that an infant or child is in full arrest should not be much of an inconvenience or burden to investigators or their agencies. This early notification may actually be an asset to investigators when investigating these complicated deaths.

Case Example 3.1 This communications system has been implemented in Charleston County, S.C. EMS dispatch personnel, text page the on-call coroner after a call is received about an infant or child whose condition is life-threatening. The following information is provided in the text page: the age of the child, the address at which the child was found, and the name of the hospital to which the child is being transported or was pronounced dead on scene. The coroner then places a phone call to the EMS dispatch center, notifies dispatchers that the page has been received, and inquires as to any change in the infant's status. Depending on the information received, the coroner will either call the emergency room to check on the infant's status, begin to respond to the hospital, or begin to respond to the scene. The coroner will notify the back-up on-call coroner of the infant's status and will initiate a double-team approach for infant death investigations, which will be discussed in detail later in this chapter.

3.5 FOLLOWING DEATH NOTIFICATION

In jurisdictions where investigators are not provided a courtesy call notifying them of an infant or child in distress, the MDI will usually be notified of the death by phone. If the death occurred on scene, notification may be made by law enforcement. If the child died in a hospital, a hospital representative, often the charge nurse or nursing supervisor, will call.

Once the MDI receives notification, the MDI's immediate role is to obtain information, provide instructions, and communicate with other involved professional personnel as noted in Table 3.1. Investigators should first obtain demographic data and basic information regarding the circumstances by which the infant arrived at the hospital. Second, information and instruction may need to be provided to the agency representative notifying the investigator of the death. Finally, the MDI should communicate with investigative personnel, hospital personnel, and any additional involved professionals to initiate and organize this infant death investigation.

3.5.1 DEMOGRAPHIC DATA AND BASIC CASE INFORMATION

Demographic data, including information about the caller, the infant, specific locations, and other basic case information, should be acquired immediately upon receiving notification of the infant death and is outlined in Table 3.2. Investigators should document the name, title, and agency of the person providing the notification as well as the date and time of the notification. The name, age, and date of birth of the infant; the current location of the deceased; the infant's home address; and the

TABLE 3.1
Immediate Role of MDIs Following Notification of Death

Immediate Role of MDI When Notified of an Infant Death
• Obtain demographic data and basic case information
• Provide information and instruction to notifying agency
• Communicate with investigative agencies, hospital personnel, and additional MDIs

TABLE 3.2
Demographic and Basic Case Information

Demographic and Basic Case Information to Be Immediately Obtained When Notified of Death

- Name and title of the individual notifying the MDI of the death
- Name and contact information for the agency that individual represents
- Date and time of the notification
- The infant's name, age, and date of birth
- The infant's current location (i.e., emergency room, scene)
- The infant's home address
- The incident location at which the infant became unresponsive
- The mode of arrival by which the infant arrived at the hospital (i.e., private vehicle vs. ambulance)
- Location of caregivers or witnesses (i.e., remained on scene or at hospital)

incident location address should be documented. The incident location is often the location from which the 9-1-1 call was made or to which EMS personnel responded. The incident location may be unknown by hospital personnel. If that is the case, investigators should contact EMS dispatch directly to gather that information. Additionally, the MDI should determine which law enforcement agency has jurisdiction over the incident location.

Basic case information, including the mode by which the infant arrived at the hospital, should be obtained. The arrival mode, whether by ambulance or private vehicle, may be important during the investigation. If the infant arrived in a private vehicle, it will be extremely important for the MDI to respond quickly once notified by hospital personnel of the death. In these scenarios, investigators do not have the ability to gather information from emergency response personnel regarding the condition of the infant or the incident location. Investigators should determine the reason that caregivers transported the infant themselves to the emergency room as opposed to activating the emergency response system. The answer may be simple; for example, the infant may have become distressed or unresponsive while in a vehicle or the caregivers may have been in a remote location without a phone, requiring them to personally drive the infant in search of medical assistance. The answer, however, may be complex and require further investigation. For example, a caregiver may not want professionals coming to their residence due to fear of discovery of illegal activities such as a methamphetamine laboratory. Regardless of the reason that caregivers personally transported the infant to a hospital, hospital staff and the MDI should ensure that they respond quickly to ensure that information is not lost at the incident location.

The investigator should also ascertain if caregivers or family members of the infant are currently present at the scene or hospital. Caregivers who are present should be advised that investigators will be responding and requested to remain at the scene or hospital until the investigators' arrival. If investigators are notified and they respond in a timely manner, there should not be a problem with caregivers waiting for a short period at either location.

3.5.2 Provide Information and Instruction

Not only must MDIs obtain information, they must also provide information and instruction, as needed, to ensure that the death is investigated properly. In an ideal world, MDIs will have established working relationships with hospital facilities and assisted in the development of policies related to deaths that occur in those facilities. This type of working relationship helps ensure that laws are followed and that the needs of the investigator and the investigation are considered. Investigations are smoother when hospital personnel are aware of investigators' needs and expectations. In cases where the facility may not be aware of the investigators' needs, information and instruction may need to be provided at the time of the death notification. This helps to ensure that evidence is not lost prior to the investigator's arrival at the hospital.

Hospital staff should be provided information about the proper way to handle an infant's body after death and the reasons for those guidelines. The deceased infant should not be cleaned nor should any medical devices be removed from the infant prior to the initial postmortem external assessment, which should be conducted by the MDI. Hospital personnel should be instructed not to discard any items until the investigator has had an opportunity to inspect and collect those items, as needed, to include diapers, suction contents, and tubes of blood that may have been drawn. The infant's personal effects to include clothing, jewelry, or other items should not be released to family until the items have been inspected and collected as dictated by the case.

Many hospitals have programs in which footprints, handprints, and locks of hair are taken from deceased infants in order to compile a memory book for the parents. These programs were initially designed to be used on obstetric units following stillbirths or deaths that occur shortly after birth. These are treasured memorials for parents. However, hospital staff should not initiate this program for infants who die suddenly and unexpectedly in an emergency room setting until after the MDI has had an opportunity to examine the body, or until the MDI authorizes hospital personnel to proceed with the memory book. In most jurisdictions, once the postmortem assessment is complete, hospital personnel can obtain the memory book items from the infant. There may be cases, however, in which the investigator determines that the items should not be obtained immediately; the items can be obtained by the MDI after the autopsy or by a representative from the funeral home chosen by the family.

Investigators may want to consider asking hospital staff to assign a chaplain or other individual to stay with the family at all times until the infant investigator arrives at the hospital. This request serves two purposes. First, the family is comforted by the presence of a caring professional who is willing and able to assist them during this time. Second, their continuous presence with the family is an investigational approach that prevents those persons who may be culpable for the infant's death an opportunity to discuss the situation with other witnesses. This prevents one witness from instructing another witness what to say and prevents them from agreeing on what information they should provide investigators who are en route to the hospital.

3.5.3 Communications

After obtaining information and providing information and instruction as needed, the death investigator should communicate with hospital personnel, other investigative agencies, and peers regarding the case to develop an organizational plan and ensure that all persons are working together to thoroughly investigate the infant's death. As a professional courtesy, investigators should provide hospital personnel with an estimated time of their arrival. Hospital personnel must make clinical decisions that affect the operation of the emergency room. Decisions, such as whether to leave the infant's body in the examination room where the infant was treated and subsequently pronounced dead, whether to move the infant's body to another examining room, or whether to move the infant's body to the hospital morgue, may need to be made. These decisions may be determined by the number of patients waiting to be treated, the number of staff present, and how a move will affect the operation of the emergency room and the treatment of other patients.

Investigators should also communicate with the law enforcement agency that has jurisdiction where the incident occurred. The MDI should ensure that this law enforcement agency is aware of the death and request that an investigator or detective from that agency respond to the hospital and that a uniform officer secure the scene if that has not already occurred. The MDI should obtain the name of the detective that will be responding to the hospital.

The MDI who received notification of the infant's death should also communicate with a peer, a MDI representing the same agency to ensure that time delays do not occur and that evidence is not lost or altered. This technique, the double-team approach to infant death investigations, if implemented, will require communication with an additional investigator to plan the investigation.

3.6 DOUBLE-TEAM APPROACH

Timely investigations are important in all death investigations to ensure thoroughness and completeness. As time passes, evidence is lost, witness accounts become blurred, and changes occur in the body. One way to accomplish a timely and thorough investigation is for investigators to implement a double-team approach for infant and child death investigations. There is an old adage, "Two heads are better than one," which basically means that when two people collaborate on a problem they have a better chance of solving the problem as their combined resources and abilities are more likely to produce a better result than if only one person were working alone.[9] Two death investigators working in tandem to investigate the circumstance of an infant's death are more able to quickly identify problems, red flags, and inconsistencies than investigators who are working alone.

This approach is a new concept for most ME, coroner, and law enforcement agencies and will require agencies to organize infant and child death investigations in a different way. This team approach, however, provides a more complete and timely investigation, ensuring that more information is acquired quickly and with less chance for loss of evidence. This approach may be beneficial in other types of death investigations as well, but has been found to be extremely valuable and efficient if used during infant and child death investigations.

The next two sections compare the current and most common investigative approach, using a single MDI, to that of the double-team approach, which uses two MDIs.

3.6.1 Single Investigator Approach

After being found unresponsive, most infants who die are transported to a local emergency room. In the majority of cases, death investigators are notified of the death by hospital personnel. These investigators may or may not immediately respond to the hospital to examine the body or to interview caregivers present there, and there does not seem to be any consistency in this regard. Some ME, coroner, and law enforcement agencies make it a priority to respond to the hospital while others do not. The same is true for the incident location; there is no consistency as to whether investigators respond to the incident location and even less consistency about when they respond.

In cases where the MDI responds to the hospital, it may be hours or sometimes days later, before they are able to visit the scene. By that time, the scene or incident location may have been altered. The lack of timeliness regarding the scene investigation may have negative consequences for the investigation as it is more difficult to recognize and identify inconsistencies. The longer the time delay between the postmortem assessment, interviews with witnesses, and the scene investigation, the greater risk information will be lost.

3.6.2 A New Approach

Instead of the above scenario, the double-team approach uses two MDIs who collaborate their efforts to investigate an infant's death. The goal of the double-team approach is for two MDIs to work independently at their respective locations, one at the hospital and one at the incident location, while maintaining communication with each other. Consistencies and inconsistencies in information gained from the infant assessment, persons present at the hospital, the scene investigation, and persons present at the scene are more likely to be quickly identified and, therefore, immediately addressed. Any concerns should be noted and accurately documented.

These MDIs should be from the same agency. They will respond to two separate locations and will have different responsibilities during the investigation. One investigator will be considered the "infant investigator" and the other the "scene investigator." Both investigators need to be able to interview, assess circumstances, photograph, and have knowledge of infant growth and development, because both will use all of these skills during their independent investigations. For medicolegal death investigations to be thorough and complete, both of these persons should be investigators from a coroner's or ME's office and should be separate from law enforcement crime scene technicians who typically do not interview witnesses.

The role of each investigator will differ, yet both are vital to a thorough investigation. As each investigator conducts part of the investigation, it is crucial that the two investigators communicate with each other. They should discuss their findings and develop a plan for the remainder of the investigation prior to leaving their respective locations. For cases in which the infant is not transported to the hospital but pronounced dead at the incident location, the on-call investigator may determine that a double-team approach may still be beneficial. In some cases where there are many witnesses at a scene, it may be beneficial for two MDIs to collaborate on the case and both respond to the incident location. In some small jurisdictions, there may be limited personnel who are able to respond to an infant's death; as a result, agencies may want to consider contracting with a medicolegal investigator who has medical or nursing experience to respond and assist with infant and child death investigations.

3.6.3 How It Works

When an infant death is reported to the appropriate agency, the MDI on-call should immediately determine the location of the infant. If the infant was pronounced dead in an emergency room, then the on-call investigator should determine the address of the incident location and notify a back-up investigator to initiate the double-team approach. These two investigators must communicate with one another to determine who should respond to which location. It is recommended that each should respond to the location to which they are closest to in order to decrease further time delays. If there is not a significant difference in distance, it is recommended that the on-call investigator respond to the emergency room as the infant investigator and the back-up investigator respond to the incident location as the scene investigator.

The initial on-call MDI will be the primary investigator for the infant death investigation and will be responsible for the other aspects of the case following the immediate investigations that occur at the hospital and scene. The primary investigator will be responsible for ensuring that information is provided to the forensic pathologist; that all medical, social service, and criminal records are obtained; and that the investigative child death review is organized and implemented along with other responsibilities as dictated by the case. It will be necessary for the second investigator to attend the investigative child death review and provide information and insight to the primary investigator as may be needed.

3.6.4 Infant Investigator: Roles and Responsibilities

The roles and responsibilities of the infant investigator, as listed in Table 3.3, are paramount to the infant death investigation. The information that will be gathered by the infant investigator and the manner by which the information is obtained will impact the entire investigation. Each item of responsibility will provide different types of information that will ultimately help determine the COD and MOD. When the information that is obtained by the infant investigator is then compared and contrasted, in a timely fashion, to the information obtained by the scene investigator, other aspects of the investigation may be impacted.

The order information will be obtained by the infant investigators during their investigation at the hospital will be dictated by the specific characteristics of each case. A recommended format is provided; however, investigators must be flexible

TABLE 3.3
Infant Investigator: Responsibilities

Infant Investigator: Responsibilities
• Interview all professional personnel present at the hospital who have information regarding the infant or circumstances of the death, including professional first responders (EMS, fire department, and law enforcement) who responded to the incident location and either assisted in the treatment or transportation of the infant and hospital personnel (physicians, nurses, social workers, chaplains, and hospital security) who may have knowledge regarding the infant or caregivers (Chapter 4).
• Ensure a strong investigational working relationship with law enforcement personnel who respond to the hospital.
• Complete the initial postmortem external assessment (Chapter 5).
• Conduct initial interviews with caregivers or witnesses present at the hospital (Chapter 7).
• Prepare primary witnesses for scene walk-through and doll reenactment (Chapter 8).
• Obtain permission from caregivers or witnesses to enter the scene or incident location, if indicated.
• Communicate findings with the scene investigator.
• Conduct clarification interview as needed after communicating with the scene investigator (Chapter 7).
• Begin to plan investigative child death review and communicate with appropriate persons as dictated by the case (Chapter 11).
• Arrange for transportation of the infant's remains to the forensic pathologist's office for autopsy and communicate with the forensic pathologist regarding circumstances surrounding the infant's death.

as there will be times when circumstances will not allow the recommended format to be followed. In those situations, investigators must use their professional judgment and determine the best course of action for the remainder of the investigation.

3.6.4.1 Infant Investigation: Recommended Format

Upon arrival at the hospital, the infant investigator should notify the emergency room charge nurse or nursing supervisor and determine if a detective from the law enforcement agency that will also be investigating the death has arrived. The investigator should also determine if professional first responders, such as EMS and fire personnel who were involved in the initial assessment, treatment, and transportation of the infant to the emergency room, are still present at the hospital. These emergency response personnel may be dispatched at any time to another emergency call; therefore, it is important for the infant investigator to interview them as soon as possible. Investigators who do not interview these professionals while they are present at the hospital may not get an opportunity to interview them until hours later. In those jurisdictions in which investigators respond quickly to the hospital, EMS personnel often remain at the hospital, before going back into service, in order to speak with the responding investigator and provide information regarding what they observed at the scene. There are times when emergency calls prohibit EMS personnel from remaining at the hospital; in those jurisdictions, however, the professional first responders will often contact the investigator once they are available.

Not only is it recommended that emergency response personnel be interviewed immediately in the event they are called to another case, but it is also often helpful to the investigator if they are interviewed prior to performing the postmortem external assessment and prior to interviewing caregivers that are present at the hospital. This allows the investigator to begin to form a mental picture of the circumstances that occurred from the vantage point of professional personnel who were at the incident location, observed the infant on scene, and may have interacted and, therefore, witnessed reactions of other persons present at that scene. The information provided by emergency response personnel may be extremely valuable during the initial interviews with caregivers. Discrepancies between the professional first responder's interviews and caregiver's interviews may be recognized and addressed immediately. The investigator may need to clarify the caregiver's statement or assess for additional discrepancies prior to departing the hospital.

The information that emergency service personnel provide should not be left out, discredited, or disregarded. Information provided by emergency personnel has often led MDIs down an investigative trail that was important to a case. EMS personnel have a vast array of experience and knowledge. They have often seen and experienced much more than MDIs realize and are a valuable resource, not just for medical information but for factual and subjective information as well.

In situations where the professional first responders have already departed the hospital, it may be necessary for the infant investigator to contact the dispatching agency and have them call the infant investigator as soon as possible. It is desirable that they call while the investigator is at the hospital, especially if the infant investigator has immediate concerns regarding the infant or information provided by caregivers. A comprehensive list of questions and information that the investigator should obtain from professional first responders is provided in Chapter 4.

Once the infant investigator has interviewed the emergency response personnel who are present at the hospital, the investigator should interview hospital personnel that provided resuscitative treatment to the infant and may have knowledge about the circumstances that brought the infant to the hospital. Usually this information can be obtained by interviewing the physician who treated and pronounced the infant dead, the charge nurse in the emergency room, and the staff nurse who was assigned to the care of the infant. These persons should have a general understanding of the circumstances that brought the infant to the emergency room as reported by caregivers. They should also be able to provide information about the medical treatment that was administered to the infant during resuscitative attempts.

Hospital personnel who cared for the infant and interacted with the family may be able to provide the investigator with subjective, as well as factual information. Hospital personnel may have overheard statements made by caregivers when they arrived at the hospital or statements made by caregivers after they were notified of the death. Hospital personnel may also be able to provide subjective information such as noting the smell of alcohol on caregivers or observing strained relationships between caregivers. Prior to departing the hospital, investigators should obtain a copy of the infant's emergency room medical record as well as a copy of the EMS run sheet if available. Both of these items will be discussed later.

After interviewing professional first responders and hospital personnel, the infant investigator should examine the remains of the deceased. The initial postmortem external assessment, which is covered in Chapter 5, should be completed prior to interviewing caregivers and witnesses. This external physical examination of the infant will provide information and perhaps raise additional questions that may need to be asked during caregiver and witness interviews. If physical findings, such as marks or injuries, are noted on the body, the investigator may be able to determine if the information that is being reported by witnesses correlates with those findings. It is important to note if caregivers and witnesses fail to mention old injuries that are found on the body. The more information available to the investigator prior to interviewing witnesses, the better. An informed and knowledgeable investigator is a much more efficient and thorough interviewer.

After assessing the body, the infant investigator should request that a hospital representative introduce them to the caregivers who are present at the hospital in preparation for conducting initial interviews with those caregivers. The art of interviewing caregivers and grieving family members as well as considerations that should be taken into account prior to conducting these interviews are discussed in detail in Chapter 7. Interviews with caregivers may be lengthy, and investigators must be prepared to spend as much time as necessary to ensure that complete initial interviews are conducted prior to their departure from the hospital.

After interviewing all caregivers and witnesses who are present at the hospital, the infant investigator should communicate with the scene investigator to compare their findings. The investigators should discuss what they learned and how their findings either differ or are corroborated. In cases in which the information obtained does not match, it may be necessary for the infant investigator to return to the caregivers and initiate a clarification interview to determine if a misunderstanding occurred or if inaccurate information was intentionally provided.

After the completion of the postmortem assessment and all interviews, the infant investigator should communicate with the law enforcement representative about the need for a scene walk-through and doll reenactment, which is discussed in Chapter 8. Plans for the remainder of the investigation, which includes the autopsy schedule, record review, and the investigative child death review (see Chapter 11), should also be discussed. After ensuring that all necessary information has been provided to all appropriate personnel, the infant investigator should communicate the postmortem and interview findings to the forensic pathologist and arrange for transportation of the infant's body to the autopsy facility.

3.6.5 Scene Investigator: Roles and Responsibilities

The roles and responsibilities of the scene investigator are listed in Table 3.4 and are just as crucial as those of the infant investigator. Information that is available at the scene or incident location may be lost or altered if an investigator does not respond immediately to that location to assess the infant's environment and interview professional persons and caregivers or witnesses who may have remained at the scene. In jurisdictions where the double-team approach is implemented and investigators respond quickly, caregivers, other witnesses, and law enforcement personnel are often at the scene, and the investigator is able to acquire information from each of them.

The ability of the scene investigator to enter the incident location will vary from jurisdiction to jurisdiction, based on the laws in those areas. Many states have statutes

TABLE 3.4
Scene Investigator: Responsibilities

Scene Investigator: Responsibilities

- Establish rapport with professional persons who are on scene and gather information. Work closely with law enforcement investigative personnel to develop a plan for investigating the infant death and determine if a search warrant is needed.
- Interview professional and nonprofessional first responders who are still present at the incident location (Chapter 4).
- Complete the infant death scene investigation (Chapter 6).
- Conduct initial interviews of witnesses or caregivers that are present on scene (Chapter 7).
- Complete scene walk-through and doll reenactments with primary witnesses present (Chapter 8).
- Communicate findings to the infant investigator.
- Conduct clarification interviews as needed after communicating with the infant investigator (Chapter 7).
- Begin to plan investigative child death review and communicate with appropriate persons as dictated by the case (Chapter 11).

that address the death investigator's right and ability to enter the incident location where a child died to investigate the circumstances surrounding that child's death. In some states, this applies to the incident location, even if the child was removed from that scene by professional responders and later died at another location, such as a hospital. Agencies should review their state statutes to determine the extent to which the scene investigator may enter the scene.

The scene investigator is also in a unique position to obtain permission from caregivers or witnesses that are present at the scene. These persons, if they are the legal owners or occupants will often provide MDIs access to the incident location to identify the potential cause of the infant's death. If the legal owners or occupants of the incident location responded to the hospital, it may be necessary for the infant investigator to obtain permission from them for investigators to enter the scene. If permission is not granted, investigators may need to obtain a search warrant and may consider this refusal a red flag.

After being notified by the on-call investigator that an infant death has occurred, the scene investigator should immediately respond to the incident location: the location where the infant was found unresponsive by caregivers and where emergency medical services personnel responded to assist. The scene investigator should request that a uniformed officer from the law enforcement agency within that jurisdiction also respond to the incident location, if it has not already been requested.

After arrival at the scene, the scene investigator must assess the situation and determine the best course of action for investigating this infant's death. A recommended format is provided; however, the scene investigator will need to be flexible as circumstances at the scene may dictate the order in which the investigation occurs. In jurisdictions where the double-team approach has been implemented and in which state statues provide a means to enter the incident location, law enforcement agencies will dispatch crime scene technicians to the location to process that scene. The scene investigator and crime scene technicians should work together to assess and process the scene (see Chapter 6).

3.6.5.1 Scene Investigation: Recommended Format

Upon arriving at the incident location, the scene investigator should introduce themselves to the professional personnel on scene; obtain their names, agencies, and professional titles; and begin to develop rapport with them. It should be determined which law enforcement agency and officer is in charge of the scene and who will be the contact person during the investigation. Communication between the MDI and the law enforcement investigative officer is a crucial component in all infant death investigations. It is important that both agencies have an understanding of the other's role and work together to ensure that the death is investigated in a concise, organized, and thorough manner.

Working with law enforcement, the scene investigator should establish a list of persons that were present when the infant was found, a list of persons who are currently on scene, and those persons that departed the scene. It is crucial to determine which persons currently at the scene were present when the incident occurred and which persons responded to the scene afterward. It is also critical to determine which persons were present during the incident but are no longer present at the scene. Those persons may have responded to the hospital, or they may have fled the scene and gone to another location.

Prior to entering the incident location, the scene investigator should interview all professional first responders who remain on scene and obtain their names, titles, and agency affiliation. The scene investigator should complete interviews with professional first responders such as EMS, fire department, and law enforcement soon after arriving on scene in the event they may be dispatched to another location. The professional first responders may be able to provide basic information about caregivers and witnesses who are on the scene, including their relationship to the infant and the type of information each may be able to provide. In particular, the scene investigator should identify whether or not the person who found the infant, or the last person to see the infant alive, is present at the scene; the first responders may have that information.

The scene investigator should determine if there were any nonprofessional first responders who arrived on scene. The scene investigator should interview these persons if they are still present at the incident location. These nonprofessionals may include neighbors or other bystanders who were not present for the incident but responded to calls for help or responded to the scene after seeing an ambulance. These persons may have heard screams and offered their assistance in the treatment of the infant, but are not professional responders.

In most incidents, it is possible for the scene investigator to obtain permission from the owner or occupant of the residence to enter the residence and complete the infant death scene investigation. However, if the investigator has not been given permission to enter the residence, it may be necessary to obtain a search warrant. Investigators should discuss this with the law enforcement officer on scene. If it is determined that a search warrant is needed, an officer should remain at the incident location until one is signed. It will be critical to the investigation to be able to investigate the death scene prior to its being disrupted or altered, whether intentionally or unintentionally.

The scene investigator, after receiving permission from the owner or occupant of the residence or via search warrant, will complete the infant death scene investigation and photodocumentation of the scene. This will be covered in Chapter 6. After completing the death scene investigation, the scene investigator will conduct the initial caregiver and witness interviews as covered in Chapter 7, and any doll reenactments and scene walk-throughs with those caregivers or witnesses as covered in Chapter 8.

Prior to departing the scene, the scene investigator must communicate with the infant investigator. These two MDIs will discuss each of their findings and determine if there are any discrepancies between the information or details that each obtained. If there are discrepancies, each investigator may need to complete a clarification interview (Chapter 7) to clarify information obtained initially or to establish whether there is missing information that may have been intentionally or unintentionally omitted. After all interviews are complete, the incident location or scene has been investigated, and the scene and infant investigators have communicated, the scene investigator should provide information to the other investigative personnel regarding the autopsy schedule and the investigative child death review.

Case Example 3.2 During the initial interview with an infant's caregiver at the hospital, it is reported that the infant slept in a crib each night. The caregiver reported she found the infant unresponsive in the crib. At the incident location, the scene investigator observed that the crib in the home was full of clothing and toys and appeared to be used as a catchall, making it improbable that the infant slept there. The scene investigator also observed a playpen that had an adult-sized pillow in the bottom that appeared to have a purge pattern. After receiving this information from the scene investigator, the infant investigator may want to immediately clarify the information received from the caregiver. It is possible that the infant slept in the playpen; however, the family referred to it as the "crib."

Case Example 3.3 At an emergency room, the infant investigator interviewed the mother of a 6-week-old baby who was found unresponsive by his mother. During the interview, the mother stated she placed her baby "on his back in a crib" around 0300. She awoke around 0700 to go to work and found the infant unresponsive. The mother stated the baby was "on his side" when she found him and that he was "blue." She reported that she screamed and that her mother, the baby's grandmother, came into the room and then called 9-1-1. At the scene, the scene investigator interviewed the baby's grandmother. The grandmother stated that she last saw her daughter and grandchild around 2300 in the living room. The grandmother then went to bed. At around 0700, she entered her daughter's room to awaken her so she could go to work. When she entered the room, she observed the baby in bed with her daughter, who was asleep and partially covering the baby. The scene investigator asked the grandmother to demonstrate during the doll reenactment the position she observed the baby and the mother. The information obtained from the grandmother was communicated to the infant investigator who then reinterviewed the mother again.

3.7 SUMMARY

The method by which infant death investigations begin and the approaches used by investigators will impact the investigations' outcomes. Infant deaths are complicated

BOX 3.2
Exercise in Thought: Answer

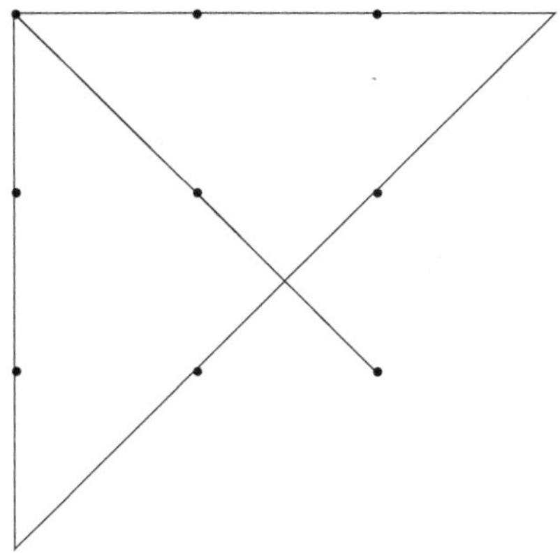

to investigate. As a result, investigators should think outside the box and utilize techniques and investigational approaches that may not be used for other types of deaths but are extremely effective when used during infant and child death investigations.

Advanced techniques and approaches, such as early notification of an infant or child in distress and the implementation of the double-team approach, are extremely effective in ensuring that information regarding the circumstances of the death are obtained and assessed in a timely fashion. Without early notification and the double-team approach, evidence may be lost, witness accounts may fade, and information and details may fall through the cracks. Changing our investigative perspective regarding these deaths can and will impact the way they are investigated and the accuracy of the COD and MOD determinations.

REFERENCES

1. Hall, W.L., Myers, J.H., Pepe, P.E., Larkin, G.L., Sirbaugh, P.E., and Persse, D.E., The perspective of paramedics about on-scene termination of resuscitation efforts for pediatric patients, *Resuscitation,* 60 (2), 175–187, 2004.
2. Young, K.D., Gausche-Hill, M., McClung, C.D., and Lewis, R.J., A prospective, population-based study of the epidemiology and outcome of out-of-hospital pediatric cardiopulmonary arrest, *Pediatrics,* 114 (1), 157–164, 2004.
3. Tham, L.P. and Chan, I., Paediatric out-of-hospital cardiac arrests: Epidemiology and outcome, *Singapore Med. J.*, 46 (6), 289–296, 2005.
4. Sirbaugh, P., Pepe, P., Shook, J., Kimball, K., Goldman, M., Ward, M., and Mann, D., A prospective, population-based study of the demographics, epidemiology, management, and outcome of out-of-hospital pediatric cardiopulmonary arrest, *Ann. Emerg. Med.,* 33 (2), 174–184, 1999.

5. Schindler, M.B., Bohn, D., Cox, P.N., McCrindle, B.W., Jarvis, A., Edmonds, J., and Barker, G., Outcome of out-of-hospital cardiac or respiratory arrest in children, *N. Engl. J. Med.,* 335 (20), 1473–1479, 1996.
6. Donoghue, A.J., Nadkarni, V., Berg, R.A., Osmond, M.H., Wells, G., Nesbitt, L., and Stiell, I.G., Out-of-hospital pediatric cardiac arrest: An epidemiologic review and assessment of current knowledge, *Ann. Emerg. Med.,* 46 (6), 512–522, 2005.
7. Young, K.D. and Seidel, J.S., Pediatric cardiopulmonary resuscitation: A collective review, *Ann. Emerg. Med.,* 33 (2), 195–205, 1999.
8. Gerein, R.B., Osmond, M.H., Stiell, I.G., Nesbitt, L.P., and Burns, S., What are the etiology and epidemiology of out-of-hospital pediatric cardiopulmonary arrest in Ontario, Canada? *Acad. Emerg. Med.,* 13 (6), 653–658, 2006.
9. Hirsch, E.D., Kett, J.F., and Trefil, J., *The New Dictionary of Cultural Literacy,* 3rd ed., Houghton Mifflin Company, Boston, 2002.

4 First Responders: Their Observations Are Important

4.1 INTRODUCTION

A thorough and complete investigation into the death of any infant will include a comprehensive review and detailed description of events that occurred from the moment the infant was found unresponsive up to the time the infant is pronounced dead and an investigator arrives at the hospital or scene. It is extremely important that investigators document the events that occurred during this significant period as valuable information; details and insight may be obtained from persons who first responded to the scene, attempted resuscitative efforts, or offered another form of assistance. Hospital personnel who provided care to the infant or family may be able to provide important pieces of information that investigators may miss if these professionals are not interviewed. The 9-1-1 call, which activates the emergency response system and puts all of these professionals in motion, is another crucial piece of evidence that should be reviewed during all infant death investigations as it may provide details about the infant's death that may not be revealed by any other source.

4.2 9-1-1 EMERGENCY CALLS

The 9-1-1 call is a vital and often overlooked piece of evidence. 9-1-1 calls are recorded by most jurisdictions and investigators should immediately seek to preserve those recordings. Information provided by a 9-1-1 caller, during an emergency, may reveal truths that may not be reported to investigators during an interview. Once the caller has had an opportunity to gain their composure, they may either unintentionally leave out details that should be disclosed or intentionally fail to disclose information they do not want known. Witnesses may not recall what they stated when they called 9-1-1 and often do not realize that their call was recorded.

Case Example 4.1 During the investigation of the death of a 3-month-old, the investigator suspected the death was the result of overlying and believed that the mother and infant had been sleeping in an adult bed. The mother denied doing so in all interviews and the doll reenactment. The investigator reviewed the 9-1-1 recording. The mother placed the call to 9-1-1 and stated, on the recording, that she and her baby were sleeping in the same bed.

A review of the 9-1-1 recording will help establish who was present at the time of the infant's death and may provide additional information about the death other than just the words spoken by the caller. Investigators should determine who placed the call to 9-1-1 and their relationship to the infant. Background noise on 9-1-1 recordings may also provide information about persons that were at the scene at the time of the incident that may not have been reported during interviews. The 9-1-1 recording is a piece of evidence that should not be overlooked as a means of determining who was present at the scene.

Case Example 4.2 Investigators had suspicions that a babysitter, who was caring for an infant that died in her care, was not being truthful regarding other persons who were present at the time of the infant's death. The babysitter stated that she was alone with the infant; however, on the 9-1-1 recording, two male voices were heard in the background and the caller acknowledged their presence on the recording.

To obtain a copy of a 9-1-1 recording, the investigator should contact the communications department for the emergency dispatch center that has jurisdiction over the incident location. In some jurisdictions, a subpoena may be needed to obtain a copy of the 9-1-1 call; in other jurisdictions, a subpoena may not be necessary. The difference is often related to the working relationships that have been established between the medical examiner's (ME) or coroner's office and the emergency communication department. Regardless of how it is obtained, the 9-1-1 recording should be reviewed during all infant and child death investigations. It is recommended that the recordings be reviewed as soon after the death as possible and be played during the investigative child death review.

4.3 FIRST RESPONDERS

First responders who arrive on scene to assist with the care and treatment of an infant that was found unresponsive or in distress may be professional first responders or nonprofessional first responders. *Professional first responders* (PFRs) are dispatched to an emergency after a 9-1-1 call has been made. They are trained in some type of emergency response and respond to the infant emergency in either a professional or volunteer capacity as fire, law enforcement, or emergency medical service (EMS) personnel.

Nonprofessional first responders (non-PFRs), sometimes referred to as good samaritans, are individuals who may not be trained in any type of emergency response, however, due to their proximity to the scene, respond and offer assistance. For example, these persons may be neighbors or bystanders who are not otherwise involved in the case, yet respond and try to offer their assistance.

Investigators should interview all PFRs and non-PFRs. Their observations of the infant, the scene, and other witnesses may be crucial to the investigation. These individuals may have valuable information that could impact the investigation and none of their observations or statements should be discounted. When responding to an emergency call, PFRs are continually assessing the situation for scene safety and the general welfare of all persons present. Non-PFRs, although not trained in emergency response, may be very observant and may be able to provide important and specific details about their observations.

4.3.1 Professional First Responders (PFRs)

After a 9-1-1 call is placed, emergency dispatchers assess the caller's complaint and dispatch the appropriate agencies and personnel to the incident location. Depending on the complaint, only one agency may be dispatched or multiple agencies may be dispatched. Investigators should determine which agencies were dispatched, the dispatch date and time, the arrival date and time, the names of all responding personnel, and each agency's report or case number.

As part of the investigation, all reports from PFRs and their agencies should be obtained and reviewed. Reports from professional responders contain demographic information about the patient and a description of the events that occurred. Emergency response personnel document factual information in a sequential format to include details about their assessment, observations, and actions. These reports rarely include subjective data, which may be valuable in an infant death investigation. EMS reports, for example, include demographic information, physical assessment findings of the patient, the treatments initiated, and the patient's final disposition. The report will often not contain subjective data or specific information that may be helpful to investigators. To obtain that information, investigators should ensure that PFRs are interviewed.

PFRs located in jurisdictions where there is a strong working relationship with the ME's or coroner's office often feel confident notifying investigators when they have specific concerns regarding an infant's death or have observed something they believe may be helpful or of interest to the investigation. These professionals have often witnessed events or heard pieces of information that may be crucial to the investigation; however, in some jurisdictions, they may not realize how vital the information they have may be to the investigation. If medicolegal death investigators (MDIs) also fail to recognize their important role and the value of the observations of emergency response personnel, the information may never be revealed. Investigators should always interview the PFRs who responded to the incident location or interacted with either the infant or the caregivers. The information they provide may change the direction of an investigation.

4.3.1.1 Interviewing PFRs

Through interviews, investigators may be able to obtain additional information that may not be documented in their formal reports. The emergency response professionals should be interviewed as soon after the death as possible to document their initial impressions, their observations of the scene and persons present on scene, as well as comments or statements overheard by caregivers or witnesses. There are general questions that should be asked of all PFRs as well as specific questions that may need to be directed toward specific individuals. PFRs have knowledge, training, and skills in different emergency response specialties that lend each to be more attuned to important yet different details or pieces of information. For example, EMS may be able to provide detailed information about the physical condition of the infant that the other PFRs may not have recognized and vice versa.

The initial impressions and observations when they arrived on scene are vital to the investigation and investigators should have a clear understanding of the scene circumstances when PFRs arrived. Critical to a complete and thorough investigation are a description of their initial observations, a description of the external and internal scene environment, their recall of persons present at the scene, the condition of the infant, and other abnormal or unusual observations. Their actions should also be documented to ensure that all information regarding the infant and scene are obtained. Investigators should use a combination of direct and open-ended questions, encouraging PFRs to provide as much information as they can recall about the scene, infant, and family. General interview questions that should be asked of PFRs are located in Table 4.1.

4.3.1.1.1 PFR Initial Observations

The PFRs initial observations, when they arrived on scene, may provide information about a witness's demeanor, a caregiver's reaction to finding the infant unresponsive, or the condition of the infant and incident location. For example, on arrival, a PFR noted that the infant's caregivers were located outside of the residence. The infant, however, was located inside the residence, alone and unresponsive. In another example, a PFR reported that on their arrival to the scene, the infant's father was at the street corner trying to help direct emergency personnel to the residence while the mother was inside the residence attempting cardiopulmonary resuscitation (CPR). The information provided in both of these scenarios is important and helps investigators form a mental picture of the events surrounding the infant's death.

4.3.1.1.2 Environmental Observations

The PFRs description of the scene environment is vital as the incident location may intentionally or unintentionally be altered during the time lapse after PFRs arrive on scene to the time investigators arrive on scene. Investigators should ask specific questions regarding the incident location in an effort to determine if the scene had been altered prior to their arrival. Incident location and scene descriptions may not be included in their formal reports and should therefore be addressed during interviews.

Case Example 4.3 The MDI arrived at the incident location and met with fire personnel who remained on scene. They reported that on their arrival, a large number of empty beer cans and liquor bottles as well as dirty ashtrays were located in several rooms; however, during the scene investigation, the investigator did not observe any beer cans or liquor bottles and clean ashtrays were located in the kitchen sink. The residence was cleaned after emergency personnel left the incident location by caregivers who did not respond to the hospital. The scene was not secured and, as a result, alterations were made. Caregivers may have either intentionally tried to clean the residence to rid any signs of drug or alcohol use or may have been cleaning the residence due to anxious energy not intentionally trying to hide anything. Either way, the information may not have been revealed had investigators not interviewed the PFRs about their observations of the scene environment.

TABLE 4.1
Interview Questions for PFRs

	Sample Interview Questions for All PFRs
Demographic Data	• Name, professional title, agency, and case or report number. • Dispatch date and time, arrival date and time. • Note date, time, and location of interview.
Initial Observations	• What did you observe when you arrived on scene? • When you arrived on scene was anyone trying to direct you to the incident location? • Did anyone meet you at the door when you arrived, if so whom?
Environment Observations	• Describe the external environment. • Describe the internal environment. • Describe the temperature inside the incident location. • Describe any unusual odors (drugs, gas, mold). • Observations of tobacco, alcohol, or drug paraphernalia. • Describe any insect or vermin activity. • Describe any animals (pets) observed at the scene.
Observations of Persons on Scene	• Describe the persons present on scene, including the number of males, females, and children, along with physical description of each (i.e., approximate age, race, physical characteristics). • Describe the actions or reactions of the persons present at the scene (e.g., crying, arguments, confrontations, stoic). • Describe any statements overheard.
Condition of Infant	• Describe the infant's location at the scene (i.e., inside or outside, which room [i.e., living room, bedroom, porch] and where in that room [i.e., crib, couch, floor]) • What position was the infant in (i.e., supine, prone, side)? • Was anyone caring for the infant when they arrived? If so, who and in what manner? (I.e., mother was holding baby in her arms; adult female was trying to perform CPR on the bed.) • Was anyone administering CPR? If so, who? • If CPR was being administered on PFR's arrival was it being done correctly? If not, describe technique. • Describe the clothing the infant was wearing. • Describe the infant's appearance (e.g., color, temperature, marks, bruises, secretions). • Describe items in the immediate vicinity of the infant (e.g., pillows, bedding, toys).
Actions of the PFR	• Describe the PFR's actions after arriving on the scene. • Did the PFR remove any items from the infant prior to the infant being transported to the hospital? If so, what items were removed and where were the items placed?
Additional Observations or Impressions	• Any other observations, intuitions, or concerns that the PFR may have in regard to the infant, caregivers, or scene.

On arrival, emergency response personnel may sense that something is amiss. Based on their experience and intuition, a PFR's gut reaction should be taken seriously as their skills and experience may tell them that something about the circumstances of the infant's death is concerning. PFRs may be able to provide information regarding identifiable observations as they report, for example, that the incident location was unusually hot or cold; they may note an unusual or recognizable smell or report hearing or seeing something out of the ordinary.

4.3.1.1.3 Observations of Persons on the Scene

Determining who was present at the incident location when the injury or death occurred is crucial in any death investigation. Accurate information about the number of people present, their names, relationship to the deceased, and their involvement in the case is vital to ensuring that all persons involved are identified and interviewed. PFRs should not be omitted when seeking this information. Although PFRs may not know the names, relationships, or roles of the persons present, they may be able to provide information about the number of people on scene as well as a physical description for each. The investigator may need to reinterview or clarify the information regarding the persons present on scene if there is a discrepancy between information provided by PFRs and witnesses.

4.3.1.1.4 Condition of the Infant

The infant's location, position, and condition, when found unresponsive by caregivers, is needed to accurately identify the cause of death (COD) and manner of death (MOD). Just as important, however, is the description of the infant's location, position, and condition when first observed by PFRs. The PFR's description may corroborate statements of caregivers, reveal inconsistencies, or require further inquiry by investigators if discrepancies occur between the PFR's account, evidence at the scene, or witness reports. The information obtained should include a description of the infant's location, position, type, and amount of clothing worn by the infant, the infant's color, temperature, and physical findings. Investigators should also inquire if any items were located on or near the infant to include pillows, bedding, and toys to name a few.

4.3.1.1.5 Actions of the PFR

The actions of PFRs who arrived on scene should be noted and documented. These questions are not designed to assess the quality of care provided by them, but rather to ensure that the investigator has an understanding of their actions and how their actions may have affected the infant and the scene. The scene or body may have been altered while performing their professional duties. Investigators should determine what may have been altered, preferably prior to conducting the initial postmortem assessment and the scene investigation.

Case Example 4.4 An emergency medical technician (EMT) reported that on arrival, the infant was lying supine on a couch bundled in a blanket. Prior to transporting the infant to the hospital, the EMT removed the blanket and noted the infant was wearing multiple layers of clothing. The EMT removed two layers of clothing to assess the patient and left the blanket and clothing on the floor, next to the couch. Had the EMT not been interviewed, investigators may not have known that the infant was wearing those items when found unresponsive even though these were noted during the scene investigation to be on the floor next the couch.

4.3.1.1.6 Other Observations

PFRs are in a unique position to witness behaviors and reactions of witnesses. First responders may have observed an individual who appeared to be under the influence of alcohol or drugs and may have overheard arguments or witnessed confrontations between witnesses. PFRs may not observe anything inappropriate or unusual; that information should also be reported to the investigator.

4.3.1.2 Fire Department Personnel

Fire personnel are trained to respond to a multitude of emergency situations and scenarios. Response and recognition of safety and environmental hazards is one of their specialties; as a result, they may be able to provide information about environmental safety concerns they observed at the scene. Fire personnel are often the first to arrive on scene and may have initiated resuscitative efforts or provided assistance in another way. They may assist EMS personnel during medical emergencies and may offer to drive the ambulance to the emergency room (ER) while EMS personnel provide emergency medical care in the back of the ambulance. In some jurisdictions, a parent may be allowed to ride in the ambulance with a minor child. If this occurs, the fire personnel may be able to provide information about statements made by the caregiver while en route to the hospital.

4.3.1.3 Law Enforcement Personnel

The observations of the first responding law enforcement officer may also be crucial in an infant death investigation. The first responding officer is often familiar with the neighborhood and may be knowledgeable about prior calls to the incident location or familiar with persons present at the scene. On arrival, the first responding officer attempts to maintain crowd control, secures the scene, and gathers basic information about the incident. They may be able to provide information regarding suspicious persons, criminal activity noted, observations of the scene and witnesses, and statements made by persons present on scene.

4.3.1.4 Emergency Medical Service (EMS) Personnel

EMS personnel may be able to provide the most specific and crucial information during an infant death investigation. Due to their profession, EMS personnel may likely have the greatest opportunity to interact with the infant and family and, as a result, may be able to provide significant information. During interviews with EMS personnel, the investigator should gather factual information, such as the medical treatment provided, as well as subjective information.

Although EMS personnel document all medical treatment provided to patients in their formal reports, these reports may not be immediately available after the death. To ensure that the treatment information is noted, prior to the postmortem

TABLE 4.2
Questions for EMS

Additional Questions for EMS Personnel

- What time did you depart the scene?
- Describe the infant's physical condition (e.g., no respirations, agonal breathing, asystole, pulseless electrical activity, or other cardiac rhythm).
- Was CPR performed during transit?
- Did the EMS crew intubate the infant? (Insert breathing tube.)
- What medications and dosages were given? What were the times and routes?
- Did EMS crew attempt to insert intravenous catheters? How many attempts were made? Where on the body were the attempts made?
- Did EMS crew attempt to insert an intraosseous catheter? How many attempts and in what locations on the body?
- Were any contents suctioned from the infant? Is so describe substance and estimate the amount.
- Describe the personal effects that were located on the infant. Were they removed at the scene or during transit? If so, what was removed and where are they now, or who were they transferred to?
- What was the final disposition of the infant? (E.g., transferred the care of the infant to ER staff; resuscitative efforts ceased at the direction of medical control; the body was transported to a funeral home; dead on arrival at scene.)

assessment and autopsy, the investigator should verbally obtain the information from them if their report is not available. Investigators should obtain a description of the infant's physical condition when they arrived on scene, a list of medical and emergency procedures attempted, a list of medications administered, a description of the infant's personal effects, and the final disposition of the infant. A sample list of specific questions for EMS personnel is located in Table 4.2.

In some jurisdictions, a parent or caregiver of a minor child may be allowed to ride to the hospital in the front of the ambulance with the ambulance driver while EMS personnel attempt resuscitative measures in the back. Other jurisdictions, however, do not allow anyone to ride in the front or the back of the ambulance other than the patient. In jurisdictions that do allow a parent to ride with a sick or injured minor child, investigators should determine who, if anyone, rode in the ambulance. If no caregiver rode in the ambulance with the infant, the investigator should inquire as to the reason. There are three possible reasons why a parent or caregiver may not ride in the ambulance with the infant and EMS personnel. First, it may be EMS policy that no one, other than the patient, ride in the ambulance. Second, the EMS crew may not have provided the parent or caregiver the opportunity to ride with them; although it may have been allowed had the caregiver asked. Third, the EMS crew may have provided the opportunity to the parent or caregiver to ride in the ambulance but they declined.

Case Example 4.5 A single mother of four children found her infant unresponsive and called 9-1-1. EMS personnel offered her an opportunity to ride in the ambulance; however, she declined due to the fact that she was the only adult present on scene and needed to find someone to care for her other children before she could respond to the hospital. In this example, it is understandable why the mother did not ride in the ambulance with the infant.

Case Example 4.6 EMS personnel responded to a 9-1-1 call for an infant who was found unresponsive by the parents. This is the couple's only child, however neither rode with EMS to the hospital. The investigator should inquire as to the reason neither of them rode in the ambulance if this is a jurisdiction that would have allowed it. EMS personnel may report that they acted so quickly that they did not give the parents an opportunity to ride along, or EMS may report that they did provide the opportunity, however the parents declined. Further inquiry may be needed, and a description of the scene may provide additional information regarding the case. For example, if PFRs report the presence of drug paraphernalia at the residence, it is possible that the parents declined to ride in the ambulance in order to remain at the scene and rid their residence of those items.

4.3.2 Non-PFR

Non-PFRs are individuals who may or may not have training in emergency response however offer assistance to other persons during an emergency situation. These responders may be bystanders, neighbors, coworkers, or other persons that are in the vicinity of the emergency. Non-PFRs may be able to provide investigators with information about the incident that is under investigation or may be able to provide information about prior incidents at this same location or involving the same witnesses.

Investigators should obtain the non-PFRs' names, dates of birth, addresses, and phone numbers as well as details about their involvement during the incident. Investigators should determine how the non-PFR became aware of the emergency; their actions after becoming aware of the situation; and their observations of the scene and other involved persons. The non-PFR may be able to provide investigators with factual objective information as well as subjective information. Investigators should determine if the non-PFR had prior involvement with the infant or caregivers or has additional information or knowledge about prior events at the incident location or with the persons involved.

Case Example 4.7 A non-PFR, the neighbor, reported that after hearing screams for help, she responded and assisted with the unresponsive infant. The non-PFR reported that 2 days prior, she overheard an argument coming from inside the infant's home. She stated that it sounded as if items were thrown against a wall. The information regarding the incident 2 days prior may be important as it may explain scene findings.

Non-PFRs, which may not be trained in emergency response, may have attempted to provide emergency medical treatment. It may be important to identify the way they offered medical assistance. If the non-PFR attempted CPR, the investigator may need to have this person describe and possibly demonstrate how they performed it. Minor injuries may be found on the bodies of children following resuscitation efforts. If CPR was performed by untrained personnel, it may be important to establish their technique for doing so.[1]

4.3.3 Hospital Personnel

Hospital personnel may be able to provide investigators with information that can impact an infant death investigation. Hospital personnel will interact with the infant while providing medical treatment and are very likely to interact with caregivers and other witnesses who respond to the hospital. They may observe reactions and interactions between caregivers, overhear statements made by caregivers, and may obtain details about the death.

Hospital personnel from many different departments may interact with the infant or the family in many areas of the hospital. The interactions may occur in the ER or in an inpatient area of the hospital. When an unresponsive child is brought to the hospital, it is first examined in the ER. If the death occurs there, the investigator should interview emergency room staff or persons who interacted with the infant or caregiver while in that setting. If the infant was stabilized, transported, and admitted to another area of the hospital, investigators may need to interview ER personnel as well as staff in the inpatient setting. In either scenario, investigators should consider interviewing physicians, nurses, social workers, clergy, and hospital security personnel.

4.3.3.1 Physicians

MDIs should routinely interview the physicians who treated the infant immediately prior to death. The ER physician, who attempted lifesaving resuscitative efforts, should be interviewed if the infant was pronounced dead in an ER. In rare cases, infants are stabilized and admitted to the hospital. The investigator should then interview the inpatient physician, which may be a pediatrician or an intensive care specialist, who treated the infant.

Investigators should document the physician's understanding of the circumstances that brought the infant to the hospital. The condition of the infant on arrival to the hospital, the physician's initial physical assessment, the medical treatment rendered, and the infant's response to that treatment, if any, should be obtained from the physician. The physician's interactions with caregivers and any concerns about the infant or the circumstances of the infant's death should be reported to investigators.

MDIs and law enforcement officers may feel compelled to solicit the ER physician's opinion regarding the cause of the infant's death. The question, in and of itself, is not wrong; however, the investigator should not let that opinion direct the investigation. ER and inpatient physicians may have opinions about the cause and manner of an infant's death; however, that opinion is often based on limited information as they have not investigated the scene, interviewed witnesses, or obtained autopsy results.

Case Example 4.8 A 5-month-old was brought to an ER in full arrest; lifesaving techniques were to no avail; and the infant was pronounced dead. The ER physician did not note any signs of injury. After speaking briefly with the mother however, the physician learned that the infant had minor respiratory problems a few days prior. The law enforcement investigator asked the ER physician his opinion about the cause of death. The physician responded that there were no signs of injury and that the death was natural, probably due to sudden infant death syndrome (SIDS). The law enforcement investigator, as a result of the physician's opinion, did not proceed with the scene investigation. The MDI, however, conducted a thorough scene investigation, witness interviews, and postmortem assessment. The autopsy did not reveal any cause of death. Toxicology tests revealed the infant died of an overdose of diphenhydramine and methadone. The MDI's scene investigation documented the presence of Children's Benadryl® Allergy Liquid (Pfizer Consumer Healthcare, Morris Plains, New Jersey) and an empty bottle of methadone. Both were located near the infant's sleep area. Further investigation determined that the mother administered both medications to the infant to keep the baby quiet. The death was ruled a homicide.

4.3.3.2 Nurses

In the hospital setting, nurses may be able to provide information about the condition of the infant and treatments rendered as well as peripheral information that may be important to the investigation. Investigators may need to interview the staff nurse assigned to care for the infant, the ER charge nurse, or the nursing supervisor.

The *ER staff nurse* is the primary nurse assigned to the care of the infant. Although many medical and nursing personnel may provide care to the infant, one individual is designated the primary care provider. The *ER charge nurse* is a registered nurse who has been assigned, for that day and that shift, to oversee the operation and care administered to all patients in the ER. The staff nurse and charge nurse may have information about the condition of the infant and both may have interacted with caregivers and witnesses as well as the PFRs who transported the infant to the ER.

The *nursing supervisor* is the nurse administrator responsible for the general operation of the facility and oversees the care of all patients in the hospital. This individual is notified of all problems or concerns in the hospital and is available to assist with issues that arise in the facility. The nursing supervisor is always notified of deaths that occur in the hospital and will usually respond to the location to offer assistance to staff, family, and third parties. Third parties who may respond to the hospital include law enforcement officers, death investigators, organ donor agency representatives, and funeral home or morgue personnel. The nursing supervisor may not have been present in the ER when the infant arrived at the hospital and, as a result, may not have any information in regard to the condition of the infant but many times has interacted with the family and third parties.

4.3.3.3 Social Workers

When an infant is brought to a hospital in critical condition, nursing staff may request that a social worker respond to offer assistance to the infant's caregivers. The social worker may have spent time with the caregivers and, as a result, may have witnessed or overheard communication between them. If the infant was born at the same facility, a social worker may have visited the infant and the family after the infant's birth and prior to discharge from the hospital, especially if the infant was considered high risk for complications. A social worker may have assisted the family and may have followed up with the family after being discharged from the hospital.

4.3.3.4 Clergy

Hospital clergy are often asked to respond to a unit in which an emergency or death has occurred. This individual will often sit with and offer assistance to the family or caregivers during the emergency crisis at the hospital and, therefore, may have information that could be beneficial to the investigation.

4.3.3.5 Hospital Security

Hospital security is another group of professionals who may be able to provide information to investigators. After the death of a child, some families or caregivers may act out in such ways that nursing staff may call security. Hospital security is often located in the ER to assist with a patient or caregiver who has become dangerous or difficult. In those cases, security officers may have heard or witnessed persons say or do something that may be important to the investigation.

> *Case Example 4.9* A 9-month-old infant was found unresponsive by her mother while the father was at work. The infant was transported to an ER. The parents, both sets of grandparents, and distant relatives on both sides of the family responded to the hospital. Before the infant was pronounced dead, the two families became verbally and physically aggressive toward one another and security had to break them up. While doing so, hospital security officers heard members of one side of the family yelling, "We knew this would happen! What did she do to her?"

4.4 SUMMARY

The activation of the emergency response system sets in motion first responders and professional persons who may be able to provide detailed information about the circumstances of the infant's death that will assist in the COD and MOD determination. Investigators who interview these individuals will obtain significant pieces of information as some of these responders may have arrived at the incident location minutes after the 9-1-1 call was received, may have interacted with the infant and family and, as a result, may be able to provide investigators crucial information and details.

Thorough and complete infant death investigations will include a comprehensive review of the events that occurred at the incident location from the moment the 9-1-1 call is placed to the time the infant is pronounced dead and an investigator arrives on scene. Observations by first responders and hospital personnel along with the 9-1-1 recording may redirect an investigation, provide information regarding suspicious circumstances, and ultimately help identify the cause and manner of the infant's death.

REFERENCES

1. Ryan, M.P., Young, S.J., and Wells, D.L., Do resuscitation attempts in children who die, cause injury? *Emerg. Med. J.*, 20 (1), 10–12, 2003.

RESOURCES

Centers for Disease Control and Prevention, Guidelines for death scene investigations of sudden, unexplained infant deaths: Recommendations of the Interagency Panel on Sudden Infant Death Syndrome, *Morbid. Mortal. Wkly. Rep.,* 45, RR-10, 1996.

National SIDS/Infant Death Resource Center (NSIDRC), Sudden, Unexpected Infant Death: Information for the Emergency Medical Technician, document, available at www.sidscenter.org (accessed June 15, 2006).

SIDS Foundation of Washington, Infant Death Investigation. Responding to Sudden Deaths in Infants and Young Children: Interactive Training Guide for Death Investigators, Law Enforcement, and Emergency Medical Personnel, CD-ROM, ELN Communications, Seattle, WA, 2003.

5 Initial Postmortem External Assessment

5.1 INTRODUCTION

An initial postmortem external assessment is a head-to-toe external physical examination with photodocumentation that is completed by the medicolegal death investigator (MDI). This assessment is crucial and should be completed prior to interviewing the infant's caregivers or witnesses of the incident and prior to the deceased being transported from the scene or hospital to the forensic pathologist's office. The information obtained during the initial assessment provides the investigator with information that may directly impact the initial interviews of caregivers and witnesses and, therefore, may help determine the cause and manner of the infant's death.

5.2 LOGISTICS

The initial assessment should be completed at the location where the infant is pronounced dead. This may be in an emergency room (ER) or at the incident location if professional first responders did not transport the infant. The Committee on Child Abuse and Neglect for the American Academy of Pediatrics recommended in 2001 that a child maltreatment specialist should examine infants who were pronounced dead in an ER before the child is removed from the ER.[1]

In some jurisdictions, once an infant is pronounced dead, the body is transported to a forensic pathologist's office prior to the MDI having an opportunity to complete an assessment. There are a number of concerns associated with this practice. First, the initial postmortem assessment provides the investigator an opportunity to assess the infant's body prior to interviewing witnesses. Without this assessment information, the investigator is unable to interview the witnesses as effectively as if the assessment information was available. Second, the initial postmortem assessment provides an opportunity for the investigator to examine the infant's remains before additional, possibly advanced, postmortem changes take place. These findings help narrow the time frame in which the death may have occurred. Third, examining and photographing the remains prior to transport ensures that if something were to happen to the infant during transport to the forensic pathologist's office, such as a motor vehicle collision, documentation of the initial physical findings is available. Fourth, if the infant is pronounced dead at the scene, there may be findings on the body that can be immediately compared to the environmental and situational circumstances at the scene, including room temperature, pattern injuries from sheets on the sleeping surface, purge patterns, and insect activity among others.

If the assessment is completed in an ER, it is a good practice to ask hospital personnel to allow the infant to remain in the room in which the death occurred and to leave all medical equipment that may have been used in the resuscitation effort in the room with the deceased. There will be times when the ER will be extremely busy, requiring hospital staff to move the infant to another examination room or to the morgue. If this is the case, all clothing, personal items, and records should accompany the body.

If the infant is assessed at the scene, two possible locations are suitable for the location of that assessment. The first location is where the infant is found when the MDI arrives on scene. The infant may be in a crib, lying on a bed, couch, or on the floor. The other location would be the back of an ambulance. It may be desirable to assess the infant in the back of an ambulance if there are many people present at the incident location; if caregivers and witnesses are being difficult to work with; or if it would be difficult to do a proper assessment at the scene due to poor lighting, space, or insect activity or infestations.

The initial postmortem assessment should be completed as soon as possible following the death. Each agency should establish policies and procedures in regard to response time, including response time to infant deaths, by investigators. Postmortem changes can occur rapidly in infants; therefore, it is important to assess the infant as soon after the death as possible. Documenting the infant's injuries, or lack of injuries, prior to advanced postmortem changes is crucial to the investigation.

The investigator should ensure that all nonprofessional personnel leave the immediate vicinity while the assessment is being completed. If the family is on scene, investigator should be introduced to the family or caregivers, explain the investigator's role and that the infant will be examined, and the investigator will return to speak with them and answer questions. This examination should not be conducted in the presence of caregivers or other witnesses; they should be asked to wait elsewhere, such as another room, for a short period of time. In the hospital setting, family and caregivers may be relocated to a different room upon the investigator's arrival. Therefore it may not be necessary for the investigator to be introduced to the family prior to beginning the assessment. If the family or caregivers are located in the same room as the deceased infant, it will be necessary for the investigator to be introduced to the family, explain the investigator's role, and then ask the family to step out of the examination room briefly while the assessment of the infant is completed prior to speaking with them further.

The initial postmortem assessment is best completed by a MDI who has a medical background such as a physician, a physician's assistant, a registered nurse, emergency medical services personnel, or other person with experience in medicolegal infant death investigation. Knowledge of normal infant anatomy and growth and developmental milestones is also helpful. Investigators who lack knowledge in these areas may be less likely to recognize abnormal findings that may be critical to the case.

5.3 PHOTODOCUMENTATION

Photodocumentation of the initial postmortem external assessment is an important component of the infant death investigation. Photodocumentation of this assessment is crucial as it provides permanent documentation of the location and position of the

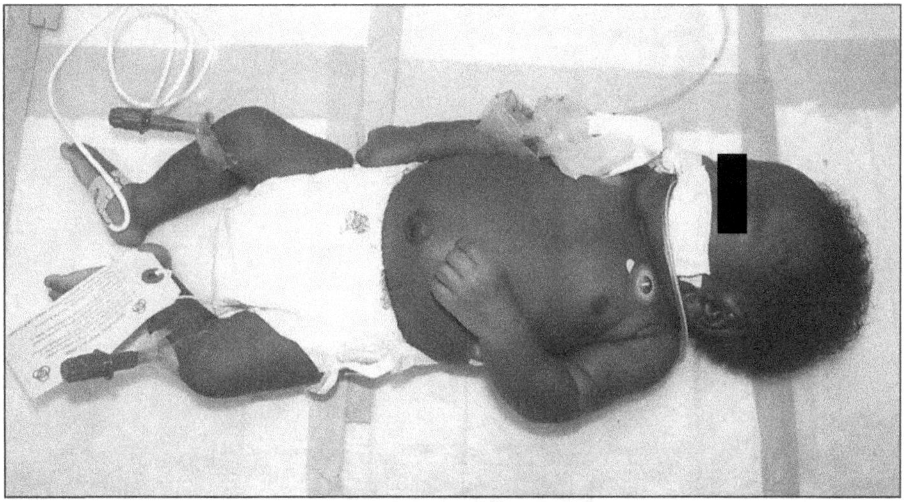

FIGURE 5.1 Full-body photo of infant in supine position with all medical equipment intact. (Photo courtesy of Medical University of South Carolina [MUSC] Forensic Pathology Department. With permission.)

infant when first examined by the MDI; the clothing and medical equipment located on or near the body; and the normal, abnormal, and postmortem changes observed.

As in all death investigations, if the infant is pronounced dead at the incident location, the body should not be moved until scene photographs are taken by the MDI and law enforcement, which will be discussed in Chapter 6. After the scene investigation has been completed, the body may be moved to conduct the external assessment. If the infant is pronounced dead in the hospital setting, the death investigator should photograph the infant as found upon their arrival. This photodocumentation provides a permanent record of the infant's location, the medical equipment, clothing and any injuries noted on the infant when the MDI arrived.

After the scene and initial photographs are taken, the infant should be placed on a flat surface in the supine position (on the back) in a well-lit location. A full-body photograph should be taken (Figure 5.1) followed by a close-up photograph of the infant's face.[2] Additional close-up photographs should be taken of any area in which there are abnormal findings. After the exam is complete in the supine position, the infant should be turned to the prone position (on the stomach) and another full-body photograph taken. Close-up photographs should again be taken of any abnormal findings noted on the infant's backside.

5.4 PERFORMING THE EXTERNAL ASSESSMENT

A head-to-toe, external assessment includes an examination of the infant from the top of the infant's head to the bottom of its feet. The exam can be done in a number of different ways, and different investigators may have different techniques. It is important, however, that each investigator examine infants the same way every time,

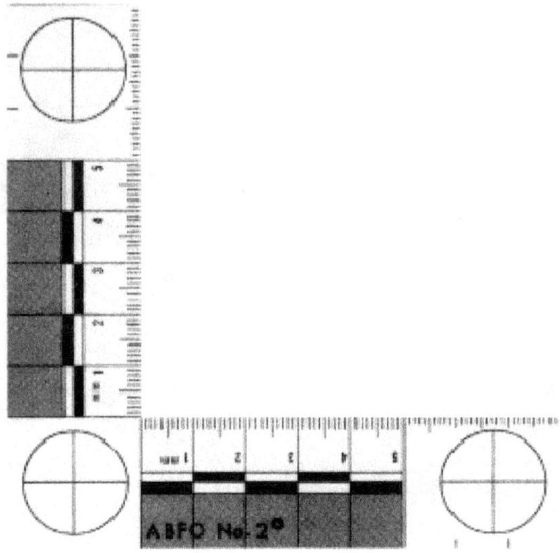

FIGURE 5.2 ABFO No. 2 scale.

ensuring that a consistent method is utilized and that nothing is missed or inadvertently left out.

Most medical personnel will begin assessing the body at the head and proceed downward to the feet. Their assessments will focus on the middle of the body and move outward, examining the trunk prior to the extremities. While performing the assessment, if any abnormalities are noted, the investigator should immediately document those findings photographically or on an infant body diagram. Clothing, as well as the diaper, should not be removed during the initial postmortem assessment. The diaper and clothing should remain on the body though it is necessary to look under those garments to assess the areas of the body that are covered by those garments.

5.5 EQUIPMENT NEEDED

Investigators performing the initial postmortem external assessment will need to ensure that they have with them the equipment needed. This will include personal protective equipment (PPE), a camera, a thermometer, and measuring instruments such as a tape measure, ruler, American Board of Forensic of Odontology (ABFO) No. 2 scale (Figure 5.2), or other type of measurement device to document the size of any abnormal findings. Investigators should also have available all investigative forms, including an infant body diagram, specimen containers for trace evidence, and paper bags for transporting evidence to the forensic pathologist's office.

PPE, such as gloves, should be worn when assessing the remains of any deceased, including infants and children, and all investigators should observe universal precautions. *Universal precautions,* strategies used to prevent the transmission of human immunodeficiency virus, hepatitis B virus, and other blood-borne pathogens, should be used when having physical contact with living or deceased persons. Under universal precautions, blood and certain body fluids are considered potentially infectious; therefore, gloves and other protective equipment should be worn when assessing deceased persons, including infants and children.[3]

5.6 ASSESSING THE INFANT'S GENERAL APPEARANCE

The assessment should begin with investigator's noting the general appearance of the infant; this should include weight, nutritional and hydration status, temperature, color, cleanliness, medical equipment, postmortem changes, and clothing and jewelry the infant is wearing. Following an assessment of the general appearance, the investigator should complete a skin and head-to-toe external assessment, examining and documenting any abnormal findings in each area of the body.

5.6.1 Weight

The weight of an infant provides the investigator with general information regarding the health and well-being of the infant. After obtaining the weight of the infant, the investigator may want to compare the infant's growth and development to that of other infants the same age on the weight-for-age growth chart (see Chapter 2) to determine what percentile the infant is in.

If the infant died in an ER, a weight may be documented on the ER triage or admission assessment. ERs will routinely weigh infants and children prior to providing medical treatment to determine the correct dosage of medications to administer, if necessary. If the child was brought to the ER in full arrest, the staff may not have had an opportunity to weigh the infant; instead they may have used a Broselow® Pediatric Emergency Tape (Armstrong Medical Industries, Inc., Lincolnshire, IL) to quickly estimate the weight of the child prior to administering medications. Prior to autopsy, the infant will be weighed by the forensic pathologist; however, the MDI may want to weigh the infant prior to interviewing caregivers if the general appearance of the infant raises questions or the infant appears emaciated, thin, or obese.

5.6.2 Nutritional/Hydration Status

The nutritional and hydration status of the infant can be estimated by assessing the skin turgor and the mucous membranes. *Skin turgor* is assessed by grasping the infant's skin between the thumb and index finger, pulling it up and then releasing the skin quickly, thus observing its elasticity. Adequate hydration is noted when the skin quickly returns to its original position, referred to as good skin turgor. If the skin remains in a tented position for a few seconds, prior to slowly returning to its original position, the skin turgor is considered to be poor, possibly the result of dehydration. An assessment of the infant's mucous membranes can also help gauge hydration. Mucous membranes are those areas inside the mouth, which include the cheek, gums, and tongue. If the membranes are dry, dehydration may be the cause, while moist mucous membranes may indicate adequate hydration.

5.6.3 Temperature

The MDI should assess the infant's temperature, also known as *algor mortis*. This may be completed by touch or with a thermometer. Many jurisdictions have policies regarding how investigators should assess the temperature of an infant and whether or not they may assess the temperature with a thermometer. The investigator should feel the infant's skin to assess the skin temperature; however, this is a subjective finding. Remember what may be considered warm to one person may feel hot to another. When assessing temperature by touch, the investigator should feel the skin on the trunk or torso, noting if the body feels cool, warm, or hot, and also assess the skin temperature of each part of the body, including the upper and lower extremities.

If the infant died in an ER, a temperature may be recorded at the time the infant was brought into the facility. An actual temperature reading may be more critical in those cases in which the infant remained on scene. Temperature readings may be obtained via rectal temperature or digital ear thermometers. Investigators should follow the policies and procedures in their jurisdictions prior to inserting a thermometer into a deceased infant to obtain a temperature. If a temperature is obtained via a thermometer, the investigator should note the procedure and the temperature in their report and notify the forensic pathologist prior to autopsy.

5.6.4 Color

During the assessment of the infant's general appearance, the investigator should document the infant's color and any color differences from one area of the body to another. The color may vary along a color spectrum from white to purple. The color of the infant may provide information to the investigator and the pathologist regarding the cause of death (COD), time of death, and possibly the position of the infant. For example, if the skin is cherry-red in appearance, the COD may be the result of carbon monoxide poisoning. Postmortem color changes that may help determine the time of death and the infant's position at death will be discussed later in this chapter.

5.6.5 Cleanliness

The cleanliness of the infant and the infant's clothing is another area that should be assessed and noted in regard to the general appearance of the infant. Cleanliness may be an indicator of the type and appropriateness of care given by the family or caregivers. The investigator should note if various articles of clothing that the infant is wearing are of the same condition and cleanliness. For example, an investigator noted that the infant's shirt appeared newly washed, while the infant's pants and socks were extremely dirty. The investigator may need to determine if the infant's shirt was changed prior to their arrival.

5.6.6 Medical Equipment

Medical equipment that was used during resuscitative efforts by medical personnel should be noted during the assessment of the infant's general appearance. This may include intravenous lines (IVs), intraosseous catheters (IOs), electrocardiogram and defibrillator pads, as well as oxygen administration methods, including nasal cannulas or face masks. Resuscitative efforts may leave physical marks on the body; as a result, it is important to have documentation of all equipment used, the number of attempts made by medical personnel to insert IVs and IOs, and information regarding any medical equipment that may have been removed prior to the investigator assessing the infant. However, the best practice is not to remove medical equipment prior to the MDI assessing the infant or prior to autopsy.

5.6.7 Postmortem Changes

Postmortem changes should be noted and documented during the assessment of the infant's general appearance. The areas that should be assessed include algor mortis, rigor mortis, livor mortis, and purge. Algor mortis is an assessment of the infant's temperature (Section 5.6.3). As mentioned, jurisdictions may have different policies governing the assessment of algor mortis. There is much debate regarding the use of skin, rectal, ear, or liver temperatures, which is beyond the scope of this text. Investigators should follow the policies in place in their jurisdictions.

Rigor mortis is the temporary stiffening of muscles following death. An assessment of rigor mortis can be subjective. However, investigators should attempt to move the extremities of the infant to assess the amount of muscle stiffening, which may provide information regarding the time of death.

Livor mortis is the amount of settling or blood pooling that is present in the dependent areas of the body following death. This settling of blood results in a purplish-red discoloration. Investigators should note whether the livor will blanch, turn white when pressed, or is not able to be blanched and is therefore "fixed." Noting the livor pattern may provide information about the position of the infant at the time of death, and that information should be compared to statements made by caregivers and witnesses.

Case Example 5.1 An infant is pronounced dead on scene and livor mortis is noted on the front side (stomach) or prone side of the infant during the initial postmortem external assessment. During the initial interview with caregivers, it is reported that the infant was placed on its back to sleep and that the infant was found in that same position. The investigator's findings and the information obtained during interviews do not correlate. As a result, the investigator will need to further assess and investigate the circumstances surrounding this infant's death.

Investigators should also document any purge that may be evident from the mouth or nose. *Purge* is a discharge that is expelled from the mouth and nose of deceased persons. This discharge is often blood tinged and may be found at the location in which the death occurred, such as in the crib, bassinet, or other sleeping surface. Noting the presence of purge on the infant will lead investigators to look for evidence of purge at the scene.

5.6.8 Clothing/Jewelry

The clothing, along with any jewelry, should be noted and documented on the body diagram. The investigator should list all pieces of clothing, making sure that if there are layers of clothing on the infant that all information is documented. Overbundling of the infant may lead to hyperthermia; just as infants may suffer from hypothermia if they are not dressed appropriately. It will be important for the investigator to assess the scene temperature to determine if the amount of clothing and blankets around the infant may have contributed to overheating. Noting whether the diaper is clean or dirty may also play an important role in the investigation, and the diaper should be opened and examined. Many caregivers place jewelry, such as earrings, necklaces, and bracelets, on infants. Those items should be documented on the body diagram yet remain on the infant until autopsy.

5.7 SKIN ASSESSMENT

Throughout the initial postmortem assessment, the infant's skin will be assessed for scars; scratches; bruises; rashes; abrasions; lacerations; petechiae; pinch, grab, or slap marks; burns; and insect, animal, or human bite or suck marks. Any and all injuries or trauma should be photographed with a measuring device, such as an ABFO no. 2 scale, and documented on the body diagram. Specific areas of concern for each part of an infant's body are listed in Table 5.1. Bite or suck marks should be processed according to each agency's protocol as soon as the mark is recognized. This may include swabbing the mark with a cotton-tipped applicator to try to obtain deoxyribonucleic acid (DNA) from the possible perpetrator.[4]

Experienced infant death investigators will be able to complete this initial postmortem assessment in a short period of time. Cases in which many injuries or abnormalities are noted will take longer. This initial assessment will have little or no value, however, if the investigator does not have an understanding of the significance of their findings or does not communicate their findings to the pathologist. Information gathered from the assessment should be used and considered by the investigator while interviewing caregivers and witnesses. As a result, it is important that the individual who performs the assessment also be the person to complete the initial interview with caregivers and witnesses. This investigator should be trained and skilled, not only in the physical assessment of infants, but also in interviewing.

5.8 BODY DIAGRAM

Documenting the initial external physical findings on an infant body diagram is an important step in documenting the assessment. For smaller jurisdictions that may not have access to high quality cameras, the documentation, or lack of documentation, on the body diagram may be very important to a case. During or immediately after the external assessment, the investigator should document their findings on an infant body diagram. An example of an infant body diagram is available on the newly revised Sudden Unexplained Infant Death Scene Investigation Report Form, which was developed by the Centers for Disease Control and Prevention (CDC). This infant body can be found on the CDC Web site at http://www.cdc.gov/SIDS/PDF/SUIDIforms.pdf.[5] The investigator should draw on and label the diagram, which should bear the date and time the examination was completed, the name of the infant, the case number and the name of the investigator completing the diagram. All medical equipment, clothing, and jewelry attached to or on the infant as well as any abnormal physical findings should be drawn and labeled on the diagram.

TABLE 5.1
Initial Postmortem External Assessment: Areas of Concern

Head and Neck Assessment	• Assess the shape and symmetry of the head. Note if the head is rounded or elongated. Newborns may have an elongated head, which is referred to as molding. Molding occurs when the cranial bones overlap during a vaginal delivery as the infant is moved through the birth canal. Note any flattening of the head. Flattening of one part of the head may indicate the infant continually lies in one position. • Palpate the head (skull) for any fractures, depressions, or crepitus. • Assess the fontanels, often referred to as soft spots. These soft spots are the areas where the skull has not completely fused together. The posterior fontanel, located toward the back of the head, will usually close by 2 months of age. The anterior fontanel closes between 12 to 18 months of age. Note whether the fontanels are present, and whether they appear sunken in, bulging, or flat. Fontanels that are sunken in may be signs of dehydration; bulging fontanels may be signs of increased intracranial pressure. • The head circumference will usually be measured at autopsy. If the investigator has concerns, however, that the size of the infant's head either appears overly small or large, it may be helpful to take a measurement during this initial assessment and then compare that measurement to the national growth charts. To measure the head circumference, a tape measure should be placed just slightly above the eyebrows and ears and around the back of the head. • Assess the face for symmetry. Note any pressure marks, especially lividity and blanching patterns. If the infant was found face down, or if something was lying over the infant's face, there may be areas of color differences. Some areas may appear blanched (white) while other areas appear darker. Note if there is any mucous or emesis (vomit) around the face and mouth. • Assess the eyes. Note if the eyes appear sunken as that may indicate dehydration. Open the eyes and look at the sclera (the white part of the eye) and note any unusual color or hemorrhages. Assess the pupils of each eye for size and shape. The pupils should be round and about the same size. Photodocumentation of the infant's eyes is of utmost importance regardless of the findings. It may be necessary for the investigator to ask for assistance in holding the eyes open in order for photographs to be taken. The photographs will document the presence or absence of hemorrhages or other findings in or around the orbits. • Assess the mouth. If possible, open the mouth and note if there is any mucous, froth, blood, or vomit in the mouth. Note whether the mucous membranes appear moist or dry and any teeth that may be present. Assess the lips and tongue for any cuts or lacerations; children who suffer from seizure activity may bite their tongues or lips if they have teeth. Assess the frenulum, the thin piece of tissue that connects the gum to the upper lip, by gently pulling the upper lip upward to see if it is torn.

continued

TABLE 5.1 (continued)
Initial Postmortem External Assessment: Areas of Concern

Head and Neck Assessment (continued)	• Assess the ears. Note the cleanliness and any drainage from the ears. Look behind the ears for any lacerations, abrasions, bruises, or skin tears. • Assess the nose for any drainage, mucous, froth, or foreign bodies and note if the membranes are moist or dry. • Assess the neck. Note any ligature or pressure marks or other unusual findings.
Chest and Stomach Assessment	• Assess the symmetry of the chest and stomach. Palpate the abdomen for distention or tightness. • Assess for pressure marks on the surface of the chest and stomach, noting any abrasions, discolorations, or pattern injury (Figure 5.3A and Figure 5.3B). • Assess umbilical cord healing for infants less than 1 month of age.
Arms and Hands Assessment	• Note the number of puncture wounds and presence of IVs, which may indicate attempts by medical personnel to start intravenous therapy. • Open the hands and assess the palms for any burns, abrasions, or other deformities. • Note the length of the fingernails. If the infant has long fingernails, the infant may have self-inflicted scratches, especially to the face. • Assess for grab marks to the arms.
Legs and Feet Assessment	• Note and document any puncture wounds or the presence of an IO. An IO is a medical device that is inserted into the long bones of infants' legs to administer fluids or medication (Figure 5.4A and Figure 5.4B). • Assess the bottom of the feet; note any burns, cuts, or other deformities to the feet. • Assess for grab marks to the legs.
Perineal or Perianal Assessment	• If the infant is wearing a diaper, the investigator should open the diaper to assess the perineum for blood, edema, discoloration, or trauma. • Note the contents of the diaper. If there is fecal material in the diaper, note the color and consistency. • Assess the external genitals. Normal female newborns may appear to have enlarged and darker colored external genitals, and normal male newborns may have an enlarged, darker colored scrotum. Note whether male infants are circumcised and if so whether healing has occurred in infants under 1 month of age.
Back Assessment	• After completing the examination from the supine position (on the back), the examiner should assess the backside of the infant by gently placing the infant in the prone position (on the stomach). A photograph should be taken to document the back prior to completing the assessment. • Assess for symmetry, pressure marks, and color differentiations. Mongolian spots are darkened areas of pigmentation that can be found anywhere on the body; however, they are often noted on the back and buttocks of dark-skinned infants. These spots may be misinterpreted as signs of abuse; they should be documented, photographed and evaluated further by a forensic pathologist to determine if the discoloration is natural or from abuse.

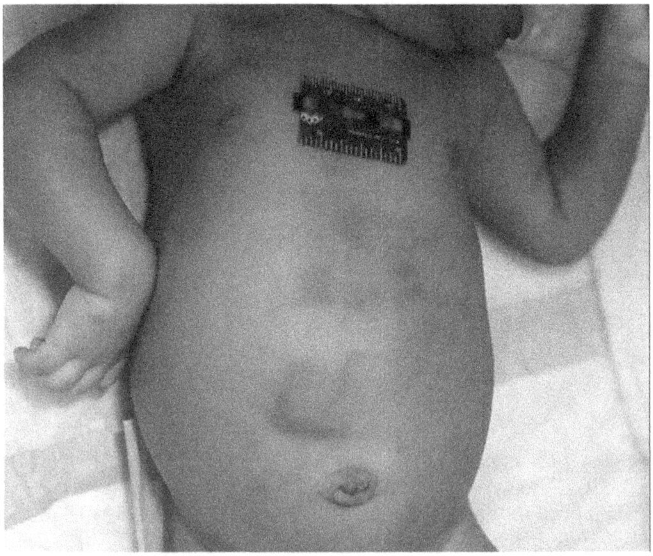

FIGURE 5.3A Pattern injury found on the abdomen of a 3-month-old infant. (Photo courtesy of MUSC Forensic Pathology Department.)

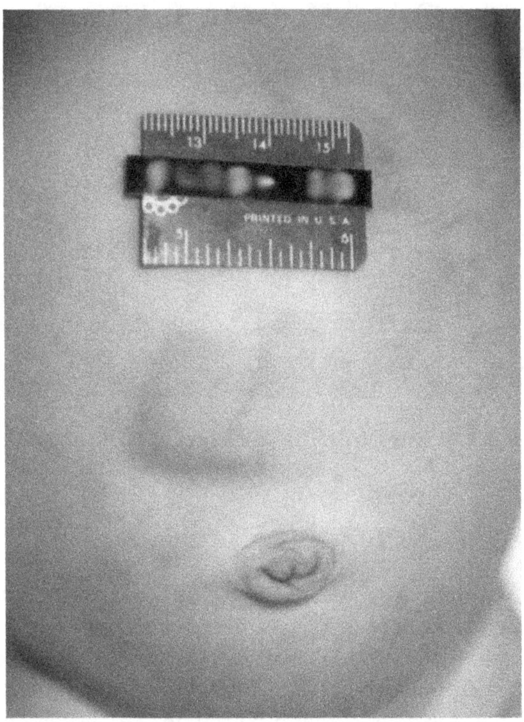

FIGURE 5.3B Close-up photograph of abdominal injury. (Photo courtesy of MUSC Forensic Pathology Department.)

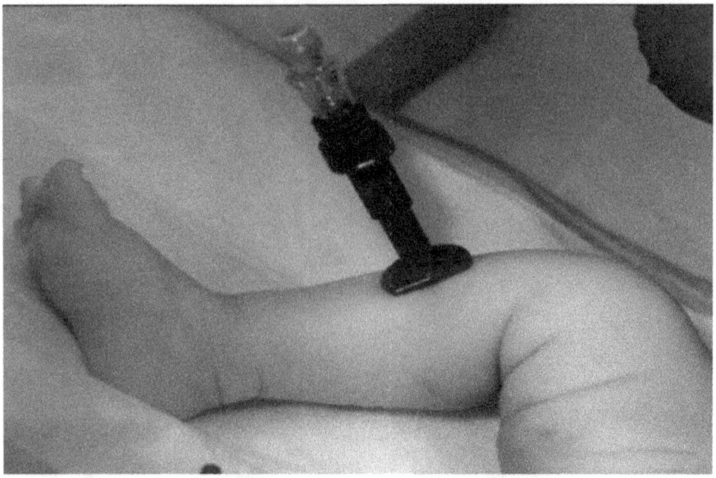

FIGURE 5.4A IO placed in the right leg of an infant. (Photo courtesy of MUSC Department of Forensic Pathology.)

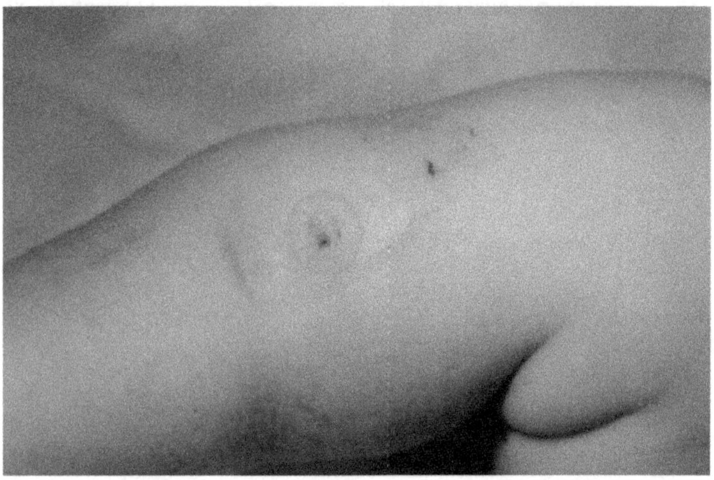

FIGURE 5.4B This photo depicts the investigator's finding on the right leg following removal of an IO. (Photo courtesy of MUSC Forensic Pathology Department.)

5.9 PHYSICAL EVIDENCE

Following the photodocumentation and initial postmortem external assessment, the investigator may need to collect evidence that is either on the body or came from the body prior to the body being transported to the forensic pathologist for autopsy. Most pieces of evidence found on the body should not be removed prior to autopsy, However, if the evidence is considered to be fragile (i.e., it may be lost, altered, or contaminated), then it should be properly collected and preserved in a way to maintain a proper chain of custody. Such items may include hairs, debris, and other foreign objects. However, these items should be present at autopsy for examination and evaluation by the forensic pathologist.

When the infant was transported by emergency medical personnel to a local hospital, evidence may have been removed in the course of treating the infant that now must now be collected. These items may be external pieces of evidence or internal pieces of evidence.

5.9.1 External Physical Evidence

External pieces of evidence will include items that were transported with the infant to the hospital. This includes all clothing the infant was wearing, pacifiers, bottles, medications, and any medical devices that were inserted during the transportation and treatment of the infant. It is important for the investigator to determine what the infant was wearing when transported by emergency medical personnel and to locate all of those items. The diaper the infant was wearing when transported from the scene should be collected. If the infant is still wearing that diaper when the investigator arrives, it should remain on the infant until autopsy. If the diaper has been removed, the investigator should locate and secure the diaper for evaluation at autopsy. Often the diaper may be found in the trash; however, it still should be located and transported with the infant to autopsy.

5.9.2 Internal Physical Evidence

Internal pieces of evidence that need to be transported to the autopsy include any items that were removed from inside the infant. These items may include blood samples, suction contents, or any foreign object that may have been recovered during emergency intervention.

When a patient is first admitted to an ER, admission blood samples are often drawn for laboratory testing. These tubes of admission blood may be kept in the hospital for a number of days, depending on each hospital's specific policy. The investigator should request and secure these tubes for further testing. These tubes of blood, which can be acquired by contacting the laboratory department of the hospital, should be provided to the forensic pathologist or forensic laboratory for testing as indicated by the case and in keeping with departmental policy.

Suction contents may be recovered from either emergency medical personnel or from ER staff. Suction contents are usually discarded fairly quickly so it may be helpful to request that the contents not be discarded when advised of the death. If the material is still available, the suction contents should be measured, described, and transported to the autopsy where the contents can be further examined and tested as needed.

Foreign objects may be recovered from the infant's body during resuscitative efforts and should be considered internal evidence. These foreign objects, such as items that caused choking or any item that was removed from the infant's nose, ears, mouth, or vaginal or anal orifices, should be collected, secured, and available for evaluation at autopsy and transferred to law enforcement personnel, maintaining proper chain of custody and departmental policy.

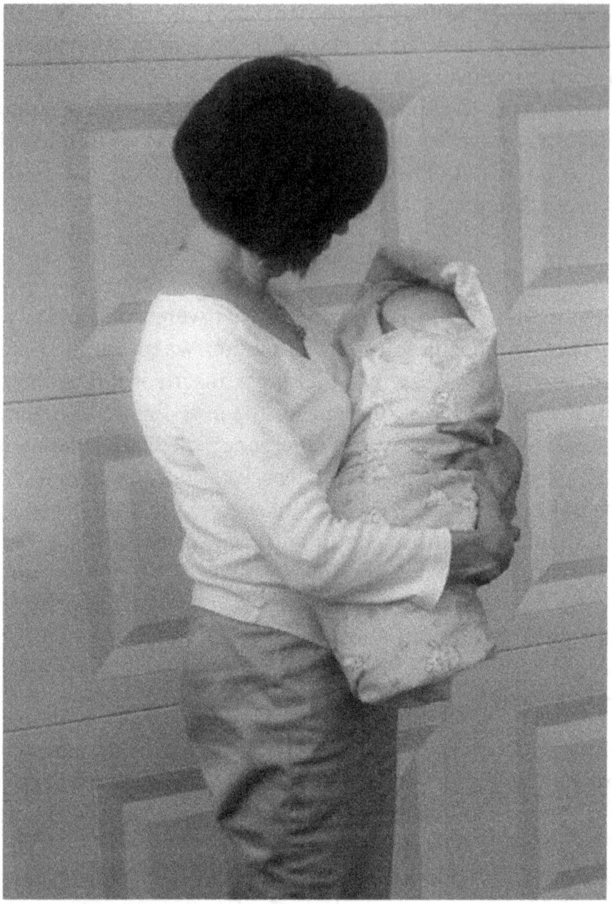

FIGURE 5.5 Investigator swaddles and carries the deceased infant in a caring manner when departing the scene or hospital.

5.10 TRANSPORTING THE BODY

Whether transporting the body from the ER or scene to the forensic pathologist's office for autopsy, the investigator should handle the infant's body with respect and care, being sure to handle and carry the infant as if the infant were alive. Caregivers and families are often present when the body is removed from either location or are comforted knowing that the person transporting their baby is doing so with care and compassion. It is suggested that the baby be swaddled in a blanket and then either carried in the arms of the investigator (Figure 5.5) or placed in an infant carrier (Figure 5.6) as opposed to placed on a large gurney or stretcher. Investigators should not underestimate the importance of handling the infant gently during transport; family and caregivers will appreciate the thoughtfulness as will others who may be watching.

FIGURE 5.6 Investigators may consider using an infant carrier when removing a deceased infant from the scene or hospital. Located in a baby carrier, the infant will be secure while in transit to the autopsy facility. Note: the depicted carrier has been noted to be an unsafe sleep environment for infants to sleep in. This carrier should not be used with living children.

5.11 SUMMARY

The initial postmortem external assessment is a crucial investigative tool for the complete and thorough investigation of sudden and unexpected infant deaths. The assessment, when completed prior to interviewing caregivers and witnesses, provides physical evidence information that may guide the interview process, the scene investigation, and the doll reenactment. Communication with law enforcement and the forensic pathologist regarding any abnormal findings is paramount to the investigation. Investigations that do not include an initial postmortem external assessment completed by the MDI immediately after the death of the infant may be negatively impacted as physical and trace evidence may be lost.

REFERENCES

1. American Academy of Pediatrics Committee on Child Abuse and Neglect, Distinguishing sudden infant death syndrome from child abuse fatalities, *Pediatrics,* 107 (2), 437–441, 2001.
2. National Medicolegal Review Panel, Death investigation: A Guide for the Scene Investigator, report, U.S. Department of Justice, Washington, D.C., 1999.
3. Nolte, K.B., Taylor, D.G., and Richmond, J.Y., Biosafety considerations for autopsy, *Am. J. Forensic Med. Pathol.,* 23 (2),107–122, 2002.
4. American Board of Forensic Odontology, ABFO bitemark methodology guidelines, available at http://www.abfo.org (accessed July 2, 2006).
5. Centers for Disease Control and Prevention, Sudden Unexplained Infant Death Investigation Reporting Form. Additional Investigative Scene Forms: Body Diagram, forms, available at http://www.cdc.gov/SIDS/PDF/SUIDIforms.pdf.

6 Infant Death Scene Investigation: It Tells a Story

6.1 INTRODUCTION

The incident location where an infant became unresponsive or was found dead may provide investigators with information that may help determine the cause, manner, and circumstances surrounding the infant's death. This scene can speak volumes about the living conditions of the infant and family, environmental factors, lifestyle decisions, and other risk factors that may have played a role in the infant's death. Investigators should assess and document the scene to identify physical factors that may have contributed as well as physical evidence that may identify who was involved and how their actions or lack of actions may have contributed to the infant's death.

As with other aspects of death investigations, time is of the essence as persons who have access to that location may intentionally or unintentionally alter scenes. Investigators should make it a priority to visit the scene following every unexpected infant or child's death. The amount and type of information obtained when assessing the scene environment has the ability to alter the course of the investigation and the cause and manner of death determination.

The incident location or scene should be investigated in layers beginning with the most general and broad perspective referred to as the *macroenvironment*. The focus then shifts to a more specific and smaller area, the *microenvironment*. A detailed and comprehensive examination of both is critical to a thorough death investigation. Investigators should have basic knowledge of death scene management, and agencies should establish policies and protocols to ensure appropriate response to, and the investigation of, infant death scenes. National guidelines were developed and released in 1999 by the U.S. Department of Justice in "Death Investigation: A Guide for the Scene Investigator."[1] Investigators should be aware of the national guidelines and implement them into all death scene investigations. The infant death scene should be evaluated and documented in accordance to state and national guidelines as well as agency policy and protocol.

Infant death scenes provide a unique challenge to investigators. They must assess the scene for potential environmental and physical hazards. These hazards, which may not affect adults, may have increased the infant's risk to injury or death. The scene should be assessed from the "infant's perspective," taking into consideration the infant's size, growth, and developmental level, and vulnerabilities. Investigators who fail to recognize that infants have a greater risk of succumbing to environmental and physical hazards or the mistreatment of others may not recognize important scene findings.

This chapter will focus on specific aspects of the scene that investigators should consider when investigating an infant death. Cases in which the infant was pronounced dead on scene and, therefore, not transported by first responders to a local emergency room and deaths that occurred in day-care settings pose a unique challenge to investigators. Specific questions and areas of concern will be addressed when investigating deaths in these scenarios.

6.2 DEATH SCENE INVESTIGATION: WHEN DOES IT BEGIN?

All death investigations begin when investigators are notified of an incident in which a life-threatening event or injury has occurred. The investigation of a death begins immediately. In jurisdictions in which advanced notification is provided to investigators or the double-team approach is used, the infant death scene investigation begins when the scene investigator is notified of the situation and prepares to respond to the incident location. The scene investigator begins to assess the circumstances with the first piece of information received: the address and description of the incident location.

When notified of an infant's condition, the scene investigator will obtain the address of the incident location and will determine if the incident location is a private residence, business, day-care center, or other location. The neighborhood in which the scene is located may provide some information. Investigators must ensure they are not biased by that information, however, and should be aware of additional risk and safety factors that may be associated with certain locations.

Investigators should be observant when arriving at the scene to note neighborhood and community dynamics, hazards, or other concerns. Prior to arriving at the exact location, the investigator should be observant of the condition of the homes (dwellings), the socioeconomic status of the area, bystanders who are in the vicinity, and the general upkeep of the neighborhood. After arriving at the incident location, the scene investigation begins with the comprehensive assessment and documentation of the macroenvironment followed by the microenvironment.

6.3 MACRO VS. MICRO: WHAT IS THE DIFFERENCE?

There are distinct differences between the macro- and microenvironmental assessments and investigations. Although the two may be intertwined and the investigation of each may occur at relatively the same time, investigators should be aware of the differences to ensure that they do not leave out or fail to document important aspects of each. One is an assessment of the entire incident location while the other is a detailed assessment of the area in which the death or injury occurred. Until investigators examine the scene and interview witnesses, it may not be known where the microenvironment is located.

The macroenvironment, also referred to as the "big picture" is a broad, large-scale description of the incident location. This information is crucial to the documentation of the external and internal scene location, which will include the type, layout, and condition of the dwelling as well as environmental findings and hazards that may be noted during the scene walk-through. The macroenvironmental findings should be documented in photographs or scene diagrams to ensure that a permanent record of the investigator's observations is preserved.

The assessment of the microenvironment includes a detailed examination of the area in which the infant was known to have become unresponsive or was found dead. If the infant died and remained on scene, the microenvironment would include the immediate area around the infant. In cases in which the infant was transported and died in another location, the microenvironment may be unknown until interviews have been completed with the primary witnesses. After completing the scene walk-through, however, investigators may be able to identify a probable incident location, which may be a crib, bassinet, couch, playpen, adult-sized bed, or other locations that should be examined thoroughly (Section 6.5.2).

Investigators should follow agency and jurisdictional policy and protocols prior to entering a scene and conducting a scene investigation. Depending on the circumstances of the case, investigators may need to obtain permission from the legal owner or resident of the location or may need to obtain a search warrant, as indicated by state law, prior to entering the incident location.

6.4 DOCUMENTING THE MACROENVIRONMENT

A general assessment of the entire incident location is best accomplished during a scene walk-through, which provides investigators an opportunity to get a sense of the big picture. During the macroenvironment assessment, investigators should evaluate the external and internal areas of the scene. The external area includes a description of the location, type, and ownership of the dwelling, while a description of the internal area includes the layout and condition of the dwelling, documentation of animal activity, the presence of alcohol and drugs, environmental hazards or concerns, as well as the inspection of other specific areas of interest.

The macroenvironment is first assessed by conducting a scene walk-through. According to the U.S. Department of Justice, a scene walk-through is "an initial assessment conducted by carefully walking through the scene to evaluate the situation, recognize potential evidence, and determine resources required," which "provides an overview of the entire scene, identifies any threats to scene integrity, and ensures protection of physical evidence."[2] In essence, a scene walk-through is an initial assessment or preliminary survey of the death scene. During a scene walk-through, investigators mentally outline how the scene should be examined and identify the areas of the scene that should be focused on during the microenvironmental assessment.

Upon arrival at the scene, investigators should introduce themselves and obtain a brief description of the circumstances from professional responders present. If the infant's body is on scene, the medicolegal death investigator should confirm the death of the infant and then conduct the scene walk-through. The scene walk-through is often best completed in conjunction with an officer from the law enforcement agency with jurisdiction over the case. The scene walk-through is an opportune time for investigators to photodocument the macroenvironment providing permanent documentation of the overall scene environment.

The general overall condition of the incident location should be noted during the scene walk-through to include the size and layout of the building, the cleanliness of the location, the presence of domestic animals, and the presence of environmental hazards. Prior to the incident location being disrupted or cleaned, investigators should note the presence of ashtrays, liquor bottles or cans, prescription and over-the-counter medications, herbal and cultural remedies, and the presence of medical supplies such as humidifiers and apnea monitors. The walk-through provides information regarding the overall condition of the home, including the temperature, the type of utilities, as well as the presence of mold, vermin, and other potential physical dangers to the infant.

6.4.1 External Macroenvironment

Investigators should document the address of the incident location along with a description of the dwelling (i.e., one- or two-story single family home, mobile home, apartment complex, private business, day-care center). Information regarding the age of the dwelling (i.e., new construction vs. older home) may be important as some deaths may be the result of risk factors associated with the age of the dwelling, such as lead paint. Photographs should be taken of the exterior of the dwelling and it is recommended that a photograph include a picture of the dwelling's address if possible (Figure 6.1A, Figure 6.1B, and Figure 6.2)

6.4.2 Internal Macroenvironment

An assessment of the internal macroenvironment provides important information about the layout of the building, the condition of the dwelling as well as environmental factors or hazards that may have contributed to the death or its sequela. Infants are more vulnerable to environmental risk factors than adults or older children; as a result, investigators should take time to evaluate all aspects of the internal macroenvironment to identify potential risk factors and how they may have contributed to the infant's death.

The layout of the dwelling includes documenting the size and design of the location as well as potential entry and exit points. Investigators should note the number of rooms in the dwelling, the location of each, and the specific use for each room. In particular, it should be determined which residents sleep in which rooms, which bedroom belongs to which persons, and where in that room each person sleeps. For example, if a bedroom has a twin bed as well as a set of bunk beds, it will be important to determine who slept in each of the three locations in that room. A scene diagram may best depict the layout of the dwelling. Many agencies have a form that may be used to draw scene diagrams. If a form is not available, however, investigators can use a blank piece of paper to draw the basic layout of the incident location. Investigators must be sure to document the name of the deceased, the agency case number, the date and time the diagram was drawn, as well as the name and title of the person drawing it.

An assessment of the condition of the internal area is also a component of the macroenvironment assessment. The condition will include a description of the type of utility systems in the dwelling. Investigators should note if the dwelling uses city

FIGURE 6.1A Investigators should photograph the external environment of the incident location to permanently document the type and condition of the dwelling. This example is a two-story single family home.

FIGURE 6.1B The dwelling's physical address should also be photodocumented if available. This address was located on the mailbox not on the dwelling itself.

FIGURE 6.2 The physical address will be available on some dwellings and should be photodocumented during the scene investigation.

or well water, and if the heating system is powered by electricity or gas. It should also be determined if those systems are working and if they are not, the reason why. For example, it may be noted during the scene investigation that there are no working lights. It should be determined why there is no electricity (e.g., the occupant did not pay the electric bill, or there are no light bulbs in the fixtures). The ambient temperature at the incident location should be noted. During the scene investigation, the thermostat setting should be photographed (Figure 6.3).

The cleanliness of the incident location should also be noted as investigators assess the condition of the incident location. Although cleanliness is a subjective description, investigators should describe the incident in their narrative report and photograph examples of the description to include excess trash, dirty ashtrays, alcohol containers, and the general upkeep of the area. Insect and rodent activity or infestations should be documented in the narrative report as the infant may have injuries associated with them (for example, the body of the infant may be noted to have numerous ant and roach bites). A description of the insects identified at the scene may help explain those findings.

An assessment of environmental hazards noted at the incident location should be documented. These hazards may include the presence of carbon monoxide or other noxious gases or fumes, lead paint, mold and illegal drugs to name a few. The presence of domestic animals in the home should be documented during the investigation, including a description of the animal's type and size. Documentation regarding domestic pets that reside in the home may be important if the pet is able to get

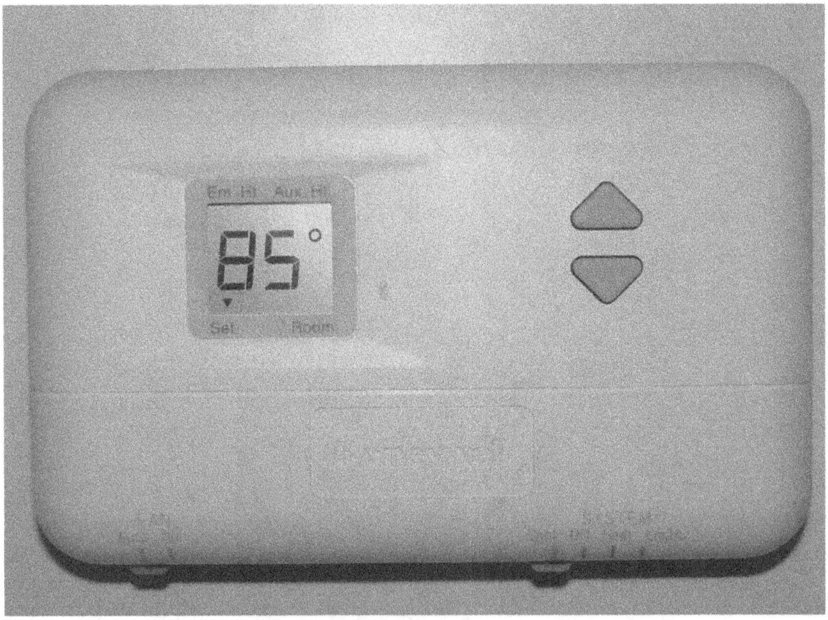

FIGURE 6.3 Thermostat setting at an incident location.

into the sleeping area of the infant; for example, the infant slept in an adult bed with the parents and a large dog, or a cat who resides in the home is able to jump into the playpen with the infant. Investigators should photograph environmental hazards that are recognized during the scene investigation. These hazards may or may not have contributed to the death, however, should be documented so that appropriate follow-up and referrals can be made if the hazard places other persons at risk for injury or death.

During the macroenvironmental scene investigation, investigators should be sure to look for evidence and scene information in three additional areas. At every death scene, investigators should look in the trash, the toilet, and the refrigerator. Each trash can located in the incident location should be looked through to see if evidence of any kind may have been thrown away. Investigators may locate all kinds of evidence or items in trash cans that provide information and details about the death. Some items that may be found include illegal drugs, empty prescription bottles, empty liquor bottles, receipts, and written notes to name a few. The number of dirty diapers in the trash may also provide information about the circumstances surrounding the death. The toilet is another area in which information can be gained as individuals may put items in the toilet with the intention of getting rid of them. The refrigerator should be inspected during the scene investigation. Items in the refrigerator may reveal information about the living conditions of the infant and family. Investigators will be able to assess if there is adequate food for the infant or family or assess the presence of alcohol and the presence of medication or drugs that may be stored in the refrigerator (Figure 6.4).

FIGURE 6.4 Refrigerator contents. In this example, investigators noted many alcohol containers, a few baby bottles, and very little food.

6.5 DOCUMENTING THE MICROENVIRONMENT

The microenvironment is the area within the larger macroenvironment in which the infant either became unresponsive, was in distress, or died. This area should be the focal point of the scene investigation unless scene evidence directs the investigation otherwise. The organization of the scene investigation will depend on the presence or absence of the infant's body. On arrival to the incident location, the scene investigator should first determine if the infant's body is or is not on scene.

6.5.1 The Process

The infant's location, when investigators arrive on scene, may not be the location in which the incident occurred. For example, on arrival the infant may be lying on a couch in the living room although the infant was found unresponsive elsewhere in the residence. The infant may have been moved to the living room prior to a first responder arriving on scene, or first responders may have moved the infant's body to better assess the infant. The scene investigation, postmortem assessment, and interviews with primary witnesses will provide information about the infant's location that will, for most cases, be the focal point of the scene investigation.

On arrival to the death scene, investigators should not touch or move the infant's remains until the location and position of the infant is photographically documented. The location and position of the infant when first observed by investigators will, in most cases, not be the location or position in which witnesses, or professional first responders, first observed the infant. Although the infant was probably moved, investigators should photodocument the infant's location and position when the investigator first arrived on scene. Photographs should include a distance overall shot of the room where the infant was located. Close-up photographs of the infant should also be taken to document the infant's head or face and any items that may be in close proximity of the infant.

The initial postmortem assessment should be completed after the infant's body is photodocumented. Depending on the case specifics, it may be beneficial to move the infant to another location within the scene prior to conducting the postmortem assessment. Moving the infant to another location within the scene ensures that purge or other fluids, which may be excreted during the examination, do not contaminate the location in which the infant was found by investigators. The body, when turned during the assessment, may excrete fluids that may inadvertently leave transfer marks on the surface. To prevent later confusion with regard to the marks present on arrival and which were caused during the physical assessment, the body should be moved to a clean, noninvolved location prior to conducting the assessment.

After the infant's body is moved, the location in which the infant was located should be assessed again, documenting any items that were under the infant or marks or patterns left by the infant. A photograph of the area underneath the infant should be taken to document the location of decomposition or purge fluid and the item on which the infant was lying. Investigators should assess all items that were in the immediate vicinity of the infant and the material that was located under the infant.

Once investigators have assessed the macroenvironment, documented the infant's location and position when they arrived on scene, conducted the initial postmortem assessment, and examined and documented the area under the infant, investigators should complete the microenvironment scene investigation. Investigators must use their observation, assessment, and interview skills to identify the area within the incident location in which the infant was last known to be alive and was found unresponsive. The area may contain physical evidence that may explain circumstances that contributed to the death. Investigators should complete a scene walkthrough to identify those areas in which the infant may have been located, look for evidence that may confirm that location and position, and interview witnesses to determine consistency between the scene findings and witness reports.

Photographs should be taken of the location believed or reported to be where the infant was last known to be or found. The area should be assessed for any physical findings such as blood, mucous, or purge fluid. Items in the reported location should be described and photographed, including pillows, toys, the type and amount of bedding, bottles, pacifiers, and such. Investigators should also assess the infant location for additional safety factors to ensure that all items around the infant are in good condition. During the examination of the infant's location, investigators

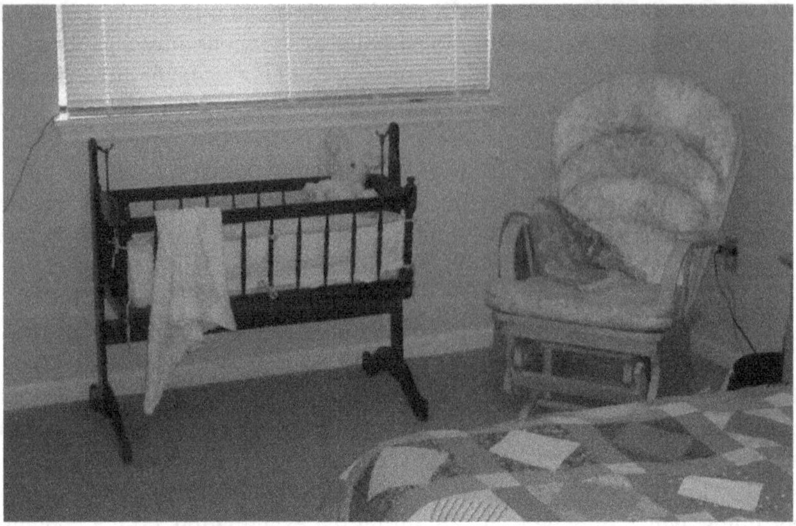

FIGURE 6.5A First responders present on scene reported that the infant was found in a bassinet located in the parent's bedroom.

should assess for physical findings on the surface as well as those items that may have been under the infant. Investigators should describe and document the type and amount of material under the infant. This will include a description of the surface and the layers below the surface. The infant may have been placed facedown on a blanket in a bassinet. Investigators should assess under the blanket and identify and document the surface under the infant. Under the blanket may be pillows, an egg crate mattress, sheepskin, or other layers of soft bedding; any of which may have contributed to the death (Figure 6.5A through Figure 6.5C).

6.5.2 Common Infant Death Locations

There are endless possibilities of locations and positions in which infants may have been placed and where they were found unresponsive. Common infant death locations include cribs, bassinets, playpens, couches, and adult-sized beds. The following sections provide specific information regarding these locations and areas of concern for each that investigators should be aware of during the scene investigation and subsequent doll reenactment.

6.5.2.1 Cribs

Infant deaths are often referred to as *crib deaths,* although the number of infant deaths that actually occur in cribs each year is unknown. During the investigation, the investigator should inquire as to the age of the crib and determine if it meets national safety guidelines. The U.S. Consumer Product Safety Commission (CPSC) recommends that antique and vintage cribs be disposed of as they may be unsafe environments, especially if there are cutouts in the headboard or footboard in which the infant's head may become trapped. The commission also suggests that the

FIGURE 6.5B Close-up photograph of the location where the infant was reported to have been found.

FIGURE 6.5C The sleep surface should be assessed as investigators should look under the area where the infant was located. In this example, an adult pillow was located in the bassinet.

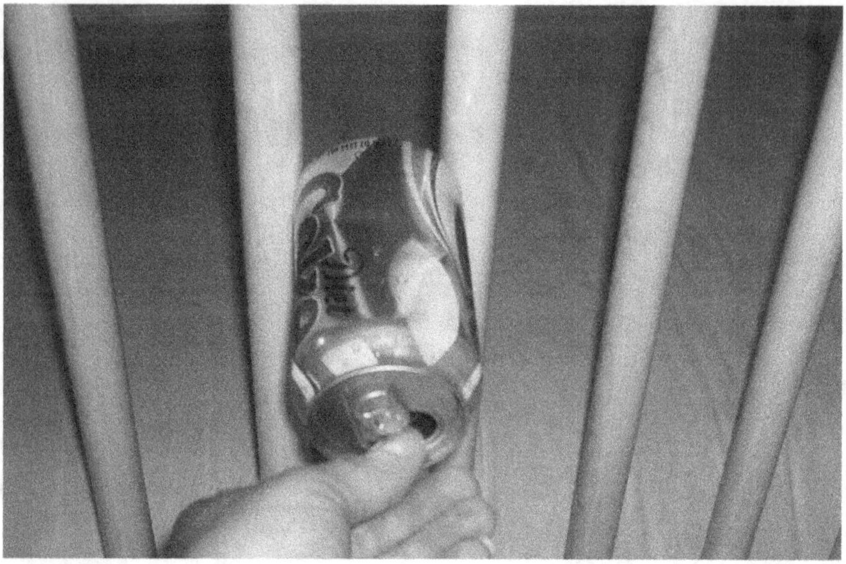

FIGURE 6.6A Investigators assessed the distance between crib slats. This crib is considered safe as the soda can is not able to fit between the slats.

FIGURE 6.6B Investigators were able to insert a soda can between the slats of this crib, which is considered an unsafe sleep environment.

distance between the slats be no more than 2 3/8 inches (about the width of a soda can) and that there are no broken or missing slats (Figure 6.6A and Figure 6.6B). Investigators should note any missing, broken, or loose hardware on the crib or mattress support, and the mattress in the crib should be firm and tight-fitting, which should prevent the infant from becoming wedged between the mattress and the slats (Figure 6.7A and Figure 6.7B). Investigators should also document the location of

FIGURE 6.7A Broken or missing hardware should be photodocumented. In this case, the corner of the crib was being held together with wire, which is noted at the bottom of the corner slat.

the crib as the CPSC and the National Safety Council recommend that cribs be kept away from windows. Infants that are in cribs, next to windows, may become entangled in the strings that hang from blinds or shades.[3,4]

After assessing the safety features of the crib, the investigator will need to assess the sleep surface layers that the infant may have been placed or found on. The CPSC recommends that pillows, quilts, comforters, sheepskins, pillowlike bumper pads, or pillow-like stuffed toys not be placed in the crib with an infant.[3] The type and amount of surface layers as well as all items in the crib should be documented.

6.5.2.2 Bassinets/Cradles

Bassinets and cradles are small minicribs that provide a smaller sleeping area for infants. The investigator should assess the condition of the bassinet or cradle to determine if the item meets national safety guidelines, which include a sturdy bottom

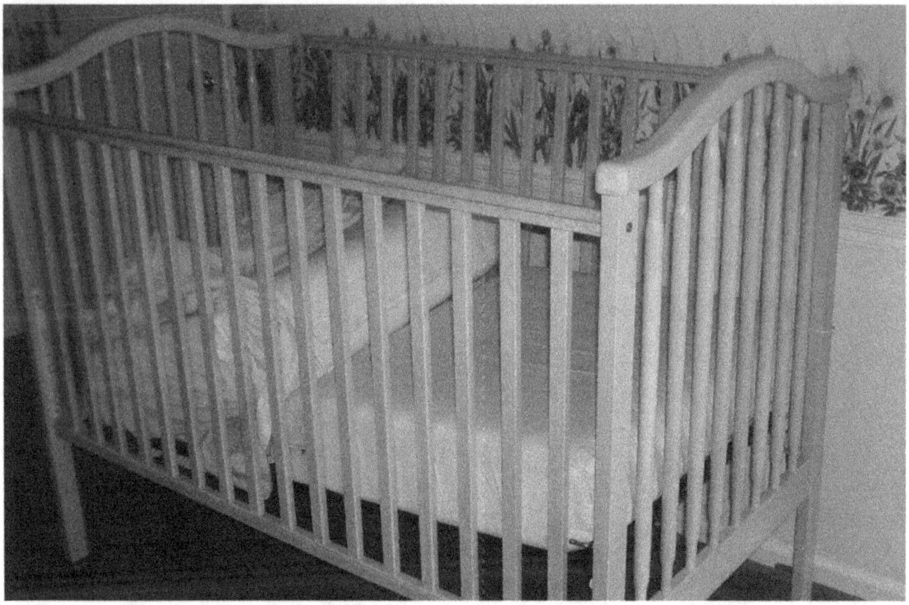

FIGURE 6.7B The sleep surface in this crib is couch cushions that were placed there. These cushions do not meet the recommendations that a firm tight fitting mattress should be used.

with a wide base for stability, smooth surfaces on the inside with no protruding staples or other hardware that may injure the infant, and a firm mattress that fits snuggly in the bottom of the bassinet or cradle. During the scene investigation, the investigator should note the location of the bassinet or cradle, the layers of bedding present in the bassinet, as well as any items located in the bassinet such as pillows, bedding, and stuffed animals.

6.5.2.3 Playpens

Playpens, which may be referred to as play yards or portable cribs, that have mesh sides should also be assessed during the scene investigation. CPSC recommends that the holes in the mesh not exceed 1/4 inch and that there be no tears, holes, or loose threads in the mesh that could entangle an infant.[3] The layers of bedding placed in the playpen as well as items that were present in the playpen should be described and photographed (Figure 6.8).

6.5.2.4 Couches

Infants may be placed to sleep on a couch or may be lying on a couch with another person when the death occurs. Infants can become wedged between the back cushion and a seat cushion or in other crevices. During cosleeping circumstances, the infant may become wedged between cushions and another person's body. Couches are considered to be unsafe sleep locations for infants and the risk of injury is increased if there is also cohabitation on the couch. The height of the couch should be measured

FIGURE 6.8 A caregiver reported that the infant slept in the playpen. During the scene walk-through, the playpen was noted to be full of clothes.

if a witness reports the infant rolled off the couch. The ground surface on which the infant landed should also be documented (Figure 6.9A through Figure 6.9C).

6.5.2.5 Adult Beds

During the scene investigation, investigators should document the size and type of bed (e.g., twin, full, queen, or king size, standard mattress or waterbed) as well as the firmness of the surface if the infant was placed or found on an adult bed. The investigator should document the layers of bedding material along with items on the bed. The number of pillows should be counted and the location of each item photographed. Deaths may occur due to wedging between the bed and the wall; therefore, the space between the bed and wall or furniture where the infant became wedged should be measured (Figure 6.10A and Figure 6.10B). The height of the bed should be measured during the scene investigation and the ground surface described for cases in which a witness reports that the infant fell or rolled off the bed.

6.5.2.6 Other Possible Infant Death Locations

There are numerous locations where an infant may become unresponsive. The most common have already been addressed; however, there are others that warrant mentioning. Infant deaths may occur in any location where an infant may be placed. In addition to the locations previously mentioned, an infant death may occur in a chair, car seat, baby carrier, stroller, or in the arms of a caregiver (Figure 6.11). Regardless of the location, investigators must take time to assess the location for

FIGURE 6.9A A witness reported the infant was sleeping on a couch and rolled off onto the floor before becoming unresponsive.

FIGURE 6.9B The witness was asked to place the doll where the infant was located after rolling off the couch.

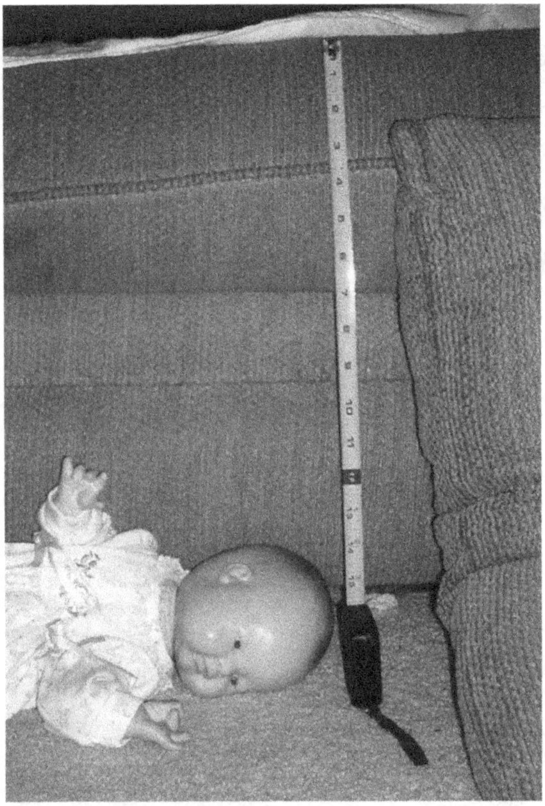

FIGURE 6.9C Investigators should measure the distance from which the infant reportedly fell.

features that may place an infant at an increased risk for injury or death. Investigators determine if the item is in good repair, what items were located around the infant, as well as the surface of the item on which the infant was placed. Cases in which the infant was in the arms of a caregiver may be particularly difficult to investigate.

6.5.3 Cosleeping and Bed-Sharing Scenarios

During the investigation of an infant's death, it may be reported that the infant shared a sleep surface with another individual. Sharing a sleep surface with an infant or child is sometimes referred to as cosleeping or bed sharing. Both of these descriptions can be misleading. *Cosleeping* implies that both the child and the other individuals were asleep, where the description *bed sharing* is only an accurate description if they were actually on a bed. There are a number of locations in which an infant may have been on the same surface as another person. Some examples of surfaces that may be shared include beds, couches, loveseats, the floor, beanbag chairs, and such.

Investigators should thoroughly assess and document the area in which the infant was reported to have shared a surface with another person. The area should be

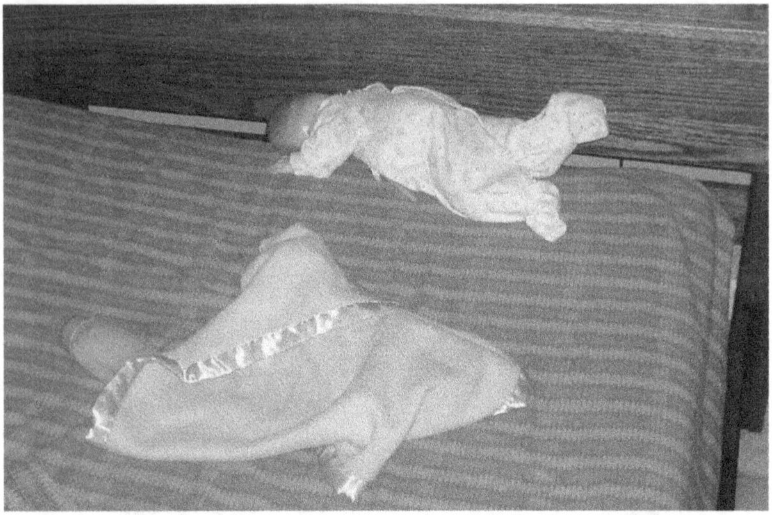

FIGURE 6.10A A witness reported that the infant was found wedged between the mattress and a headboard. The witness demonstrated the infant's position during a doll reenactment.

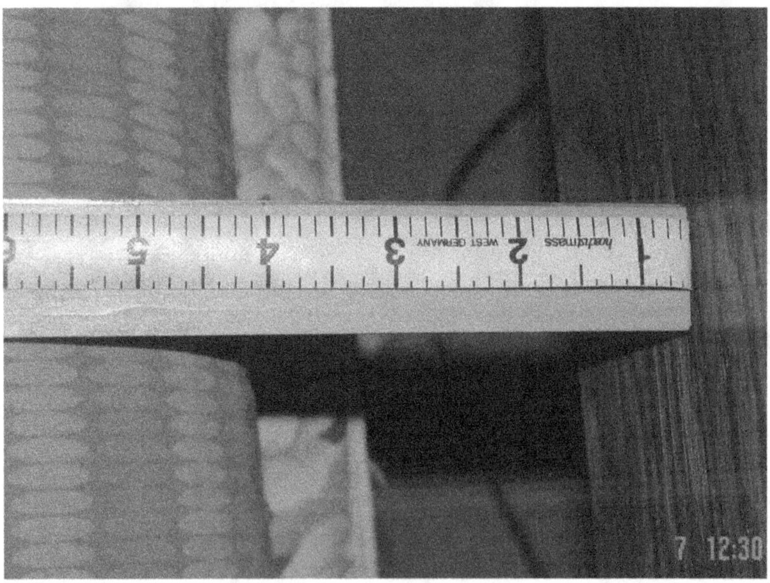

FIGURE 6.10B A measurement should be taken to document the distance between the mattress and headboard.

assessed for physical evidence that may confirm the presence of each individual. Investigators should obtain the name, age, height, and weight of each person sharing the surface with the infant, as well as a description of each person's position. Each person may also be asked to demonstrate their position during the doll reenactment (Figure 6.12A through Figure 6.12D).

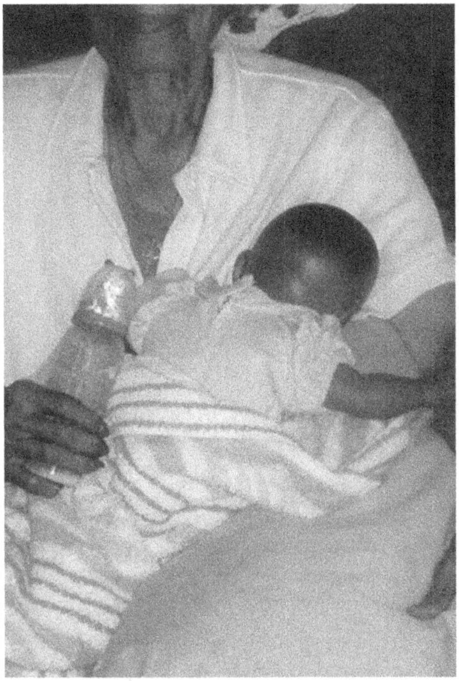

FIGURE 6.11 Infant deaths that occur in the arms of a caregiver should be demonstrated during a doll reenactment.

FIGURE 6.12A During an infant death investigation, it was reported that the infant and a caregiver were sharing a sleep surface on an adult bed. Investigators should photograph the bed as observed during the scene investigation.

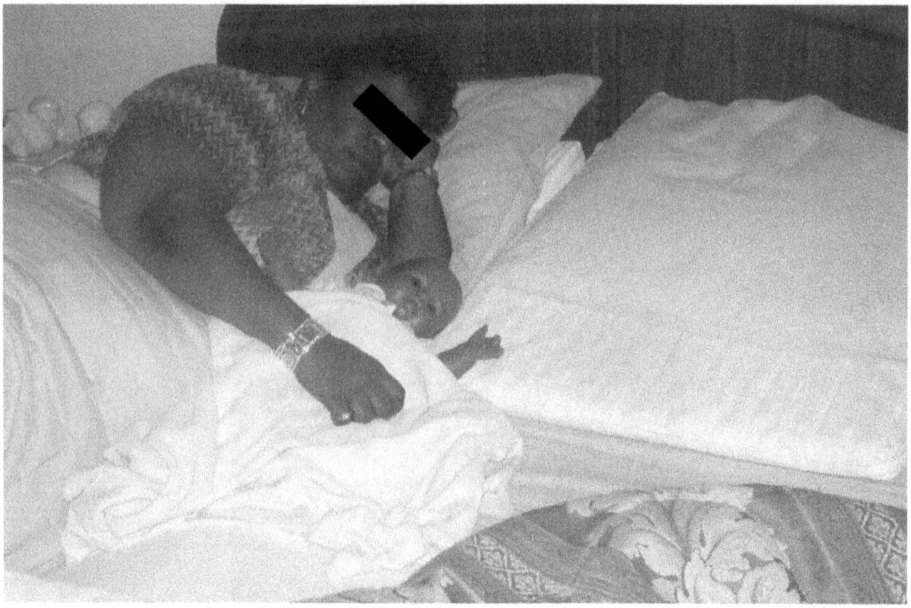

FIGURE 6.12B During the doll reenactment, investigators asked the witness to demonstrate his or her position and the infant's position on the sleep surface when the infant was last known to be alive.

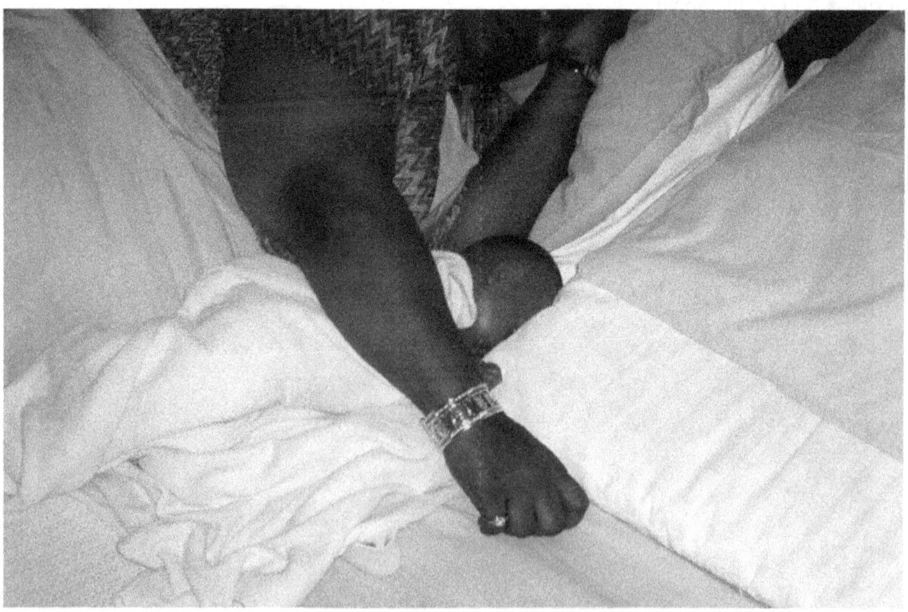

FIGURE 6.12C The witness should be asked to demonstrate his or her position and the infant's position when the infant was found.

FIGURE 6.12D Photographs should document the surface on which they were located, noting any other unsafe sleep conditions.

6.6 DAY-CARE CENTERS

Infant deaths that occur outside of the family or caregiver's residence pose additional challenges to investigators. Although licensed child care facilities are fairly safe places, more and more children are in those settings, which increases the chance that an infant may die while in their care. After the death of an infant or child that is in the care of a day-care provider, investigators should obtain specific information about the facility. A death at a day-care center may highlight areas of concern that need to be addressed to promote safety in this and other day-care centers. Investigators should be aware of the agency in their state that regulates day-care licensing and the method by which that agency should be notified when a death occurs in such a facility.

6.6.1 Types of Day-Care Centers

During the scene investigation and interviews with the day-care providers, investigators should determine the type of day-care facility and if the facility is registered or licensed. Investigators should contact the licensing agency, identify when the registration or license was issued and if there have been any major violations noted with this facility. Each state has requirements regarding the licensing of home and out-of-home day-care centers; however, the requirements vary from state to state. Investigators should familiarize themselves with the type of facilities in their state and the requirements for each. Typically, states have different levels of registration or licensing which is based on the number of children that are being cared for and the standards by which the child care provider must adhere.

Often, home-based day-care providers, sometimes referred to as family child care centers, are those that operate in the residence of the individual who cares for the children. The number of children being cared for will determine what type of registration or license is required. In some states, it is not mandatory for child care providers to register with the state if they are only caring for one child that is not related to them. The child care provider in this example may not be required to register with the state or meet any requirements. Another type of day-care center are providers who offer child care services, in their home, and care for more than one child that is not related to them. Depending on the state, these home-based child care providers may have to register with the state, yet may not be required to meet specific standards. In other states, these home-based day-care providers may have to apply for a license and meet state requirements, including periodic audits to provide documentation that they are meeting the licensing standards. The last category, out-of-home day-care centers, may be licensed to care for many children and, as a result, have the strictest licensing requirements.

6.6.2 Licensing Requirements

Investigators should familiarize themselves with state licensing requirements when investigating an infant death that occurred in a day-care facility. Knowledge of the requirements helps investigators determine if the provider met the standards of care for the number of children in their care. If the child care provider failed to follow state guidelines and the death resulted from unsafe practices or from lack of supervision, the investigator should notify the licensing agency of their findings.

During an infant death investigation at a day-care facility, investigators should obtain the name of the facility, the name of the owner or operator and the type of day-care facility. Many states require that day-care providers display the license in a conspicuous place along with an emergency procedure plan. Investigators should document the information on the license and photograph it if it is available. During the investigation, the investigator should verify the license status with the licensing agency. Investigators should also determine if there have been any violations filed concerning this day-care facility, its owner, or any staff employed there. Of particular interest will be any reports of serious injury or death to any other children previously in their care.

Investigators should identify the number and ages of children present at the time of the death as well as the names of all staff persons present at the time of death. Investigators should evaluate the staff-to-child ratio to determine if state requirements were being met and if the child who died was being adequately supervised. If the day-care center is required to have separate spaces for children of different ages, the investigator should determine if the deceased child was in the right room with the correct group of children.

It may be necessary to review background information on the day-care center employees. Investigators may want to review background checks, prior work history, and verify individual staff members' work times for the incident date. Some states require that day-care providers be certified in cardiopulmonary resuscitation and first aid; therefore, it may be necessary to verify certification or other training requirements as dictated by the case. Investigators should interview all staff present at the time of death to determine if appropriate care and supervision was provided to the child.

During the scene investigation at a day-care facility, investigators should document any environmental hazards that may have placed the infant at an increased risk for injury or death. Again, investigators should document the water and heat source, the presence of animals or vermin, and the presence of other substances that may have contributed to the death such as cigarette smoking and alcohol. Investigators should assess the surface on which the infant was placed to determine if it meets with the state's safety recommendations. It is also important for investigators to determine if other children at the day-care facility have been ill. Reports of other sick children may be important if the death is the result of a contagious illness. Information regarding the signs and symptoms the other children are exhibiting may provide clues to the forensic pathologist regarding the disease process. If the death was the result of a contagious process, the caregivers for the other children should be notified so that they can take appropriate preventative action.

6.7 EVIDENCE OR CHAIN OF CUSTODY

During a scene investigation, it may be necessary for items to be removed from the scene and placed in evidence. It may also be necessary to remove items from the scene and transport them to the autopsy for the forensic pathologist to be able to examine those items and compare and contrast each item to possible marks on the infant. Investigators must be certain that they follow their agency policies and protocols to ensure that the chain of custody is maintained for those evidentiary items that are removed from the scene. Chain of custody ensures the continuous accountability of evidence. The chain of custody paper trail indicates when an item was taken into custody, who maintained control of the item, and to whom it may have been transferred for analysis or processing. Investigators must ensure that all chain of custody protocols are followed to maintain the integrity of the evidence should the evidence need to be presented in court.

6.8 SUMMARY

The death scene tells a story. It provides details about the circumstances surrounding the death, the living conditions of the occupants, as well as environmental and lifestyle factors that may have contributed to an infant's death. The scene may quickly become altered after a tragic incident, and it is crucial that investigators respond quickly to the incident location. The quicker the response, the less likely evidence will be lost.

During the scene investigation, investigators must ensure that a complete assessment is made of the area in which the infant became unresponsive (the micro-environment) as well as an overall assessment of the incident location (the macro-environment). The scene must be photographed and processed according to agency policy and national guidelines to ensure that a complete investigation occurs, which includes documentation of all physical and environmental hazards that may have placed the infant at an increased risk for injury or death.

The scene should never be overlooked and should be assessed immediately after the death occurs, usually within the first few hours. As time passes, the scene may become intentionally or unintentionally altered making it more difficult for investigators to identify potential risk factors. The scene tells a story and provides a picture of the circumstances surrounding the infant's death. The saying, "A picture is worth a thousand words," could not be more true. An investigator's observations at a death scene may be just as important and influential as the words spoken by a witness. The complex and tragic story of an infant's death may be revealed in the scene that is left behind. The investigator's goal is to be able to look at and assess the infant death scene before it is altered. Again, time is of the essence; investigators who fail to investigate the scene may just miss the story.

REFERENCES

1. U.S. Department of Justice, Death Investigation: A Guide for the Scene Investigator, Report NCJ 167568, November 1999.
2. Technical Working Group of Crime Scene Investigation, Crime Scene Investigation: A Guide for Law Enforcement, report issued by U.S. Department of Justice, Washington, D.C., January 2000, available at http://www.ncjrs.gov/txtfiles1/nij/178280.txt (accessed August 6, 2006).
3. Consumer Product Safety Commission, Crib Safety Tips: Use Your Crib Safely, Document 5030, available at http://www.cpsc.gov (accessed on June 19, 2006).
4. National Safety Council, Crib Safety Tips, document available at http://www.nsc.org (accessed on June 19, 2006).

RESOURCES

Centers for Disease Control and Prevention, Sudden Unexplained Infant Death Investigation. A Systemic Training Program for the Professional Infant Death Investigation Specialist, document 200-2005-13514, 2006.

Dix, J., *Handbook for Death Scene Investigators,* CRC Press LLC, Boca Raton, FL, 1999.

7 The Art of Interviewing

7.1 INTRODUCTION

Many resources are available that teach investigators effective interview and interrogation strategies. Publications have been written and entire businesses have been developed to train investigators in the needed skills to interview adult victims, witnesses, and suspects. Much has also been written about effective ways to interview children who have witnessed a crime or who themselves were victimized. Professionals agree that the strategies and techniques used when interviewing children should be different than those used to interview adults. Another group of interviewees may benefit from a different interview approach: the primary witnesses of an infant's or young child's death, such as the parents and caregivers. Interviewing witnesses about any death can be difficult; however, there is often an added dimension of grief and emotion associated with the deaths of young children. Even the most experienced interviewer may find it difficult to gather detailed information without feeling as if the interview process is causing pain to the survivors.

Interviewing is a skill that can be developed with training and experience. Skilled interviewers develop a plan of action prior to initiating an interview. They consider the logistics of the interview, including who, when, where, and how the interview will be conducted. The interviewer should also consider the type of interview as well as the type and amount of information that should be obtained. Experienced interviewers who use a nonthreatening tone and actively seek to develop a rapport with the interviewee are often able to defuse intense emotion in witnesses who are extremely upset. They are prepared for the unexpected and are able to adjust their plan of action as needed.

Interviews with primary caregivers or witnesses are crucial components of any infant death investigation and the initial interview sets the tone for the remainder of the investigation. A good interview is vital to the success of an investigation and can significantly impact the case; just as a poor interview may be worthless to the investigation and result in negative consequences for the case.[1] Whether or not investigators have suspicions of foul play, the initial interview should be organized in such a way that the investigator is able to obtain as much background information related to the infant and family as possible. The investigator's goal in this type of interview is to get to know the infant, the family, and the circumstances surrounding the death, and to develop a 48-hour time line of events leading up to the infant's death.

The way interviewees are approached, spoken to, and interacted with during the initial interview may affect the amount of information the investigator is able to obtain and the witness's willingness to participate in a scene walk-through, a doll reenactment, or future interviews. The organizational structure, that is, which topics are discussed first and the order of subsequent topics, may impact the investigator's ability to obtain all of the information needed to thoroughly and completely investigate the infant's death.

Following the initial interview, investigators should compare the information obtained from primary witnesses to that of professional first responders (PFRs), the scene investigation, and the initial postmortem infant assessment. If discrepancies arise, investigators should then conduct a clarification interview to clear up any areas of miscommunication or misunderstanding. Cases in which numerous, unexplained discrepancies occur may require investigators to conduct additional interviews or participate in the interrogation of a witness.

There is an art to interviewing the primary witnesses of an infant's death. This chapter will cover interviewing basics, the different types of interviews, preplanning considerations for each, as well as specific information that should be acquired during the initial and subsequent interviews as they relate to infant death investigations. The planning and forethought that goes into an interview with a primary witness cannot be understated; both are critical to the investigation of an infant's or young child's death. Investigators may need to evaluate the ways and methods used to interview primary witnesses. A new approach may greatly impact an investigator's ability to obtain necessary information during interviews with primary witnesses.

7.2 INTERVIEW BASICS

To become an effective interviewer, investigators must have knowledge of basic strategies and techniques that should be considered and put into action prior to and during each and every interview. Without this basic knowledge and understanding of how each aspect can impact a case, it will be more difficult for investigators to use advanced interview techniques that may be needed during an investigation. A review of the basics is always beneficial, as advanced techniques grow out of these fundamental skills. Interview skills are perishable if not practiced and honed. As interview skills are mastered, interviews will be more successful. It is estimated that, "ninety to ninety-five percent of all evidentiary items presented in court stem from information extracted from a victim, witness or suspect" and that "intelligent and careful questioning accounts for the solution of 99 percent of all cases."[2] Infant deaths are difficult to investigate for many reasons; therefore, it is vital that investigators not only be skilled in the basics, but also have knowledge of and experience with additional approaches.

Effective interviews have three components: the preparation phase, the implementation phase, and an evaluation phase. Interviewers, who take time to understand the importance of each phase and how each phase will impact their interview, and ultimately their investigation, will be more successful in meeting the case-specific goals of their investigation than other interviewers.

7.2.1 Preparation Phase

The preparation phase of any interview is vital, as preplanned and organized interviews are more successful. Interviewers who develop a plan of action prior to the interview will identify the goals and purposes of the interview, identify the minimum information needed, and determine the type of interview that should be conducted to ensure that the desired information is obtained. Logistics of the interview must also be considered, and interviewers should identify who should be interviewed as well as when and where the interview should be conducted.

The organizational structure and format of an interview should be determined during the preparation phase and prior to implementing any interview. The interviewer should determine how the interview will begin, what topics will be covered, the sequence of those topics, and a plan to conclude the interview. Interviewers who preplan the organizational structure are more confident during the interview and are less likely to omit anything that was predetermined to be important to the investigation. This could not be truer than when interviewing parents who are grieving over the recent death of an infant or very young child. It is absolutely vital that the initial interview with these individuals be preplanned and organized, as the amount of information needed from them and the emotions surrounding these deaths complicate an already difficult investigation.

Another consideration is determining whether it is necessary to advise a witness of their Miranda rights either prior to or during an interview. Generally, Miranda must be provided if a witness is in police custody for the commission of a crime. During the initial interview (Section 7.4), investigators try to obtain information related to the cause of death (COD) and manner of death (MOD) to determine if a criminal act has occurred. The initial interview, primarily conducted by the medico-legal death investigator (MDI), is designed for information gathering. At this time, the interviewee is not a suspect nor in police custody; therefore, Miranda rights do not need to be read. If, however, during the scene investigation, initial postmortem infant assessment, and the initial interview, investigators determine that a criminal act occurred and the witness is a suspect, appropriate action should be taken to have law enforcement personnel advise the witness of their Miranda rights.

7.2.2 Implementation Phase

The *implementation phase* is the actual interview conducted with the witness. This phase has three distinct sections: the introduction, the body, and the closure. All three sections are important, and investigators should not underestimate the effect that each will have during the initial interview and possible subsequent interviews. Some general information for each section is described below; however, specific items of interest to infant death investigations will be addressed later in the chapter as each type of interview is discussed.

7.2.2.1 Introduction

The introduction of and the method by which the interview is initiated sets the tone for the remainder of the interview. Interviewers should take great care in determining how they will begin the interview process, including how to introduce themselves, explain their role in the investigation, and build rapport with the witness. During initial interviews with witnesses, honesty is the best policy; interviewers should introduce themselves, explain who they are and the reason for the interview, and elicit the witness's assistance.

Building rapport with a witness is most likely to occur if the interviewer shows respect and empathy and takes the time needed to listen. Interviewers who rush and are not prepared or equipped to handle the interview will find it difficult to build rapport and to obtain the information needed. The interviewer should attempt to make the witness feel comfortable and reduce their anxiety. Many resources are available that address specific methods for building rapport, but they are beyond the scope of this text. Investigators should take the time to learn additional ways to incorporate these techniques into all interviews.

7.2.2.2 Body of the Interview

After the introduction in which the tone has been set for the interview, questioning begins to determine what the witness knows about the incident being investigated. Investigators should provide the witness an opportunity to describe events in a free-flowing narrative format in conjunction with open-ended and direct questions. The goal is for investigators to identify all circumstances surrounding the incident and who, what, why, where, when, and how the incident occurred. While some types of interviews begin with "Tell me what happened" and allow the witness to describe the incident in an uninterrupted narrative format followed by more direct questions from the interviewer, another approach may be more effective when interviewing primary witnesses in infant death investigations. That approach will be discussed at length later in the chapter.

7.2.2.3 Closure

The method by which an investigator closes or departs the interview is just as important as the method by which the interview began. Just as with the other sections of the interview, the closure should not be rushed or omitted, as the method by which the interviewer exits the interview will leave a final impression on the witness. This impression may affect the witness's willingness to participate in additional interviews if needed. Interviewers should provide the witness an opportunity to ask questions and should attempt to answer those questions as truthfully as possible. The interviewer should thank the witnesses for their time, let them know that they have been very helpful, and ask their permission to contact them if the interviewer should have any additional questions. The investigator should provide the witness with contact information and again offer final condolences before departing. During infant death investigations, it may be necessary to prepare the witness for a scene walk-through or doll reenactment. Preparing the witness for each of those will occur during this final section of the interview and will be discussed in Section 4.5.

7.2.3 Evaluation Phase

After the interview with a witness is complete, investigators should take time to evaluate the effectiveness of the interview. There are two aspects of the interview that should be evaluated: First, the information that was received from the witness should be evaluated to determine if the information is consistent with other aspects of the investigation. This evaluation will help investigators determine if additional interviews should be conducted, if the scene needs to be reexamined, or if additional records should be obtained. Second, the investigator should evaluate their effectiveness as interviewers, critique themselves, and learn from their experiences and their mistakes. Two interviewers may be present for some interviews. In these cases, the interviewers should work together so that each can improve their techniques and their approaches to interviews. It is through experience that investigators master the skills needed to interview effectively, and it is through honest evaluation and assessment of themselves that they may then improve upon the skills they already have.

7.3 TYPES OF INTERVIEWS

An interview is a conversation in which the interviewer tries to elicit specific information from the interviewee. Interviews are nonaccusatory in nature with questions designed to acquire factual information needed to investigate the case at hand. The interviewer's goal, the obtaining of information, may or may not be met as the interviewee may or may not have an interest in or motivation to provide accurate information. Investigators and interviewers should utilize the type of interview that meets the purpose and goal of the interview and which lessens the witness's interest or motive in providing inaccurate information.

For the purpose of infant death investigations, there are four types or levels of interviews that may be utilized. The first interview is the initial interview, which may be followed by a clarification interview, follow-up interview, or an interrogation. Each type of interview is unique in its goal, its organizational structure, its logistics, as well as the impact it may have on the determination of the COD and MOD.

During infant death investigations, investigators begin by conducting initial interviews with primary witnesses. Investigators who determine that a witness is intentionally or unintentionally providing misleading or inaccurate information may need to conduct the next type or level of interview, a clarification interview. If it is determined that the information obtained during the clarification interview is not consistent with other aspects of the investigation, the investigator may then need to conduct one or all of the other types of interviews.

Investigators may need to conduct one or more clarification or follow-up interviews with the same individual prior to an investigation being complete. The number of interviews needed during an infant death investigation is case dependent as is the type of interviews that may be needed. Medicolegal and law enforcement investigators who were present for the initial interview will help determine if it is necessary to conduct additional interviews with any or all of the other caregivers and witnesses. The role that the MDI plays in the implementation of each type of interview may vary depending on the investigator's interview skills, jurisdictional policies and practices, and the case-specific aspects of the investigation.

7.4 INITIAL INTERVIEW

The initial interview, the first interview with primary witnesses, should be conducted by the MDI. This interview, which is lengthy and often emotional for the witness, should occur as soon as possible after the infant's death and prior to the forensic autopsy. The purpose of the interview is to gather as much information about the infant, the infant's family, and circumstances surrounding the infant's death. The interviewer should use this information to develop a time line of events that occurred during the 48 hours prior to the infant's death. The investigator's goal is to get to know all of the involved persons.

This interview is best conducted in a conversational nonthreatening tone that provides the investigator an opportunity to establish rapport with the witness. This is turn may affect the willingness of the witness to participate in other aspects of the investigation. Although conversational in nature, the investigator preplans the organizational format and direction of the "conversation." In planning the interview, it may be helpful to remember that discussion of events and information furthest from the incident is easier than that nearer to death. For example the infant's medical history, including pregnancy, delivery, and vaccination information, will be addressed prior to developing the 48-hour time line and prior to saying to the witness, "Tell me what happened." Direct and open-ended questions are first used to gather specific information about the infant and family that is furthest from the incident. This structure allows the witness to gain and maintain their composure, as they focus on providing specific detailed information that is distant to the incident. This structure provides the investigator detailed background information on the infant and family that may then be compared to the witness's account of the circumstances surrounding the infant's death. Having the detailed history of the infant and family prior to gathering the incident information, investigators may be better equipped to identify inconsistencies between the two.

This organizational format also provides investigators an opportunity to identify the witness's truth-telling style. By asking a witness to provide information and details that are distant in time from the incident, the investigator can assess the witness's style for providing truthful information. Witnesses are more likely to provide inaccurate or misleading information when questioned about the circumstances surrounding the infant's death as opposed to when providing information regarding the infant's and family's medical history. As a result, investigators who have been with a witness for a period of time gathering background information may be able to note a difference in the witness's demeanor when they report specific information about the death.

Investigators who begin an interview with a primary witness to an infant death with "Tell me what happened," risk the witness being unable to maintain their composure. It is during this type of situation, when parents and caregivers are emotionally distraught, that an investigator may decide to interview the witness later. A delayed interview results in a delayed investigation. In some situations, a change in the organizational format of the interview may assist a witness to maintain their composure and, at the same time, ensure that the information needed is obtained.

In infant death investigations in which the double-team approach has been implemented, both the infant and scene investigators conduct initial interviews of primary witnesses. The infant investigator conducts initial interviews with primary witnesses who responded to the hospital and the scene investigator conducts the initial interviews with primary witnesses who remained on scene. After each investigator conducts the initial interviews at their respective locations, the two investigators then communicate with one another. If there are discrepancies in the interviews, the scene investigation, or the postmortem infant assessment, one or both of the investigators should then conduct a clarification interview.

During the preparation phase, however, the interviewer must determine the logistics of the interview including who should be involved in the interview, the order of interviews, when and where the interviews should occur, what information must be obtained, and the best method and approach to be used. Specific topics that must be covered, as well as the sequence of those topics and how they are presented to the witness, are critical to the success of the implementation phase of the interview. A recommended format for an initial interview with a parent or caregiver during an infant death investigation is provided in Section 7.4.5. Following the interview, investigators should take the necessary time to evaluate the information obtained and evaluate their effectiveness as interviewers.

7.4.1 The Initial Interview: Who Is Involved

Critical to any investigation is determining who should be interviewed, who should conduct the interview, and who, if anyone, other than the interviewee and the interviewer should be present for the interview. There are a number of people who may be interviewed regarding the circumstances surrounding an infant's death, just as there may be many individuals who want to interview or be present for those interviews. Investigators must preplan and decide which individuals will be interviewed and in what order to ensure a concise and orderly investigation.

7.4.1.1 Who to Interview

Identifying the individuals who should be interviewed during an infant death investigation is vital. There may be many people who had contact with the infant during the 48 hours prior to the infant's death, who have knowledge of the infant's medical and social histories, or who were present at the time of the infant's death. Some of these persons are primary witnesses, while others are secondary witnesses. The investigator should, whenever possible, interview the primary witnesses first.

The primary witnesses in an infant death investigation include the person who last cared for the infant prior to death, the last person who knew the infant was alive, the person who found the infant unresponsive or in distress, the primary caregivers, and the infant's legal guardians. The *primary caregiver* is the individual who has the primary day-to-day responsibility of caring for the infant. The *legal guardian,* however, is the individual who has the legal authority and duty to care for another person, in this case, an infant or young child who is incapable of caring for his or her own interests. There may be one person who fits all of the above descriptions, or in some cases, there may be multiple people who fit the above criteria.

> *Case Example 7.1* The biological mother, who is single and the primary caregiver, was at home alone with the infant. She was the individual who last cared for the infant, last saw the infant alive, and was the person who found the infant. In this case, there is only one primary witness.

Case Example 7.2 The biological mother and the biological father were at home with the infant, along with the infant's maternal grandmother. The grandmother put the infant down and heard the infant cry approximately an hour later but did not go in and check on the infant. The father then found the infant unresponsive a short time later. In this example, all three individuals are considered primary witnesses.

Case Example 7.3 A 6-month-old infant, who lived in a foster home and was the ward of the state, died while at a day-care center. One day-care provider put the infant down to sleep and another worker found the infant unresponsive. The primary witnesses include the day-care providers, the foster parents, who are the primary caregivers, and the caseworker for the children and family service agency who is the legal custodian for the child.

Primary witnesses may have many titles including biological, adoptive, or foster parent; stepmother; stepfather; grandparent; babysitter; nanny; day-care provider; or family friend to name a few. Some of these individuals will know more about the infant's medical and social histories as well as family circumstances and dynamics than others. The individuals with the most information about the infant's history may or may not have been present at the time of the death or had contact with the infant during the 48 hours prior to death. It is crucial that the investigator determine who was present at the time of the death, who had contact with the infant during the last 48 hours of the infant's life, and which other persons may have valuable information about the infant and family.

Secondary witnesses are individuals who may have additional information regarding the circumstances surrounding the infant's death and the infant's and family's medical and social histories. These individuals may or may not have been present at the incident location around the time of the infant's death and may or may not have had contact with the infant in the 48 hours prior to its death. These witnesses should be interviewed; however, it may not be necessary or beneficial to interview them in the same organizational format as that of primary witnesses.

Case Example 7.4 An infant died while at a day-care. The biological parents did not have contact with the infant during the 48 hours prior to the infant's death as the infant resided with the maternal grandmother who is the legal guardian and primary caregiver. The grandmother and the day-care provider are the primary witnesses; however, it may be necessary to interview the biological parents to gather specific information regarding the pregnancy, prenatal care, and delivery that may not be known by the primary witnesses.

Case Example 7.5 A 3-month-old infant who resided with his mother was placed by her and found unresponsive by her. A female friend from out of town spent that night at the mother's residence. The mother, who is the primary caregiver, the legal guardian, and the person that placed and found the infant, is the only primary witness. Although the friend was present at the scene and should be interviewed, she is considered a secondary witness as she did not place or find the infant and is not the primary caregiver or the legal guardian. She may have important information about the death; however, she does not need to be interviewed in the same organizational format as the mother.

7.4.1.2 Who Conducts the Initial Interview

One primary investigator should conduct the initial interview with a primary witness, while a secondary investigator observes the interview. It is ideal if one of the individuals has a medical or health care background, and the other interviewer is a law enforcement investigator. Due to the purpose and goal of the initial interview, persons with knowledge of infant or maternal health, infant growth and development, and medications and who have experience conducting health histories have a skill set that is very conducive to the initial interview of primary witnesses during infant death investigations. In most cases and jurisdictions, the MDI will be the primary interviewer. The primary interviewer's role is to introduce both interviewers, offer condolences, establish rapport with the witness, and conduct the interview. The interviewer should also answer questions the witness may have regarding the investigation, prepare the witness for future aspects of the investigation including the doll reenactment, and, after the completion of the interview, communicate with the secondary interviewer.

The secondary interviewer should be the lead investigator for the law enforcement agency with jurisdiction over the case. The secondary interviewer's role is to observe nonverbal cues, take detailed notes of the interview, and prepare to ask additional questions of the witness if there are questions that the primary interviewer failed to ask or if there are details that need to be clarified. The secondary interviewer must also communicate with the primary interviewer at the completion of the interview and be available to advise the witness of their Miranda rights should that be necessary.

The two interviewers should work as a team, in tandem, as each of their roles is important. Interview teams that work well together will develop the best rapport with witnesses and will gather more information than teams that do not work well together. When two interviewers are present, the primary interviewer can focus their attention on listening to the witness, while the second interviewer takes notes. It is vital that both investigators be present for the initial interview as it provides an opportunity for both to hear the primary witness's account of the circumstances and provides an opportunity for both to observe the witness's nonverbal cues. It eliminates the need for each witness to be interviewed multiple times by multiple people, which is beneficial to the witness and is also beneficial to investigators.

7.4.1.3 Other Persons Who May Be Present during the Initial Interview

Investigators should predetermine which other persons, if any, may be present while a primary witness is interviewed. It is best if the witness is interviewed alone, away from other primary or secondary witnesses. This should be handled tactfully so as to not add more pain to families. Some investigators may allow a support person to be present for the interview as long as those persons are not primary or secondary witnesses. This practice, however, is discouraged and, if allowed, should be done with great care. It is not acceptable for the third party to interrupt the interview or to try to answer questions for the witness. If the third party does so, he or she needs to be asked to leave the interview area. There is also the potential that information from the interview may be shared with others and possibly compromise the investigation.

Infant deaths bring out strong emotions in many people, and it may be that a third party will not understand the interviewers' questions or may feel that asking the same question more than once is harassment; as a result, the third party may try to answer questions for the witness. The third party likely will not understand the interview process or the direction of the interview and, as a result, may either intentionally or unintentionally interfere.

Case Example 7.6 The mother of a deceased infant requested that her chaplain be present with her during the interview. The chaplain was allowed to sit with her and was asked not to interject or try to answer for the witness. The interview was conducted and the interviewer had concerns regarding the mother's response to a specific question. A few minutes later the investigator rephrased the question and asked it again. The chaplain interrupted and repeated the answer the mother gave earlier, thus preventing the mother from answering the question a second time.

The presence of a third party may also prevent the witness from being forthright about circumstances or events that may be embarrassing or shameful to the witness. Some of the topics that will be covered during the initial interview are sensitive and personal in nature and difficult for the witness to discuss in private, let alone with others with whom they may or may not feel comfortable sharing information. There may be times when a friend or family member of the witness may offer to sit with the witness during the interview process even though the witness did not request this. The witness may not want them to be present, but may be reluctant to say so for fear of hurting their feelings or is too uncomfortable to ask them to leave. By planning ahead and explaining to the witness the need to speak with them privately, the investigator decreases the chance that the third party will, in some way, hinder or disrupt the interview process.

Case Example 7.7 L.J., a young mother, was interviewed following the death of her infant son. A friend, who was not identified as a primary or secondary witness, was allowed to sit with her during the interview to offer support. The mother was questioned about the infant's and family's medical history. After reviewing the infant's medical records, it became apparent that the mother failed to mention significant medical information. A few days later, during a follow-up interview in which the mother was interviewed alone, she reported the medical history that was left out during the initial interview. She explained that she did not want to talk about those items in front of her friend.

If a third party is present for the initial interview of a primary witness, investigators should provide the witness an opportunity to speak to the investigator in private. Near the end of the interview, after a rapport has been established, the investigator should let the witness and the other person know that the investigator needs to speak with the witness alone for a few minutes. The investigator should ask the witness if there is anything the witness would like to say but did not have wanted to say while the other person was present.

Case Example 7.8 A 6-month-old died while at home with the mother while the father was at work. The parents were initially interviewed together. During that interview, the father did not reveal any concerns; however, when each parent was given the opportunity to speak to the investigator alone, the father revealed to the investigator that he had concerns and questions about his wife's behavior.

7.4.2 When to Conduct the Initial Interview

Determining when to interview primary witnesses is of utmost importance to a timely investigation. The infant investigator and the scene investigator should complete initial interviews with primary witnesses as soon as they have completed the initial postmortem infant assessment and the death scene investigation, respectively. The initial interviews should not be delayed or postponed until a later time, and the more time that passes between the incident and the time of the interview, the greater the chance the witness will forget or be unable to recall important details.

In general, people recall information and details better soon after being exposed to the information, and as time passes, some information is forgotten. The first documented study to identify the rate at which memory declines was conducted by Hermann Ebbinghaus in 1885. His results, sometimes referred to as the Ebbinghaus forgetting curve, are considered one of the most important studies related to memory loss. He conducted experiments on himself and tested his memory of nonsense syllables at intervals ranging from 20 minutes to 31 days. The greatest memory loss, according to his study, occurs within the first hour after exposure and continues over the next 8 to 9 hours before leveling off. His study showed that he only remembered 40% of the information after 9 hours.[3–6]

Many other studies have been conducted to evaluate the accuracy of eyewitness accounts. Some have demonstrated that eyewitnesses can reconstruct their memories based on misleading information received from outside sources after the incident.[7] As more time passes between the incident and the time the witness is interviewed, the greater the chance that the witness will forget information or that information that occurred after the incident will alter their perceptions. The key for investigators is to interview witnesses as soon after the incident as possible, as time is of the essence. In an ideal situation, witnesses would be interviewed within the first hour of the incident. Realizing that it may not be possible to interview witnesses within the first hour, investigators must ensure that, at a minimum, the initial interviews occur within the first few hours after the incident. The goal is to interview each witness as soon after the incident as possible. With the implementation of early notification and the double-team approach, investigators are much more likely to be able to decrease the amount of time that lapses between the incident and the initial interview.

7.4.3 Where to Conduct the Initial Interview

The location where the initial interview is conducted depends on the location of the witness. It is recommended that the initial interview of primary witnesses be completed in the field, where the witnesses are located. The infant investigator should interview witnesses who respond to the hospital at the hospital; the scene investigator should interview witnesses who remained on the scene at the scene.

Some law enforcement agencies prefer that all witnesses be taken to the police station to be interviewed. Although this practice provides a controlled environment, it is not conducive for initial interviews in infant death investigations. The initial interview should be completed in the field, either at the scene or at the hospital, to provide the least threatening environment in which to gather information about the infant. The amount of time that may be lost while arranging for and transporting witnesses from the scene or hospital to the police station and then back to the scene can affect the amount of information obtained. The transportation of witnesses to the police department also interferes with the completion of a timely doll reenactment with witnesses at the scene. Interviewers, whether death investigators or police officers, who are organized and prepared will be able to conduct the initial interview effectively on scene or at the hospital. The initial interview is designed to gather as much information as possible from the witnesses. This information will then be compared to the findings of the initial postmortem assessment, the infant death scene investigation, accounts from other witnesses, and with records that will be obtained from multiple agencies. If a discrepancy occurs, it will then be necessary for the investigator to reinterview the witnesses. For these additional interviews, it may or may not be desirable to have the witness in a controlled environment; however, the initial interview should be as nonthreatening as possible to develop rapport with the witness and obtain as much information as possible from them.

At the hospital, the infant investigator should discuss with a hospital representative the need to use a small room to interview the witnesses that are present. Often the nursing supervisor, social worker, or chaplain is helpful in this regard. Most hospitals have a small, private room that may be used for private conferences with families. This room may be in the emergency room (ER) or in another part of the hospital. The closer the room is to the area of the hospital in which the infant died, the better. The goal is to find a location that is conducive to a conversation and in which the witness feels comfortable. Limiting the distance the individual has to be moved for the interview is desirable. Investigators must keep in mind that the witness's physical comfort may impact the interview, and the room should be furnished so that the witness and both interviewers can sit down at eye level. The size of the room is also an important consideration. The room should be small enough to comfortably seat four to five people; a room smaller than that size may make the witness feel cramped. On the other hand, a large room may make it difficult for the witness to have a sense of privacy, and this may make it more difficult for a rapport to be established.

The scene investigator should assess the surroundings at the scene to determine the most conducive place to interview witnesses. The scene investigator may decide to interview the witnesses inside a building, outside, or in the investigator's vehicle. The scene investigator must take into consideration the location in which interviews should occur that are conducive to the interview yet do not compromise the scene. After the MDI and law enforcement personnel have processed the death scene, it may then be appropriate to interview witnesses in a private room within the incident location. If using the incident location, the scene investigator should look for a room in which the witness and both interviewers are able to sit down comfortably. The initial interview with caregivers will be fairly lengthy, and it is important to consider the physical comfort of the caregiver when determining where to conduct interviews.

7.4.4 What Information Should Be Obtained

The initial interview is designed to help investigators learn as much about the infant that died as possible. This will include information regarding the pregnancy, prenatal care, and the delivery. The infant's medical history, including illnesses, hospitalizations, immunizations, and medications, is also important. The infant's development, including motor skills, dietary information, bowel and bladder habits, and social behaviors, should be discussed. The family dynamics and demographics, family medical and social histories, and environmental factors common to the infant should not be overlooked. The primary witnesses will be asked to describe events as they occurred in relation to the infant as well as their actions and the actions of others.

7.4.5 How to Conduct the Initial Interview

The approach that the interviewer takes to acquire all of the necessary information is crucial, and a primary factor in the amount of information obtained is the organizational structure of this planned conversation. Many witnesses will become emotional when asked to provide details surrounding the infant's death. As a result, it is beneficial to first gather information about the infant and family that is distant to the incident being investigated. This approach is a direct contradiction to techniques that recommend a witness begin by giving an open narrative about an incident. It is recommended that investigators begin with the most distant information, usually the pregnancy and the infant's birth, and then work chronologically to the present time. This provides the investigator an opportunity to gather necessary information before the witness gives an account of the immediate circumstances surrounding the infant's death. This format is easy for interviewers to follow, ensuring no information is left out. The witness is able to easily see the progression of the interview, can chronologically report the factual, less emotional information while composed, and can then focus on providing detailed information about the circumstances surrounding the death, which often proves to be an emotional time.

The investigator should plan to spend as much time with the witness as needed to ensure that the goals and purposes for the interview are met. The interview should not be rushed and should flow smoothly so that the witness does not become weary of the process. Interviewers who plan the interview will decrease their need to reinterview a witness for details or questions they failed to obtain during the initial interview. It may be necessary to interview the witnesses again; however, additional interviews should be utilized to clarify information already obtained or to move toward an interrogation if needed.

The implementation phase of the initial interview, as with all interviews, begins with an introduction. The primary interviewer should introduce the interviewers, including their names, titles, and agency affiliations. The investigator should also confirm the identity and relationship of the witness and offer condolences prior to beginning the interview as seen in Box 7.1.

The investigator should inquire as to the witness's demographics, the legal and correct spelling of name, and contact information. The relationship of the witness to the infant must be clarified, as the witness's description of the relationship may be different from how the investigator may describe the relationship.

BOX 7.1
Sample Introduction

"Ms. Jackson, my name is John Smith and I am a medicolegal death investigator with the county coroner's office. Here with me is Officer Jones from the sheriff's department. I am very sorry for your loss and that I have to speak with you; however, I need your help to learn as much as possible about what happened today. Now I understand that you are Steven's mother, is that correct?"

Case Example 7.9 Prior to the interview, it was reported that the witness was the infant's "mother." Investigators must clarify if she is the biological, adoptive, or foster mother and if she is the legal guardian. "Ms. Jackson, what is your relationship to Steven?" "I am his mother." "Are you his biological mother?" "Yes." "Are you also his legal guardian?" "No." "Who is the legal guardian for Steven?" "My mother, his grandmother is the legal guardian." In this case, the witness stated that she is the biological mother of Steven and further clarification reveals that although she is the biological mother, she does not have legal custody of the infant.

Case Example 7.10 "Ms. Riley, what is your relationship to Steven?" "I am his mother." "Are you his biological mother?" "No." "What is your legal relationship to Steven?" "I am his grandmother, but he has lived with me since he was born. I am the only mother he has ever known." "Are you Steven's legal guardian?" "No. He is a ward of the state. Child and Family Services is his legal guardian." After interviewing the witness, it was revealed that the Department of Child and Family Services had legal custody of the child, who resides with the maternal grandmother. Although the grandmother considered herself to be the child's "mother," she in fact, is not the biological mother of the child nor does she have legal custody.

Investigators must determine the infant's legal name, as well as nicknames by which the infant is known to the witness. Families and caregivers may have a number of nicknames for the infant. Investigators must determine the legal name of the infant, the name that is on the birth certificate, as well as any names by which the infant may be referred to during the investigation. The investigator should ask the witness what name they called the infant, the investigator should ask the witness if he or she may call the child by that name. If so, the investigator should then use that name during the interview.

Case Example 7.11 "Ms. Jackson, what is Steven's full legal name, the name that is on his birth certificate?" "Steven Adam Jackson Jr." "What name do you call him?" "Stevie."

Investigators should let witnesses know how important they are to the process and that with their help it may be possible to determine what happened to the infant. Investigators may want to thank the witnesses in advance for their assistance and acknowledge that the process may be long and difficult (Box 7.2).

There is a lot of background information to obtain during infant death investigations. The interview should proceed chronologically forward from the infant's birth, which is furthest removed from the incident, up to the time of the infant's

BOX 7.2
Sample Acknowledgment of Assistance

"Ms. Jackson I need to try to determine what happened to Stevie. Your help is very important, as I need to learn as much about Stevie as possible. I want to thank you in advance, as this may be a difficult process. But I want you to know that it is very important that we understand what happened so that we not only answer our questions but also yours."

death. This organizational format places the most emotional part of the interview at the end, providing the witness the opportunity to provide as much background information as possible before getting to the incident surrounding the infant's death. Starting with the less emotional topics, the investigator is able to establish a rapport with the witness before getting to the specific and often traumatic details.

One way to begin acquiring background information is to ask the witness when and where the infant was born, followed by a discussion of the infant's birth, including pregnancy history, prenatal care, delivery, and hospitalization after birth. Depending on whom the witness is and what relationship the witness has to the infant, the witness may or may not know information regarding the pregnancy and delivery. A suggested format and sample questions are provided in Box 7.3. Investigators should have a general idea of information needed and a possible sequence for asking those questions; however, interviewers must be able to adapt their plan depending on the information provided.

BOX 7.3
Maternal/Infant Health Sample Questions

"Ms. Jackson, when was Stevie born?"
"Where was Stevie born?" Obtain name and address of hospital if known.
"Tell me about your pregnancy?"
"Any complications?"
"When and where did you start to receive prenatal care?"
"Who was your obstetrician?" Obtain the name and address if known.
"Were you on any medications during your pregnancy?" Obtain names if known.
"How did you go into labor, spontaneous, induction?"
"What type of delivery did you have with Stevie?"
"Were there any complications during delivery?"
"How long did you stay in the hospital after delivery?"
"How long did Stevie stay in the hospital?"
"Did Stevie have any medical problems at birth?"
"Was he breast or bottle fed in the hospital?"
"Did Steve's pediatrician see him in the hospital?"
"Who was the pediatrician?" Obtain name and address if known.

BOX 7.4
Infant Medical History Sample Questions

"Has Stevie had any medical problems since birth?"
"What problems has he had?"
"Has he ever been hospitalized? If so, for what conditions and where was he hospitalized?"
"Who is his regular doctor?" Obtain name and address.
"Does he see any other doctors?" If so, obtain name and address.
"When was he last seen by his doctor?"
"What vaccinations has Stevie had?"
"Were there any complications with the vaccines?"
"Is Stevie on or ever been on any medications?" If so, obtain names.
"Have you ever given him any medication such as Tylenol®* pain reliever, teething medicine, or gas drops?" Obtain medication name, reason, and when administered.
"What does he take those medications for?"
"Who prescribed them?"
"Which pharmacy do you use to fill his prescriptions?"
"Has he received any over-the-counter medications?"

* Registered trademark of McNeil Consumer Healthcare Division of McNeil-PPC, Inc., Fort Washington, PA.

After obtaining all necessary pregnancy, prenatal, delivery, and birth record information, the investigator should then discuss the infant's medical history since birth. Some sample questions are listed in Box 7.4.

A description of the infant's dietary, bowel and bladder habits, growth and development, as well as the social behaviors of the infant should be obtained. Physical symptoms of illness that the infant may have recently exhibited should also be addressed. Sample questions are listed in Box 7.5.

At this time, the investigator should inquire as to the mother's prior pregnancy history if the witness is an individual that would know that information. The investigator should also inquire about the family's medical history, including the parents, siblings, and extended family. Sample questions are in Box 7.6.

The investigator should determine the living conditions in which the infant resides, including the physical environment, the persons who reside there, as well as the family structure. *Family structure* is a description of those persons that make up that family, the recognized status and position of each person, and how each family member may interact with the others. There are many different types of family structures, including nuclear, extended, or single-parent families to name a few. For large families with complicated relational ties, it may be beneficial for investigators to draw a family tree for the infant. This will provide a visual of the relational lines among all family members. Family tree diagrams have been found to be helpful during the investigative child death review, allowing all investigative team members

BOX 7.5
Infant-Specific Sample Questions

"Tell me about his diet."
"Was Stevie breast- or bottle-fed?" If breast-fed, determine for how long. If bottle-fed, determine what type of formula is used.
"What does he eat each day?" Determine what he eats, the amount, and how frequently.
"Does Stevie eat any solid food? If so, what type?"
"Have you noticed a change in his bowel or bladder habits? Any change in the consistency of his stool?"
"What was Stevie able to do?" Indicate whether he could roll over, sit up, crawl, or walk.
"What was his normal temperament? Was he a fussy or quiet baby?"
"Does Stevie sleep through the night?"
"Where does he usually sleep?"
"Had Stevie been sick recently?"
"What did you notice?" E.g., fever, cough, rash, vomiting, diarrhea, fussy, pulling at ears, inconsolable.
"What did you do about it?" Indicate whether he was taken to a doctor or medicated.

to have an understanding of the family lineage and relationships. Investigators can learn how to draw a family medical tree at the National Society of Genetic Counselors Web site, http://www.nsgc.org. Sample questions are listed in Box 7.7, and a sample family tree is in Figure 7.1.

After obtaining all necessary background information and rapport has started to grow, the interviewer should ask the witness to describe the events that led up to the infant's death. The interviewer should ask the witness to describe what happened and allow them to answer, uninterrupted, in a narrative format. An example of how to begin is in Box 7.8.

The investigator should allow the witness to answer, uninterrupted, before going back over the information provided to ensure that all of the important aspects are covered. The investigator should ensure that the information listed in Box 7.9 is addressed either in the narrative description or through direct questioning. The witness that either placed the infant or found the infant should also be asked the sample questions in Box 7.10.

The sample questions presented are designed to obtain the minimum amount of information needed, and depending on the circumstances surrounding the death, many more questions may need to be asked. It is impossible to generate complete lists of questions that should be asked of primary witnesses during an infant death investigation, however, the sample questions should generate discussion that will provide interviewers and investigators with information that will direct the remainder of their interviews and the investigation.

BOX 7.6
Family Medical History Sample Questions

"Do you have any medical problems?"
"Who is your doctor?"
"Do you take any medications: prescribed or over the counter?" Obtain names.
"We talked earlier about your pregnancy. Do you have other children?"
"How many children do you have?" Obtain names, dates and places of birth, and Social Security numbers.
"Did you have any complications with those pregnancies or deliveries?"
"Have you had any miscarriages or lost any other children?"
"Do any of your other children have any medical problems?"
"Describe their medical histories."
"Ms. Jackson, are there any medical problems in your family?"
"Are there any medical problems that are extensive in your family?" E.g., high blood pressure, diabetes.
"Have any other children died in your immediate or extended family?" If so, find out who and when.
"Who is Stevie's biological father?" Obtain name, date of birth, address, Social Security number.
"Does he have any medical problems or take any medications?"
"Are there any medical conditions that run in his family?"
"Do you smoke?" If so, find out what, how much, and where (e.g., inside the home).
"Did you smoke during your pregnancy with Stevie?"
"How much alcohol to you consume?"
"Did you drink during your pregnancy with Stevie?"

BOX 7.7
Family Structure Sample Questions

"Where does Stevie usually reside?" Obtain address.
"With whom does he live?" Names, dates of birth, Social Security numbers, and relationships to the infant.
"Does anyone who resides there smoke in the house?"
"Are there any pets?" If so, describe their type and size.
"Where in the house does Stevie usually sleep?"

After gathering information regarding the incident, the interviewer should develop a time line of events leading up to the infant's death. At a minimum, the time line should cover 24 hours prior to the death; however, 48 hours is ideal. Much of the information that will be labeled on the time line will have been gathered during the body of the interview; it may, however, be necessary to go over the time line with the witness in order for them to clarify information and fill gaps in time. An example of a 24-hour time line is in Table 7.1.

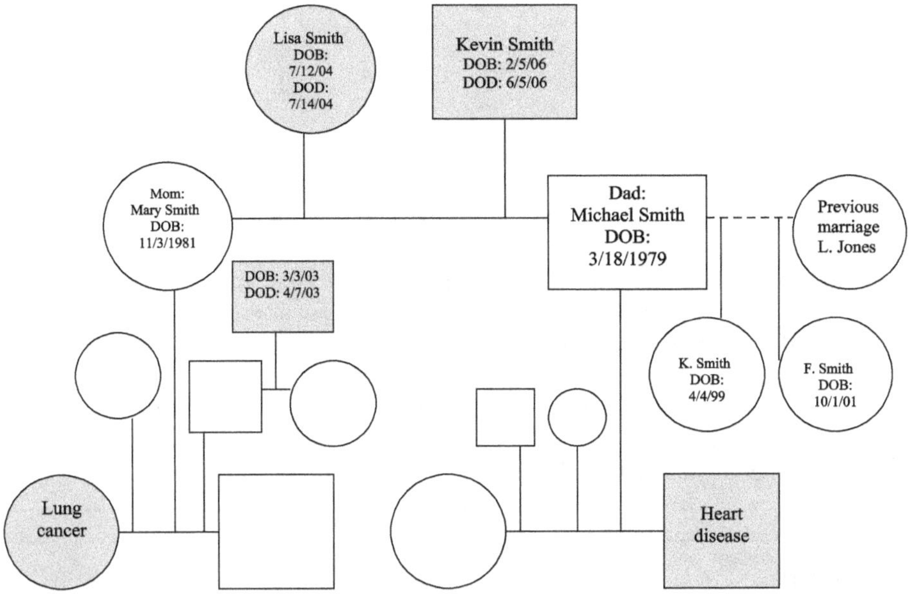

FIGURE 7.1 Family trees are visual depictions of a family's lineage. Males are represented by squares, females by circles. Shapes that are shaded represent that the individual is deceased. In this example, Michael and Mary Smith are married and have had two children: Lisa, who died on 7/14/04 and Kevin, who died 6/5/06. Michael Smith has two living children from a previous marriage. Mary Smith's brother also suffered the death of a child on 4/7/03.

BOX 7.8
Narrative Introduction 1

"Ms. Jackson, I know that this will be difficult, but I need you tell me what happened today." During the witness's account of events, the interviewer may prompt the witness by saying, "And then what happened?" or "What happened next?"

Before closing the initial interview, the primary interviewer should review any information that was not clear and should go over the incident information with the witness to ensure understanding. The investigator should then see if the witness has any questions or has any additional information that they believe may be helpful. If the witness is the next of kin, information should be provided about the next steps of the investigation. The investigator should explain the need for a forensic autopsy and provide additional information as needed. Finally, the investigator should introduce the need for the witness to conduct a scene walk-through, doll reenactment, and possible future interviews. Witnesses who are interviewed on scene may be able to participate in both the walk-through and reenactment immediately, while the witnesses who are interviewed at the hospital will have to wait until both the witness and the investigator can return to the scene. Those witnesses at the scene will progress to the doll reenactment (Chapter 9) as soon as the scene and infant investigator

BOX 7.9
Incident Sample Questions

"Where did the incident occur?"
"Who resides at the incident location?"
"Who was at the incident location before the infant was found, at the time the infant was found, and who responded to the scene afterward?"
"Who last cared for the infant?"
"Who was the last person to know that the infant was alive?"
"What time was the infant known to be alive?" Find out how they know the time.
"How did they know the infant was alive?"
"Who found the infant unresponsive or in distress?"
"What time was the infant found?" Find out how they know the time.
"Who called 9-1-1?"
"Did anyone attempt CPR? If so, who?"

BOX 7.10
Specific Questions for People Who Last Cared for, Or Found the Infant

"What time was the infant put down, last cared for, or found?" Find out how they know the time.
"Where in the residence was the infant?" E.g., nursery, living room.
"Where was the infant?" E.g., crib, playpen, adult waterbed, couch.
"What position was the infant in?" E.g., on back, on stomach, on side with wedge support.
"What was the infant wearing?"
"Describe the infant's appearance." E.g., pale, blue, rash, mucous around nose.
"How did the infant feel?" E.g., warm, cool, hot, clammy.
"What did the finder do after discovering the infant in distress or unresponsive?"

communicate. The infant investigator, however, should introduce the need and if possible escort the witness to the incident location in order to conduct the doll reenactment and scene walk-through. Prior to departing, the interviewer should thank the witnesses again for their assistance and offer final condolences. An example of a closure is provided in Box 7.11.

7.5 CLARIFICATION INTERVIEW

The goal of a clarification interview is to clear up any misunderstandings or miscommunication that may have occurred during the initial interview. Information may need to be clarified for a number of reasons, including discrepancies in information gathered by the scene investigator and the infant investigator, discrepancies that occur from one witness to another, or discrepancies between information obtained from a witness and the information that was gained by reviewing medical

TABLE 7.1
Sample 24-Hour Time Line

Date and Time		24-Hour Time Line—Case # 2006-345 Baby Doe Event
6/5/2006	0736	Pronounced dead in the ER at Sunny Hill Hospital
	0725	Arrived via ambulance at the ER
	0707	EMS crew departed scene en route to hospital. Mom and dad followed in their private vehicle.
	0659	EMS crew arrived on scene and find baby lying on the couch in the living room with dad attempting CPR.
	0651	EMS crew dispatched to incident location at 214 Kings Road.
	0649	Dad placed a call to 9-1-1 in reference to an unresponsive infant. Dad attempted CPR per instructions of emergency dispatch personnel.
	~0645	Mom found baby unresponsive face down in crib. Baby was pale, cold, with blood-tinged froth around nose.
	0630	Alarm clock awoke mom for work.
	~0230	Baby Doe awoke. Mom fed him one 8-ounce bottle of formula and changed a wet diaper. Placed him back in his crib on his stomach and covered him with a thin blanket. Slight runny nose noted.
6/4/2006	~2335	Mom and dad went to sleep after watching the news.
	2300 to 2330	Mom and dad watched the news in their bedroom.
	~2230	Dad fed Baby Doe one 8-ounce bottle of formula, changed his diaper, and placed him face down in the crib to sleep. Baby Doe went to sleep easily.
	~1900 to 2200	The family, mom, dad, and Baby Doe were at home. Baby Doe was fussier than normal.
	1815	Mom fed baby one 8-ounce bottle and a small amount of baby food. Baby was fussy. Mom noted runny nose. Baby felt warm, but mom did not take temperature.
	1800	Dad arrived home from work.
	1745	Mom arrived home with Baby Doe.
	1730	Mom picked up Baby Doe up at Lullaby Day-Care Center which reported Baby Doe had a fussier day than normal and was beginning to have a slight runny nose. They did not note a fever.
	0820 to 1730	Baby Doe was at day-care in the infant room. (Day-care provider yet to be interviewed. Will fill in time line of events after meeting with the day-care provider.)
	~0820	Mom dropped Baby Doe off at the Lullaby Day-Care and went to work at ABC Industries.
	0700 to 0800	Mom got baby up and fed him one 8-ounce bottle and baby food. Dressed him and left her house to drive him to day-care.
	0630	Alarm went off awaking mom and dad so they could go to work.

or other records and documents. The clarification interview is a nonconfrontational interview, that is organized and conducted similar to the initial interview. Usually a clarification interview is quite short, and the questions are directed toward specific aspects of the case.

A clarification interview provides the witness an opportunity to assist the investigator in gathering information about the circumstances surrounding the death that

BOX 7.11
Sample Closures

"Ms. Jackson, I want to thank you for helping me understand what happened today, and I want to answer any questions you may have."

"Ms. Jackson although the information you shared with me is really helpful, there is another way that I think you can help me. I would appreciate it if you would walk-through the 'residence' with me and show me where things happened so I can visualize what you described."

may have been misunderstood or left out, either intentionally or unintentionally. The discrepancies that were noted by the investigator may or may not be shared with the witness prior to or during the interview. It is possible that a simple, unintentional misunderstanding may have occurred during the initial interview, so the clarification interview should first give the witness the benefit of the doubt. If the discrepancies continue during the clarification interview, the investigator may need to gently question the witness's account if it appears that the witness is intentionally providing misleading or inaccurate information. This is best accomplished when the interviewer has an understanding of the witness's possible motive for providing inaccurate information. If it is believed that no one intentionally caused harm to the infant, the clarification interview can be effective in obtaining accurate information, in particular, in cases where the death may have been an accident. A clarification interview may be less effective when interviewing a witness believed to have intentionally caused harm to the infant or one who knows who did. In these situations, another level of interviewing may be necessary.

A clarification interview may be conducted anytime during an investigation; however, it is most beneficial immediately after the scene investigator and the infant investigator have had an opportunity to discuss their independent findings. Discrepancies noted in their findings may warrant an immediate clarification interview prior to one or both investigators and the witnesses leaving their respective locations.

7.5.1 Clarification Interview: Logistics

The primary interviewer for the initial interview should be the individual who conducts the clarification interview. A rapport should have developed between the primary interviewer and the witness that allows the witness to feel free to correct any miscommunications or misunderstandings that may have occurred during the initial interview. An interviewer who is genuinely trying to clear up any confusion that may have occurred is able to further develop their rapport with the witness.

During a clarification interview, it is important that the interviewee be alone. If the witness was not interviewed alone during the initial interview and discrepancies are noted, the witness should be interviewed alone. This allows the witness an opportunity to provide information that they may not have wanted to reveal in front of the individual who was present for the initial interview.

BOX 7.12
Clarification Interview 1

Effective: "Ms. Jones, I apologize that I have to ask you more questions. However, there are a couple things that I am confused about, and I want to make sure that I did not misunderstand what you said. Will you tell me again ... ?"

Ineffective: "Ms. Jones, there are some things you told me that don't add up. You said ... however ..."

Clarification interviews should be preplanned to include where and when they will be conducted. It may be necessary to conduct the clarification interview immediately after becoming aware of a discrepancy such as in the case of a discrepancy between the scene investigator's and the infant investigator's findings. Discrepancies noted early in the investigation should be clarified immediately, at the scene or at the hospital, respectively. Discrepancies that are noted later in the investigation (for example, after medical records are obtained) will require that a location and time be arranged to reinterview the witness. Clarification interviews can be conducted at a number of locations, though one of the best may be the residence of the witness, as it provides the interviewer an opportunity to assess the living arrangements of that witness.

The beginning or introduction of a clarification interview is critical to the investigator's success in getting the witness to clarify or correct information provided earlier. The interviewer's approach can make or break this interview. An interviewer who is humble and genuinely interested in clearing up any misunderstanding will be more successful than an investigator who is confrontational. An ineffective approach may put the witness on the defensive while an effective approach may motivate a witness to assist the interviewer as noted in Box 7.12.

Case Example 7.12 A primary witness, interviewed by the infant investigator at the hospital, reported that the infant was placed in a crib to sleep. The scene investigator noted that there was no crib in the home, there was, however, a playpen and a bassinet. The infant investigator should clarify with the witness, prior to either leaving the hospital, where the infant was sleeping. The caregiver may have intentionally reported that the infant was in a crib, even though they did not have one, or the caregiver may simply refer to the bassinet or the playpen as a crib. Either way, the investigator needs to clarify the witness's account to ensure that the information obtained is accurate and does not contradict what was found at the scene. An example of two approaches is provided in Box 7.13.

Case Example 7.13 At the hospital, the infant investigator interviewed a primary witness who reported that she placed the infant in a bassinet to sleep and that is also where she found him unresponsive. The scene investigator interviewed a primary witness who reported observing the infant sleeping on a couch with the primary witness who was at the hospital. The scene investigator observed a bassinet in the home that was filled with clothes and a purge pattern stain on the couch. The witness demonstrated during a doll reenactment where the infant was located, which matched the purge pattern. The infant investigator should initiate a clarification interview with the primary witness at the hospital.

BOX 7.13
Clarification Interview 2

Effective: "Ms. Jones, will you tell me again where your baby was sleeping? Will you describe it to me? Where is it located in your home?"

Ineffective: "Ms. Jones, you stated that your baby was sleeping in a crib, but you do not have a crib in your home."

Following the death, additional information will be obtained through the review of medical, social service, and criminal records. Clarification interviews may need to be conducted if there are discrepancies in the information received from primary witnesses and the information documented in the records. Discrepancies may be noted after reviewing the 9-1-1 call, after interviewing the PFRs, after reviewing medical records, or following the autopsy. In any of these situations, the investigator should attempt to clarify the information to determine if a simple miscommunication or misunderstanding occurred before confronting the witness with the discrepancy.

7.5.2 Clarifying Information from 9-1-1 Recordings

The individual who placed the 9-1-1 call may have provided information to the 9-1-1 operator that was not reported when the caller or witness was initially interviewed by the investigator. After reviewing the 9-1-1 call and noting the discrepancies, the investigator may need to conduct a clarification or follow-up interview with the witness who placed the call.

Case Example 7.14 During the initial interview, the primary caregiver, who called 9-1-1, reported that the infant was found unresponsive in a crib. The investigator reviewed the 9-1-1 recording a few days later, and in the recording, the caller stated that the infant was sleeping in an adult bed with the caller when the infant was found unresponsive. Due to the discrepancy between the witness report and the 9-1-1 recording, the witness should be reinterviewed to clarify the information that was provided during the initial interview.

7.5.3 Clarifying Information Received from Professional First Responders (PFRs)

A clarification interview may need to be conducted if discrepancies are noted between the primary witness reports and statements from PFRs; this is another reason why it is important for the PFRs to be interviewed at the beginning of an investigation. A discrepancy between the information obtained from the PFRs and the information reported by a witness may need to be clarified by the witness or the PFR. Investigators who do not interview PFRs first will not recognize this type of discrepancy until the PFRs are interviewed or their reports are reviewed, which may be many days after the death. It may be necessary to reinterview the witness and the PFRs. Investigators will have an opportunity to clarify information with the PFRs at the investigative child death review; however, it may be necessary to reinterview the PFRs prior to that review.

BOX 7.14
Clarification Interview 3

Effective: "Mr. Smith, there seems to be some confusion about the persons that were present when EMS arrived. Will you tell me again who was there so I can make sure I have it correct?"

Ineffective: "Mr. Smith, the ambulance crew told me there were lots of people there when they arrived that you did not tell me about. Tell me who was really at your house."

Case Example 7.15 When interviewed at the hospital, a PFR told the investigator that there were four adult males in the home upon their arrival. During the initial interview, the primary caregiver reported that there were two adults in the home at the time of the death and when emergency medical services (EMS) arrived. While the MDI was interviewing the caregiver, the PFRs were dispatched to another scene and, as a result, were not available for an immediate clarification interview. The interviewer should, however, conduct a clarification interview with the witness to determine if there was a miscommunication or misunderstanding. An example of two approaches is in Box 7.14.

7.5.4 Clarifying Information Received from the Record Review

Once the investigator has obtained the records, it may be necessary for them to conduct a clarification interview if discrepancies occur between the records and the information provided by the primary witnesses. The clarification interview may reveal other medical records that may be available but were not discussed during the initial interview; these may reveal information that the witness intentionally or unintentionally left out of the interview or a misunderstanding between the investigator and the witness.

Case Example 7.16 During the initial interview, the mother of the deceased infant stated that she had been pregnant two times and that this was her second child. The mother's prenatal records stated that this was the mother's fourth pregnancy, that she had experienced one miscarriage and that another child died during infancy. The investigator should initiate a clarification interview to determine, first, if there was a misunderstanding or miscommunication between the investigator and the mother and, second, to discuss the findings of the medical records. The caregiver may have misunderstood the questions and thought the investigator was inquiring about the number of living children, or the witness may have intentionally kept the other pregnancy and birth information from the investigator.

7.5.5 Clarifying Information Gained from the Autopsy

After the autopsy is completed by the forensic pathologist, questions or concerns may be raised that may be answered by witnesses during a clarification interview.

Communication between the MDI and the forensic pathologist are important during the investigation and can provide details to the investigator that contradict information provided by caregivers. That information may be able to be clarified.

Case Example 7.17 The primary caregiver of a 4-month-old infant stated that the infant drank milk and formula and was not taking any solid foods. During the autopsy, solid food was noted in the stomach contents. The investigator may need to clarify with the primary caregiver the diet that was fed to the infant, or what other persons may have fed the infant prior to death.

7.6 FOLLOW-UP INTERVIEW

Follow-up interviews, for the purpose of infant death investigations, may not be conducted until autopsy or toxicology results are available. Autopsy findings and results that are not consistent with the initial or clarification interviews may warrant a follow-up interview. Information may be provided to the primary witnesses to elicit more information from them that will provide investigators with additional information that may explain the autopsy findings and results. This type of interview may be completed after the autopsy, or it may not be completed for many weeks if laboratory results are pending. Follow-up interviews have one of two goals: The first is to provide the witness with the final autopsy results, answer questions, and offer referrals as needed. The second is to question the witness again about new information that has become available that may contradict earlier reports. This interview will usually take place after the investigative child death review.

7.7 INTERROGATION

The last type or level of interview is the interrogation, a formal, controlled questioning of a suspect that is conducted by skilled law enforcement personnel. MDIs will not conduct interrogations; however, they may play an integral part in the planning phase and preparation for an interrogation during an infant death investigation. The techniques and strategies of interrogations are beyond the scope of this text. However, the potential role of the MDI during an interrogation related to an infant's death, is important.

An interrogation is the formal, systematic questioning of an individual who investigators suspect has committed a crime, or for the purposes of this text, intentionally harmed the infant resulting in the infant's death. The interrogation is accusatory by design to match acquired, known information to a suspect in order to secure a confession from that individual.[8] The purpose of an interrogation is to obtain information that the suspect does not want to provide.[9]

Critical to the success of an interrogation is the interrogator's understanding of the case facts, including how the crime was committed, the circumstances surrounding the incident, and the motivations of the suspect. The MDI may be the individual who is able to provide much of this information and help ensure that the interrogator has all of the necessary and accurate information to conduct an effective interrogation.

In some jurisdictions, there is a team approach to investigating infant deaths and the MDI is an asset who should be present during the interrogation. The MDI's presence ensures that correct information is relayed to the interrogator, and that should there be questions about the physical findings that need to be used during the interrogation, they can be answered.

One of the major differences between an interview and an interrogation is that during an interview, an investigator seeks information. The investigator asks questions in nonthreatening ways to establish rapport and learn as much as possible about the circumstances surrounding the infant's death and about the suspect's fears, concerns, and attitudes. During an interrogation, investigators do not seek information, rather they lead the process and the suspect follows, as the goal is to obtain a truthful admission or confession.[8]

7.8 SUMMARY

The information provided by a primary witness during an infant death investigation is crucial and every measure should be taken to obtain the information immediately. Interacting with individuals, in particular parents and caregivers, who have just lost an infant can be difficult as they are experiencing one of the greatest tragedies a parent may go through. Care should be taken to ensure that the witnesses are interviewed in a compassionate and organized format that allows them to provide detailed information in a nonthreatening environment. The technique and approach investigators use to interview primary witnesses will impact the investigation. Initial interviews, conducted in an organized, empathetic, and thorough manner will benefit the investigation, the witness, and the infant's surviving next of kin.

REFERENCES

1. Ryals, J., Successful Interviewing, *FBI Law Enforcement Bull.,* March 1991. Available at http://www.crimeandclues.com/91mar004.htm.
2. South Carolina Criminal Justice Academy, Interview and Interrogation, South Carolina Department of Public Safety, Columbia, SC, 2000.
3. Ebbinghaus, H., *Memory: A Contribution to Experimental Psychology,* 1885, reprint, Thoemmes Press, Bristol, Avon, United Kingdom, 1913.
4. Rubin, D.C. and Wenzel, A.E., One hundred years of forgetting: A quantitative description of retention, *Psych. Rev.,* 103 (4), 734–760, 1996.
5. Steele, L., Trying identification cases: An outline for raising eyewitness ID issues, *Champion Magazine,* November 2004, available at the National Association of Criminal Defense Lawyers Web site at www.nacdl.org (accessed July 28, 2006).
6. Streed, T., Interviewing Psychological: The Psychological Aspects of Interviewing, paper presented at Sudden Unexplained Infant Death Investigation National Training Academy, St. Louis, MO, June 12, 2006.
7. Loftus, E.F., *Eyewitness Testimony.* Harvard University Press, Cambridge, MA, 1996.
8. Tousignant, D.D., Why suspects confess, *FBI Law Enforcement Bull.,* March 1991.
9. Vessel, D., Conducting successful interrogations, *FBI Law Enforcement Bull.,* 67(10), 1–6, October 1998. Available at http://www.crimeandclues.com/91mar002.htm.

RESOURCES

Deffenbacher, K.A., Bornstein, B.H., Penrod, S.D., and McGorty, E.K., A meta-analytic review of the effects of high stress on eyewitness memory, *Law Hum. Behav.,* 28 (6), 687–706, 2004.

Gordan, N. and Fleisher, W., *Effective Interviewing and Interrogation Techniques,* 2nd ed., Academic Press, San Diego, CA, 2002.

Jayne, B.C. and Buckely, J.P., The Investigator Anthology: A Compilation of Articles and Essays about The Reid Technique of Interviewing and Interrogation®, John E. Reid and Associates Inc., Chicago, 1999.

Loftus, E. and Ketcham, K., *Witness for the Defense: The Accused, the Eyewitness and the Expert Who Puts Memory on Trial,* St. Martin's Press, New York, 1991.

Rabon, D., *Interviewing and Interrogation,* Carolina Academic Press, Durham, NC, 1992.

Royal, R. and Schutt, S., *The Gentle Art of Interviewing and Interrogation: A Professional Manual and Guide,* Prentice-Hall, Inc., Englewood Cliffs, NJ, 1976.

Walters, S.B., *Principles of Kinesic Interview and Interrogation,* CRC Press LLC, Boca Raton, FL, 2003.

Zulawski, D. and Wicklander, D., *Practical Aspects of Interview and Interrogation,* 2nd ed., CRC Press LLC, Boca Raton, FL, 2002.

8 Doll Reenactment with Scene Walk-Through

8.1 INTRODUCTION

Doll reenactments provide valuable information during infant death investigations that may help identify the cause and manner of an infant's death. The primary goal of a doll reenactment is to thoroughly document the infant's location and position as well as the circumstances surrounding the death as reported by the individuals who last saw the infant alive, and the individuals who found the infant unresponsive. A doll reenactment provides a witness, who may have difficulty verbalizing their observations, an opportunity to demonstrate what they observed, did, or witnessed as it relates to the infant.

A scene walk-through is another investigative approach that provides witnesses an opportunity to guide investigators through the incident location and point out areas within the scene that may be relevant to the infant's death. This walk-through should be completed in conjunction with the doll reenactment. The goal of a scene walk-through with a primary witness is to provide the witness an opportunity to show the investigator the layout of the incident location, where events occurred and then demonstrate their observations with the doll.

Doll reenactments are not widely used during infant death investigations even though the technique was mentioned on the 1996 Guidelines for the Death Scene Investigation of Sudden, Unexplained Infant Death and the Investigation Report Form (SUIDIRF) developed by the Centers for Disease Control and Prevention (CDC). On that form, investigators were able to check a box, documenting whether a doll reenactment was or was not completed.[1,2] The revised Sudden, Unexplained Infant Death Investigation (SUIDI) Reporting Form released in 2006, and the training material developed to instruct investigators how to use the form, places more emphasis on doll reenactments.[3,4] The primary reason that doll reenactments may not be widely used is that many investigators may not be aware of this technique or may feel inept using it prior to being trained. Investigators must be trained and educated in this technique to ensure that doll reenactments are included in all investigations surrounding the sudden and unexpected death of an infant.

Doll reenactments and scene walk-throughs with primary witnesses are being incorporated into infant death investigation protocols by some medical examiners' (ME) and coroners' offices. As a result, more investigators are becoming aware of these techniques and are beginning to seek opportunities to develop skills in these areas. The method by which infant deaths are currently investigated will change when investigators gain knowledge regarding both of these effective techniques and incorporate them into their existing infant death investigation protocols.

8.2 THE OPPOSITION

The more information investigators obtain during an investigation of a death the better. Witnesses who are provided an opportunity to reenact the circumstances surrounding the death reveal additional information and details that were not discussed during their interview. Some investigators and agencies believe that doll reenactments add little value and will not provide any new information for their investigations. However, investigators who are experienced in the use of doll reenactments agree that the amount and quality of information gained is extremely valuable, and that without the doll reenactment, some deaths may be classified inaccurately.

Some fear that dolls used during infant death investigations will cause additional emotional pain for the family or caregiver who participate in a reenactment. Investigators who explain the procedure to the witness and are empathetic during the reenactment find that witnesses handle the reenactment very well. These persons may even appreciate the opportunity to clarify what they verbally described and the opportunity to spend more time with the investigator to ask questions and gain information from them.

The use of dolls has been controversial in other specialties, and because of that, some investigators believe that dolls should not be used during infant death investigations. For the most part, demonstration dolls used during investigations have been limited to examiners who specialize in investigating child physical or child sexual abuse allegations. Anatomically correct dolls are sometimes used when interviewing children to assess the type and amount of abuse the child may have sustained or witnessed. The controversy surrounding this practice is that some are concerned the doll is a prop that enhances or encourages leading questions by the examiner. With children, there is a concern that in order to please or agree with the examiner, the child, who may be easily led, will use the doll to act out those leading questions. Most infant death investigation doll reenactments, however, will be conducted with adult witnesses and regardless of the specialty or type of investigation, investigators should be trained to use nonleading questions during interviews or doll reenactments with adults or children.

A doll reenactment may be one of the most difficult and emotional tasks that a caregiver and an investigator may have to perform. The information that is gleaned from the reenactment, however, has the ability to greatly affect the cause of death (COD) and the manner of death (MOD) determinations. This reenactment, if done respectfully and empathetically, may also positively affect survivors following an infant's death as the survivor has an opportunity to ask questions, obtain information, and receive referral information that may help during their healing process.

New investigative techniques and scientific findings can and will change the way deaths are investigated. As new investigative techniques and procedures are introduced, implemented, and incorporated into existing death investigation protocols, the more thorough and complete death investigations will be, resulting in more accurate COD and MOD determinations. Doll reenactments and a scene walk-through greatly affect the outcome of an infant death investigation. Investigators should become familiar with the goals, benefits, and techniques of both; the equipment needed; and how to plan and implement them to incorporate them into their current practice.

8.3 BENEFITS OF DOLL REENACTMENTS

There are many benefits to utilizing doll reenactments in infant death investigation protocols. The first benefit is that it provides caregivers or witnesses an opportunity to demonstrate the location and position in which they placed or found the infant. The National Association of Medical Examiners' Ad Hoc Committee of Sudden Unexplained Infant Death noted, in 2005, that doll reenactments may be a supplemental means of gaining information regarding the infant's position at the time of death.[5] Doll reenactments provide the witness an opportunity to show investigators what their actions were, or what they witnessed others doing in regard to the infant. This demonstration provides investigators with information regarding the living and sleeping environments in which the infant was placed and found in order to identify unsafe sleep conditions or environmental hazards that may have been present and contributed to the death.

Second, there are endless ways witnesses may verbally describe the same event. Witnesses may use slang language, may name parts of the body differently than the investigator, or have difficulty putting the incident into words. The doll reenactment provides an opportunity for investigators to clarify what the witness stated during the initial interview or wrote in a statement by having them physically show the investigator the location and demonstrate the infant's position. This reenactment or demonstration provides the witness and investigator an opportunity to clarify what was described verbally during the initial interview.

Third, information that seemed accurate when explained verbally may reveal areas of concern when demonstrated. The more time investigators spend with a witness, the more information they will obtain. The reenactment provides investigators yet another opportunity to interact with a witness. After observing the doll reenactment, investigators may have additional questions for this or other witnesses, which may provide important new details about the death. Investigators who suspect a witness intentionally omitted important details during an interview may find the doll reenactment an effective technique for either confirming or eliminating those suspicions.

Finally, photodocumentation of a doll reenactment provides a permanent record of the witness's account that may be important to the current investigation or in the future. Photographs provide the forensic pathologist a visual of the infant's location and position prior to death, and a visual of the infant's location and position when found unresponsive as reported by primary witnesses that may assist in the COD and MOD determination.

8.4 PREPLANNING: DOLL REENACTMENT AND SCENE WALK-THROUGH

Prior to initiating a doll reenactment and scene walk-through with a primary witness, investigators should plan how they will incorporate this technique into their investigation. Preplanning is essential. Investigators should consider the logistics of the reenactment including the type of equipment needed and with whom, when, and where to perform the reenactment. In the preplanning phase, the investigator should also make plans to explain the procedure to other investigative personnel and explain the procedure to the witness who will be asked to complete the walk-through and reenactment.

8.5 EQUIPMENT

Two pieces of equipment are needed to perform an effective doll reenactment. The first piece of equipment is a doll and the second item is a camera. Prior to purchasing either, investigators should consider the multiple uses of each and the type of dolls and cameras that are most effective during reenactments.

It is advantageous for investigators to have easy access to both pieces of equipment and is ideal if they carry the equipment with them in their vehicles to ensure the equipment is immediately available when needed.

8.5.1 The Doll

Dolls come in all shapes and sizes. There are many dolls on the market that could be used during a doll reenactment. Some doll characteristics, however, may be more suitable during an infant death investigation than others. Investigative agencies should purchase dolls that meet their goals and budget and should consider the effects some doll characteristics may have on a witness during the reenactment. Characteristics and qualities to consider include size of the doll, movement of limbs, the appearance and lifelikeness, facial features, and the doll's ethnicity.

8.5.1.1 Size of Doll

The size of the doll is an important characteristic to consider. The reenactment will be most beneficial to the investigator, and the person asked to perform the reenactment, if the doll used is of similar size to that of the infant. Dolls come in all sizes and it is best to choose one that is approximately the same length and girth of an average 3- to 5-month-old. The similarity in size will help the witness perform the reenactment more accurately. The investigator will be able to visualize the infant in the location and position that is being demonstrated and visualize the infant in relation to physical evidence present at the death scene, such as purge patterns, pillows, toys, blankets, and other people, when the doll used during the reenactment is approximately the same size as the infant.

8.5.1.2 Movement of Limbs

Another characteristic to consider is the ability of the doll's limbs to be turned, positioned, and manipulated. It may be desirable to use a doll in which the head, neck, legs, and arms are movable. Witnesses who are attempting to demonstrate the position of the infant are able to move the limbs as needed to accurately depict the infant's position. For example, a witness may state that the infant was lying on his stomach. The investigator may need to know whether the head was turned to the left or right. If the investigator is using a doll with a moveable head and neck, the witness can accurately demonstrate the infant's position by placing the doll on its stomach and turning the head in the appropriate direction. The doll should not, however, have limbs that are removable. It would be unfortunate for the witnesses if, during the scene walk-through or doll reenactment, an appendage came off the doll.

8.5.1.3 Lifelikeness

The lifelikeness of the doll is another characteristic that is important to consider. Many stores carry dolls that are not only life-sized, but also lifelike. Desirable characteristics may include a head and face made of a soft plastic material rather than cloth, and a body that is firm yet not rigid. Some dolls are weighted, which makes them feel about the same weight as an infant.

8.5.1.4 Facial Features

The doll's facial features are another characteristic that should be considered. Two features that may affect the reenactment are the eyes and the facial expression. Eyes that roll or doll eyes that open and close may be a disturbing characteristic during a reenactment to those who have just lost a child. Dolls that are smiling may also be inappropriate for this type of reenactment as it may be upsetting to the witness. Characteristics such as the doll's facial expression or the movement of the eyes may seem like great qualities when the doll is purchased, however, may be an inappropriate doll characteristic when used during infant death investigations.

8.5.1.5 Ethnicity

For cultural sensitivity, and if budgets allow, it may be beneficial to use a doll that is the same race as the infant that died. It may be culturally sensitive to use a lighter colored doll if the infant that died was Caucasian; likewise, if the infant was African American, it may be culturally sensitive to use a darker colored doll.

8.5.2 Camera

It is important to document the location and position of the infant as demonstrated with the doll by the witness. Photodocumentation is ideal. A digital camera is most beneficial as investigators may then immediately provide the forensic pathologist and other investigators documentation of the reenactment. Investigators who do not have access to a digital camera should photograph the reenactment with whatever photographic equipment may be available. Photographs of the reenactment should be maintained in the case file and provided to the forensic pathologist prior to autopsy. If no photographic equipment is available, the medicolegal death investigator (MDI) should proceed with the doll reenactment as the information obtained from the witness will be the same. MDIs who are unable to photodocument the reenactment will need to relay the information obtained during the reenactment verbally to the forensic pathologist; provide written documentation in a narrative report; or demonstrate what was observed to the forensic pathologist, other investigators, and members of the investigative child death review team.

8.5.3 Other Equipment Considerations

Investigators should only use a doll that they bring to the scene. Dolls that are a part of the scene or that belong to a caregiver or witness should never be used in a doll reenactment. It would not be appropriate to use a doll from the scene, as that doll could then become a visual reminder of their loss weeks and months after the death.

The intention of the doll reenactment is not to add additional pain, but to gather information to investigate the death thoroughly and completely.

There are many other uses for dolls in a MDI office other than infant death investigations. Agencies should consider these additional uses when deciding to purchase dolls. Dolls are effective when used for teaching, prevention programs, court testimony, or when working with the media. There are a number of dolls on the market that would work well for doll reenactments and these additional uses. Many can be purchased at local and national chain toy stores or via the Internet. Some companies are developing and marketing demonstration dolls specifically for the purpose of prevention or education programs as well as for investigative purposes. The National Center on Shaken Baby Syndrome, for example, offers shaken baby syndrome demonstration dolls in a variety of ethnic categories.

8.6 PREPLANNING THE DOLL REENACTMENT: WHAT TO CONSIDER

8.6.1 Who Are the Primary Witnesses?

The infant death investigation doll reenactment should be performed with the primary witness who placed or last saw the infant alive and the primary witness who found the infant unresponsive. It is important for the investigator to interview each potential primary witness prior to asking them to participate in a doll reenactment and it may not be until after interviews are complete that the investigator will know who these primary witnesses are. Investigators may ask only one person to participate in a doll reenactment or they may ask many persons to participate.

Investigators must also consider who, other than the MDI and the witness, should be present for the doll reenactment. This may be determined in part by jurisdictional protocols and the working relationship between agencies to include the ME's office, coroner's office, and the law enforcement agency. Nonprofessional persons including caregivers, other witnesses, or bystanders should not be present for the scene walk-through and doll reenactment. Just as it is important to interview each witness alone, it is also important for witnesses to be alone during these times. This prevents one witness from seeing what another described or demonstrated, which may cause them to possibly repeat it back to the investigator when they are asked to do the doll reenactment themselves.

Investigators must also identify which professional personnel should be present for the doll reenactment. As with interviews, the fewer people present the better as the interviewer has a better opportunity to develop a rapport with the interviewee, and there is less distraction so the investigator and witness can concentrate on the task at hand. It may be beneficial during some investigations, however, for a second interviewer to be present for the doll reenactment. This allows both investigators to observe the doll reenactment and obtain the same information at the same time. The MDI who interviewed the witness should be the investigator who initiates and directs the doll reenactment. If a second professional is needed during the reenactment, it is best that it be the same investigator who was present during the initial interview.

A primary witness in an infant death investigation may be a minor child. The minor child may be a sibling, babysitter, friend, or other relation to the infant or caregiver. Just as with adults, these witnesses may be able to provide important information to the investigation. Prior to proceeding with an interview, scene walk-through, or doll reenactment with a minor child, the investigator should refer to their jurisdictional policies. Interviewing minor children requires additional preparation and forethought. A child's developmental level will play an important role in how and if the child is interviewed and by whom. The investigator may need to obtain permission from the legal guardian of the child or may need to request that a professional, trained to interview children, conduct the interview and doll reenactment. Investigators should refer to their agency's policies prior to initiating a child interview as it is beyond the scope of this text to provide detailed information regarding child interview protocols.

8.6.2 It Is All about Timing

Doll reenactments should be initiated after a witness has been interviewed. This allows the investigator an opportunity to gather demographic information, determine which witnesses should participate in a doll reenactment, and identify any concerns or questions the investigator needs to address during the scene walk-through and reenactment.

In some situations, the doll reenactment will take place minutes after a witness is interviewed, and in other situations, it may not take place until many hours later. The time difference has to do with the location of the witness when interviewed. The doll reenactment will likely take place shortly after the initial interview of the witnesses who were on scene with the scene investigator; however, if the interview takes place at the emergency room, there may be a delay before the witness and the investigator can return to the scene to perform the doll reenactment. Obviously, the sooner the doll reenactment is performed after the death the better; as time passes, details and memories begin to fade.

The infant death investigation doll reenactment should be initiated with a witness as soon after the death as possible but only after the scene investigation and initial interview with that witness is complete. The infant death scene should be photographed and processed by the MDI and law enforcement prior to any witness being escorted into the scene for a walk-through as this prevents contamination and relocation of any evidence that may occur during the doll reenactment. Ideally, doll reenactments should be initiated the same day the death occurred, preferably within the first few hours. In some jurisdictions, it may not be possible to complete the reenactment in that time frame. It is important, however, that the reenactment be completed with each primary witness as soon as possible after the death.

8.6.3 Location

A doll reenactment should be conducted at the incident or scene location (Figure 8.1). Reenactments are most successful and informative if witnesses are able to return to the actual incident location to demonstrate what they observed. The witness should be given an opportunity to walk through the scene to show the investigator in which rooms events occurred. During the walk-through, they may point out important aspects of the scene, provide additional details, and demonstrate how those aspects were a part of the circumstances surrounding the infant's death. For example, if an infant was found unresponsive while sleeping in a twin bed with a sibling, it would

FIGURE 8.1 Investigators should photograph the external environment of the incident location.

be important for the investigator to determine which room, which bed, and with which sibling the infant was sleeping. The walk-through with the witness at the incident location will clear up any confusion that may be present if the residence is a five-bedroom home in which more than one room has twin beds.

Witnesses often scatter after an infant's death: some remain at the scene, others responded to the hospital, and still others may leave the scene and respond to a third location. The double-team approach, if initiated, provides the scene investigator with an opportunity to immediately initiate an interview, doll reenactment, and scene walk-through with those witnesses who remained on scene, while the infant death investigator responds and interviews witnesses who responded to the hospital. It will be necessary for witnesses who were interviewed at the hospital, police station, or some other location to return to the scene to complete the reenactment and walk-through. The infant death investigator will need to return to the scene to conduct doll reenactments with those witnesses who left the scene and were interviewed at other locations.

In rare instances, it may not be possible to complete doll reenactments at the scene. In those cases, the investigator should find another appropriate location and proceed with the reenactment. Other locations may be the MDI's office, the witness's residence, the police station, or another suitable location. Although the witness will not be able to demonstrate the infant's location, the witness will be able to demonstrate the infant's position, which alone may be helpful.

8.7 EXPLAIN PROCEDURE TO LAW ENFORCEMENT

Prior to initiating a doll reenactment, MDIs should openly communicate with other investigative or law enforcement personnel their intentions to conduct a scene walk-through and doll reenactments with primary witnesses. This provides open communication between agencies and professionals, prepares law enforcement personnel for the sequencing of the medicolegal death investigation, and is an opportunity to provide teaching to young or inexperienced officers. In some jurisdictions, law enforcement personnel will want to be present for the doll reenactment; in other jurisdictions, they may not want or feel their presence is needed. Either way, infant deaths are investigated much more thoroughly when investigative agencies communicate with one another to ensure that all agencies have the same information.

8.8 EXPLAIN PROCEDURE TO WITNESSES

Primary witnesses, who will be asked to participate in a doll reenactment, should be provided information about the reenactment and given an opportunity to ask questions prior to it being initiated. The investigator will determine during the interview if it would be beneficial for the witness to participate in a doll reenactment and if so should discuss the doll reenactment with them. Hopefully, the investigator was able to establish a rapport with the witness during the interview that will make the transition to the scene walk-through and doll reenactment easier and smoother. Investigators should take time to explain the importance of a reenactment, the role of the investigator, and the witness's role in the process.

At the end of the interviews, the investigator should thank witnesses for their time and begin to set the stage for the doll reenactment. The investigator should briefly explain to the witnesses that there is another important way they can help the investigator understand the circumstances that were conveyed verbally. The interviewer should inform the witnesses that it will be helpful if they would walk-through the scene with the investigator and point out specific locations where events occurred. This will provide the witnesses an opportunity to explain the circumstances again, point out the location of incidents at the scene, and demonstrate the events as described in the interview. It is crucial that the investigator elicit the help of the witnesses and inform them that it may be difficult to identify the infant's cause of death without the witnesses' assistance. Witnesses who recognize that they play an important role in the investigation will often cooperate fully and will provide valuable information if approached respectfully.

Prior to the walk-through and reenactment, the witness should be shown the doll that will be used. This provides the witness an opportunity to become familiar with the doll and the ways it may be manipulated. A witness may inquire why it is important to use the doll. The investigator should explain that it is necessary to accurately document the infant's location and position; the doll helps investigators do that. The witness should also be informed that it may be necessary to take photographs during the scene walk-through or doll reenactment. This is not the time, however, to take scene photographs as those should have already been taken prior to initiating the scene walk-through or doll reenactment. However, if the witness should point out an aspect of the scene that may not have been photodocumented, it may be necessary to take additional photographs. Photographs of the locations and positions that the witness places the doll should be taken (Figure 8.2A through Figure 8.2D).

FIGURE 8.2A During a scene walk-through, the witness led investigators to this room in which two twin beds were located.

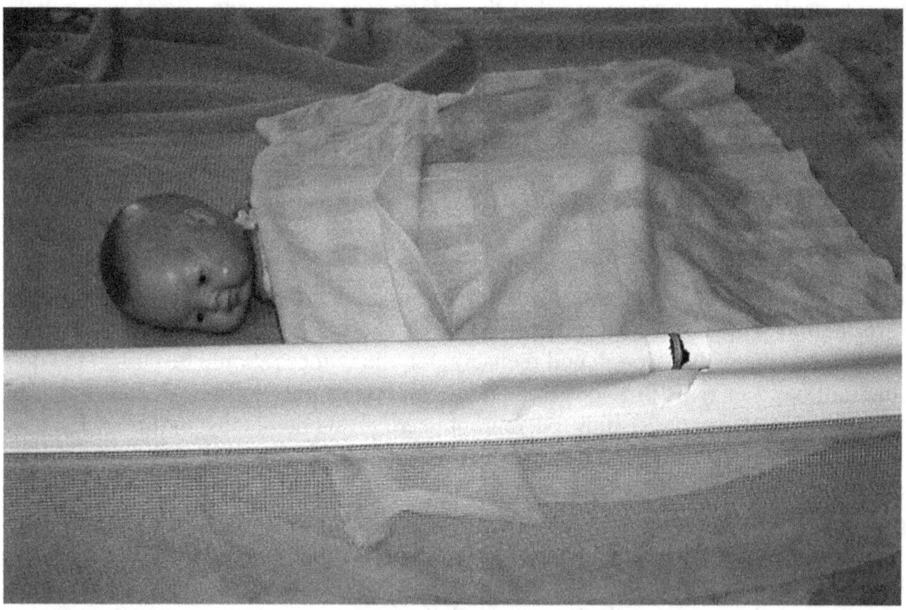

FIGURE 8.2B The witness stated that she put the infant down to sleep on the twin bed that had the safety side rails. The witness was asked to show the investigator how the baby was put down to sleep. The witness placed the doll on its back and covered the doll with a blanket.

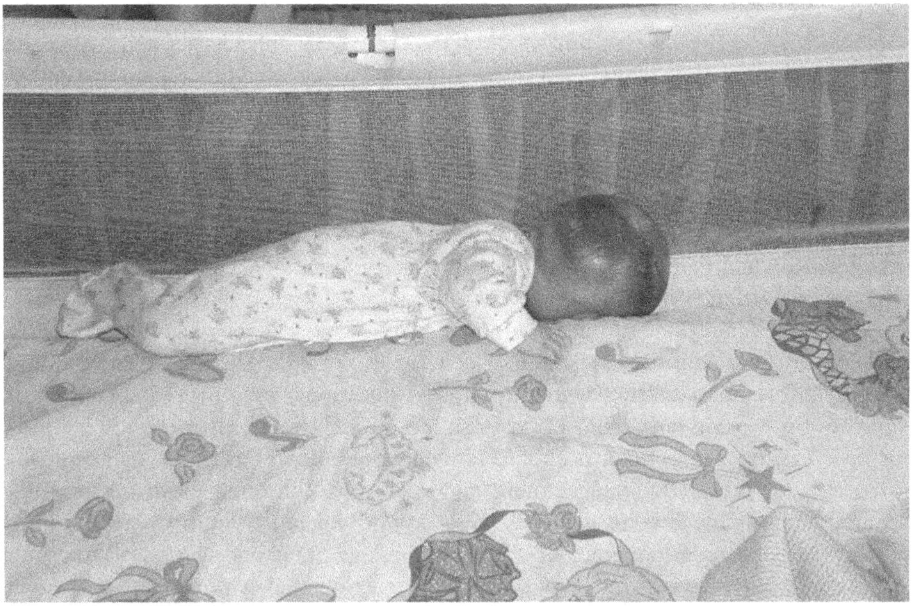

FIGURE 8.2C This witness stated that she found the infant trapped between the mattress and the safety rail. The investigator handed the doll to the witness and asked her to show the investigator where the baby was located. The witness placed the doll in the depicted position.

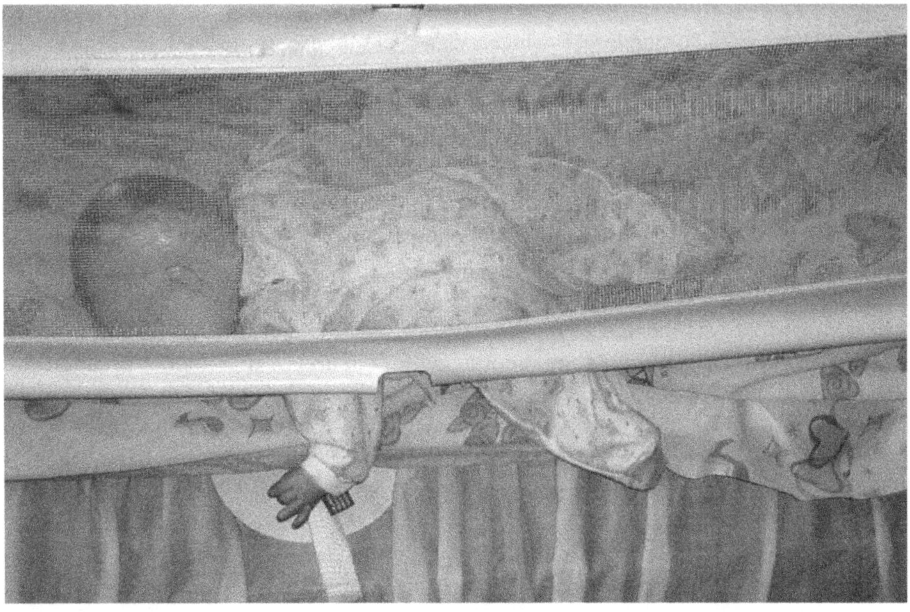

FIGURE 8.2D Investigators may need to photograph the position that the doll is placed in by the witness from multiple angles to accurately depict the infant's location and position.

The doll reenactment and scene walk-through may be a very emotional time for some witnesses. The investigator should handle the doll with respect and assure the witnesses that this procedure is not intended to cause them additional pain, but rather to help ensure that the circumstances surrounding the infant's death are understood to accurately determine what caused the infant's death. The investigator should empathize with them and inform the witnesses that they may take their time and that their willingness to assist the process is appreciated. Witnesses should be informed that these procedures are intended to help provide answers to the family regarding the infant's death and that accurate information regarding the cause of the infant's death will, in time, promote healing as they will not wonder what happened to their child.

In rare circumstances, investigators may encounter witnesses who refuse to participate in the doll reenactment and scene walk-through. The investigator should provide information and answer the witness' questions, give the witness a short period of time to compose themselves, or suggest that the reenactment be rescheduled for later that day. Investigators should be concerned, however, if a witness refuses to participate in the doll reenactment and scene walk-through even after special accommodations have been made. Witnesses who are not trying to hide anything will typically be very cooperative during a doll reenactment and scene walk-through and even those witnesses who do not want to interact with law enforcement personnel will often talk openly with MDIs from a coroner's or ME's office.

8.9 INITIATING THE SCENE WALK-THROUGH AND DOLL REENACTMENT

After explaining the procedure, the investigator should escort the witness to the scene entrance and ask the witness to walk through with the investigator. Investigators should let the witness lead the investigator through the incident location. The investigator should direct the witness by asking them to "Show me" where they saw the infant as opposed to the investigator asking, "Is this where the infant was?" The witness should lead the investigator through the scene and should not be led or asked to answer leading questions (Figure 8.3A and Figure 8.3B).

When the witness mentions the location of the infant, the investigator should hand the doll to the witness and ask the witness to show the investigator specifically where the infant was located. If the infant was placed in a crib, playpen, or bassinet, for example, the investigator should confirm the location of that item in the incident location to ensure that those items are in the same place during the scene walk-through and doll reenactment as it was during the time of the incident. After the witness places the doll in the location, the investigator should inquire as to the infant's exact position (for example, face up, face down, on side) and the position of the head, neck, arms, and legs. The witnesses should be prompted to describe any persons, animals, or other items that were in the vicinity of the infant including pillows, blankets, stuffed animals, toys, and sleeping assistive devices such as wedges. The witness should be directed to place those items near or around the doll as they were when the witness observed the infant. As the witness demonstrates how

FIGURE 8.3A A witness was asked to show the investigator where the infant was located. The witness led investigators to the infant's room.

they placed or found the infant, the investigator should clarify the location and position ensuring that any photographs taken of the doll reenactment are representative of what is being described and demonstrated (Figure 8.4A and Figure 8.4B).

During the doll reenactment, investigators should ask the witness if the surface layers are the same as when they placed or found the infant and if the items that were located near the infant are the same as those present for the walk-through and reenactment. Once photographs are taken of the location and position of the infant, the investigator should inquire as to the type and amount of material that was under as well as those items placed over the infant. It will be necessary for the investigator to pull back each layer of bedding material to properly document the surface on which the infant was placed or found (Figure 8.5A through Figure 8.5C). Layers of material that should be documented may include bedding and blankets, quilts, comforters, egg crate mattresses, sheepskin coverings, and pillows. The sleep surface layers should be confirmed with the witness to ensure an accurate description of the type and amount of material on the surface that the infant was placed or found. The scene may have been altered prior to the walk-through or doll reenactment. If the layers are not the same or the items that were near the infant have been moved, the witness should be asked to make the area look like it did when the incident occurred. This alteration may have occurred during the scene investigation as evidence may have been collected or by family or caregivers that either intentionally or unintentionally altered the incident location by cleaning out the infant's crib, washing sheets, or putting toys away in their proper place.

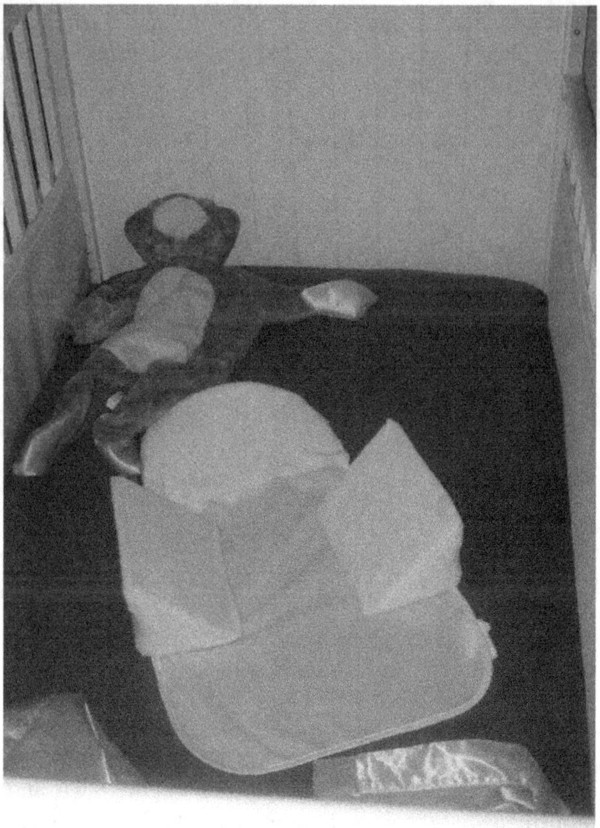

FIGURE 8.3B The witness pointed to the crib and stated the infant was put down in the crib to sleep. The investigator observed the wedge in the crib and asked the witness if the items in the crib were there when they observed the infant in the crib.

Case Example 8.1 During the reenactment, a witness placed the infant face down in a bassinet. After establishing the infant's location and position, the investigator inquired about the surface that the infant was placed on. The witness stated there was an adult-sized pillow in the bottom of the bassinet that was not present during the scene walk-through and doll reenactment. During the scene investigation, a purge pattern was noted on the pillow. Law enforcement removed the pillow from the scene and placed it into evidence. The witness provided information about the pillow once they were prompted to describe the surface on which the infant was lying. A similar pillow was located and placed in the bassinet for the reenactment.

8.9.1 Sleep Surface Considerations

It is important for the witness to demonstrate where other persons were located and positioned in relation to the infant if the scene involved the infant sharing a sleep surface with other persons. The witness should be asked to walk through the scene

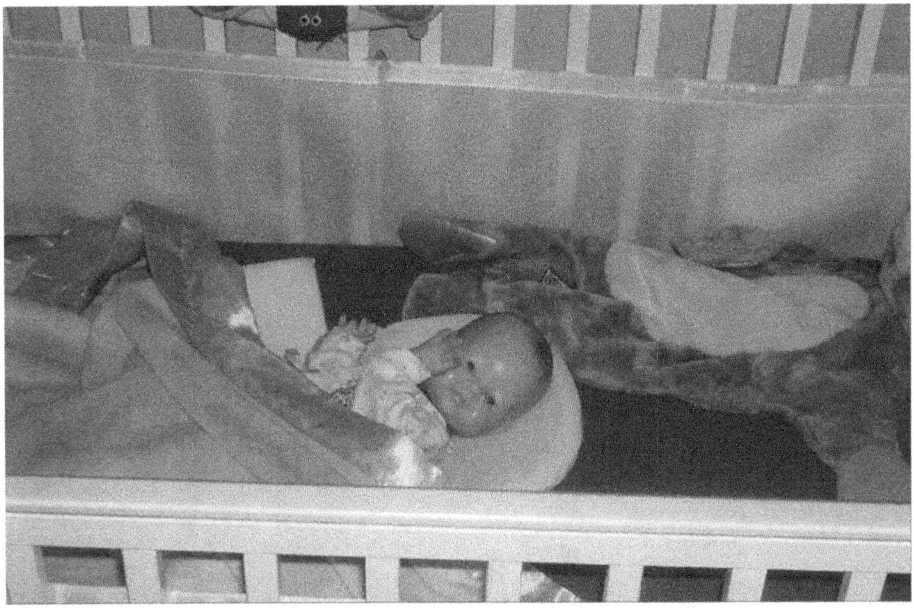

FIGURE 8.4A The witness placed the doll on its back on the sleeping device to represent the position in which she placed the infant down to sleep.

and direct the investigator to the location where the infant was placed or found. The doll should be placed in the location and position that the infant was observed, ensuring that all items, including bedding, blankets, and pillows, are in the correct position. An animal, such as a dog or cat, may have shared the sleeping surface with the infant. The investigator should inquire as to the position of that animal while on the sleep surface when observed by the witness and obtain a description of that animal including the approximate size and weight. Information regarding the ages, height, and weight of all persons known to be sharing a sleep surface with the infant should be obtained along with a description and demonstration of the location and position of each person on the sleeping surface as observed by the witness. The investigator should direct the witness to demonstrate where the other persons were positioned on the sleep surface, which may have been a bed, couch, love seat, or the floor. It may be beneficial to have the witness assume the positions of the persons they observed (Figure 8.6A and Figure 8.6B).

8.9.2 Cardiopulmonary Resuscitation (CPR) Demonstration

In some cases, it may be beneficial to have witnesses demonstrate on the doll, how they performed emergency medical treatment such as CPR. A demonstration of the method used to perform CPR may provide information regarding marks that were found during the postmortem physical assessment of the infant. If there are concerns that a witness's lifesaving attempts may have left marks or caused an injury that needs to be explained, the witness should be asked to demonstrate his or her technique.

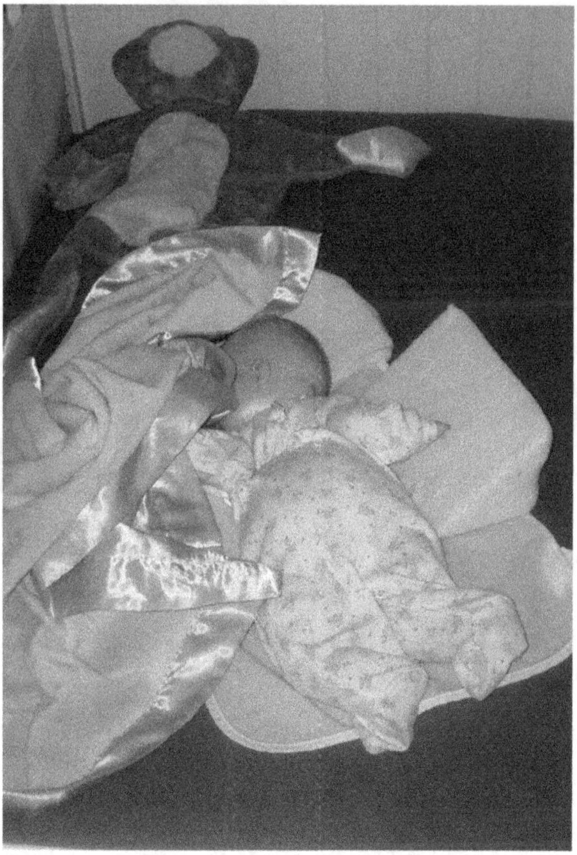

FIGURE 8.4B The witness stated that when she found the infant unresponsive, the baby was on its stomach and its face was covered by the blanket. The witness placed the doll in the depicted position to demonstrate how she observed the infant.

8.10 INVESTIGATIVE CONCERNS

During a doll reenactment, investigative questions or concerns may arise that will require the investigator to make decisions regarding how to proceed with the investigation. First, concerns may arise if the information provided by the witness does not match the evidence at the scene or statements made by other witnesses. In these situations, the investigator must determine whether to confront the witness with the discrepancies or not. That decision may be based on agency policy or protocol; however, some suggestions for gently confronting a witness will be discussed. Second, it may be necessary to request a primary witness to repeat a doll reenactment if physical findings from the autopsy do not correlate with the witness's account of events during the interview or reenactment. Third, a witness may ask difficult questions in regard to culpability of the infant's death. Investigators should be prepared to answer these questions.

FIGURE 8.5A The caregiver reported that the infant was placed faced down on an adult bed for a nap while the caregiver worked around the house. During the scene walk-through, investigators were led to this adult bed.

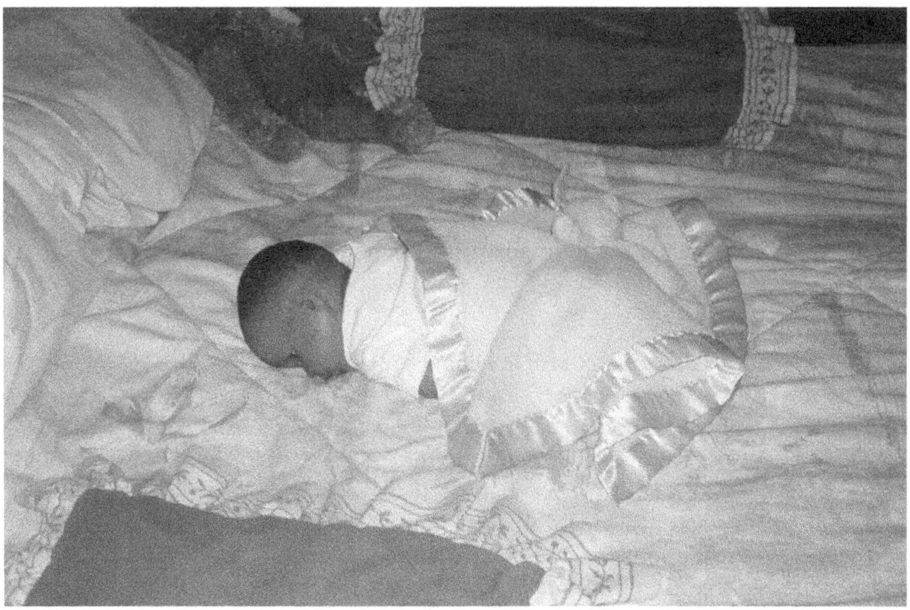

FIGURE 8.5B The witness placed the doll on its stomach in the middle of the adult bed, between two small decorative pillows and covered it with a light blanket.

FIGURE 8.5C Investigators should pull back the layers of bedding to document the sleep surface layers and determine if those present were the same during the reenactment as when the infant was found. In this case, the infant was put face down on a thick comforter that was covering many sheets and a thick soft pillow top mattress.

8.10.1 Confronting Witnesses

It may be necessary to confront witnesses if the information that they provide during an interview or doll reenactment does not match scene evidence, autopsy findings, or statements from other witnesses. Investigators must determine when, how, and under what circumstances it may be appropriate to confront a witness. Two situations will be covered here in which confrontation may be necessary: homicides and deaths resulting from accidental overlying or suffocation.

8.10.1.1 Homicides

The MDI, in most jurisdictions, will not engage in an interrogation or confrontational questioning of a homicide suspect. The MDI's role while investigating the infant's death is to develop a rapport with the potential witness or suspect, gather as much information as possible, and communicate that information to the forensic pathologist and to law enforcement investigators. It may be beneficial, however, for the MDI to be present and provide information during the interrogation or confrontation of a witness. In some jurisdictions, the MDI, if experienced, may be the individual that acts in that role. Law enforcement officials need the investigative information that was obtained by the MDI just as the MDI must rely on law enforcement to arrest potential suspects. The working relationship between the MDI and the law enforcement officials will often affect the outcome.

FIGURE 8.6A A witness stated she observed another caregiver cosleeping on a futon-type bed with the infant. The witness led investigators to this location. Investigators inquired if the pillows present during the scene walk-through were also present when the infant was found.

FIGURE 8.6B The witness placed the doll in the position she observed the infant and demonstrated the position of the individual she observed cosleeping with the infant.

8.10.1.2 Accidental Deaths

Deaths that may be the result of an overlying or suffocation due to bed sharing, cosleeping, or an otherwise unsafe sleep environment can and are often difficult for caregivers and witnesses to discuss. These individuals may fail to provide truthful information regarding an unsafe sleeping situation. There are a number of reasons they may fail to provide truthful information. First, they may fear prosecution. Second, they may be embarrassed that their actions or the actions of another may have contributed to the infant's death. Finally, it may be too difficult for them to admit, to themselves as well as to others, that their actions or decisions may have placed their child at an increased risk for injury and death.

During the interview and doll reenactment, it may become apparent that the information provided by the witness is not accurate. The investigator should assess the witness's motivation for providing inaccurate information. Seasoned infant death investigators may be able to recognize witnesses that may fear personal outcomes should the death be the result of overlying. In those cases, and depending on jurisdictional policies, it may be appropriate for the investigator to gently confront the witness regarding the inaccurate information and acknowledge the witness's possible fears and concerns.

When placing infants in unsafe sleeping environments, most caregivers are not trying to intentionally cause injury to the child. Often the caregiver believes that they are providing a safe and comfortable sleeping environment for the child and that by sharing a sleeping surface with the infant, they are able to protect their child from crib death. As a result, accidental deaths, due to overlying or suffocation, are rarely prosecuted unless there is compelling evidence that the caregiver was under the influence of drugs or alcohol. Acknowledging the witness's fear of prosecution and acknowledging that they were trying to take good care of the infant, their fears can be lessened. The investigator should reassure the witness that accurate information is needed to ensure that the death of this child is completely understood. Experienced infant death investigators who have used this technique to gently confront witnesses have found that after lessening their fears and acknowledging that they were trying to be good care providers for the infant, witnesses will often change their initial statement and will demonstrate with the doll what really happened. The information provided during their interview as well as the interviews of other witnesses, the details provided during the doll reenactment, the findings during the scene investigation, and the autopsy results should all be consistent. If they are not, it may be necessary to conduct a follow-up interview and repeat the doll reenactment.

8.10.2 Witness Questions and Concerns

During the doll reenactment, witnesses will be asked to provide the investigator with lots of detailed information. At the same time, the witness may request information from the investigator regarding his or her findings and how the witness's actions may have contributed to the death. Investigators must be prepared for difficult and emotional questions that may be asked by witnesses. It is important that investigators be truthful with their answers, provide information, and make referrals as needed based on the circumstances surrounding the infant's death. It may not be beneficial to the investigation, however, to reveal important information that is known about the infant if a homicide is suspected. Investigators may need to determine on a case-by-case basis what information is shared with the next of kin.

Infant deaths that may be attributed to bed sharing or cosleeping are often very emotional for survivors. These are cases in which the witness may ask the investigator, "Am I responsible for my baby's death?" or "Did I suffocate my baby?" The investigator's role and the policies in place by their employing agency may dictate how they answer this tough question. Some investigators provide a "nonanswer," stating that they are not the person who will make that determination, thus putting off the question. This tactic fails to acknowledge the witness's fears and closes the door on teaching opportunities with the witness. Some witnesses may view this tactic as untruthfulness knowing that their concerns are justified.

Another possible strategy for answering this tough question is to provide factual information. This factual information begins by acknowledging that the infant, based on the investigation and the investigator's experience, was in an unsafe sleeping environment that did place the infant at an increased risk for injury or death. The investigator should then remind the witness that the investigation is not complete and that when a final determination is made, the investigator will be better able to address that question. This tactic acknowledges the witness's concern, provides information that the investigation will continue, and that when a final determination is made, the investigator will provide that information to the appropriate persons. Until that determination is made, the concerns of the witness are validated, which may impact the care of other children that are in that person's custody or environment. By providing a nonanswer, some witnesses may take that to mean that their actions are not culpable; therefore, they may not alter their lifestyle in regard to bed sharing or cosleeping with other young children.

8.11 SUMMARY

A doll reenactment and walk-through are critical to determining the infant's COD and MOD and helps ensure that a complete picture of the infant's location and position are obtained. There are many aspects that should be considered prior to initiating a doll reenactment including what type of doll to use, preplanning the reenactment, and issues to consider during the reenactment. Doll reenactments may provide some of the most important pieces of information that will be obtained during an infant death investigation. As a result, a doll reenactment and scene walk-through should be included in the investigations of all infants that die suddenly and unexpectedly.

REFERENCES

1. Centers for Disease Control, Appendix Instructions for Completing the Sudden Unexplained Infant Death Investigation Report Form (SUIDIRF), *Morbid. Mortal. Wkly. Rep.*, 45 (RR-10), 7–22, 1996.

2. Centers for Disease Control, Sudden Unexplained Infant Death Investigation Report Form (SUIDIRF), 3.96, Section 5, 4. http://www.cdc.gov/epo/dphsi/mecisp/forms/suidirf3.96.pdf.
3. Centers for Disease Control and Prevention, SUIDI Reporting Form: A Guide for Investigators, document, available at the CDC Web site http://www.cdc.gov/SIDS/SUIDHowtoUseForm.htm (accessed on August 11, 2006).
4. Centers for Disease Control and Prevention, Sudden Unexplained Infant Death Investigation: A Systematic Training Program for the Professional Infant Death Investigation Specialist, document 200-2005-13514, 2006.
5. Corey, T.S., Hanzlick, R., Howard, J., Nelson, C., and Krous, H., A Functional Approach to Sudden Unexplained Infant Deaths. Prepared by the NAME Ad Hoc Committee on Sudden Unexplained Infant Death. Approved by the NAME Board of Directors on October 14, 2005. http://www.thename.org.

RESOURCES

Everson, M.D. and Boat, B.W., Putting the anatomical doll controversy in perspective: An examination of the major use and criticisms of the dolls in child sexual abuse evaluations, *Child Abuse Negl.*, 18 (2), 113–129, 1994.

Faller, K., Anatomical dolls: Their use in assessment of children who may have been sexually abused, *J. Child Sex. Abus.*, 14 (3), 1–21, 2005.

Goodman, G.S. and Aman, C., Children's use of anatomically detailed dolls to recount an event, *Child Dev.*, 61 (6), 1859–1871, 1990.

Morgan, M.K., *How to Interview Sexual Abuse Victims: Including the Use of Anatomical Dolls,* Interpersonal Violence: The Practice Series, Sage Publications, Thousand Oaks, CA, 1994.

National Center on Shaken Baby Syndrome, www.dontshake.com.

Thierry, K., Lamb, M., Orbach, Y., and Pipe, M., Developmental differences in the function and use of anatomical dolls during interviews with alleged sexual abuse victims, *J. Consult. Clin. Psychol.,* 73 (6), 1125–1134, 2005.

9 The Forensic Autopsy: The Investigator's Role

9.1 INTRODUCTION

The investigation into the cause and manner of an infant or young child's death has many crucial components, one of which is the forensic autopsy. A forensic autopsy should be conducted on all infants and children who die suddenly and unexpectedly. The autopsy findings must also be communicated to the investigator and compared to statements made by all witnesses, the scene investigation, the doll reenactment, and records reviewed. The forensic autopsy is one component of an infant death investigation. The autopsy findings cannot stand alone as they should be consistent with other investigational aspects of the case.

The forensic pathologist should have an understanding of the process by which infant deaths are investigated and should be provided details regarding the investigative findings. Specifically information about the infant, the incident scene, and the circumstances of the death should be shared with and provided to the forensic pathologist before the autopsy begins. Just as important, the medicolegal death investigator (MDI) should have an understanding of the autopsy protocol and the forensic pathologist's findings should be communicated to the investigator. Communication between the MDI and the forensic pathologist is vital to ensure that investigation of the death is thorough and complete and that the cause of death (COD) and manner of death (MOD) are accurately identified.

MDIs should have a basic understanding of the two types of autopsies, when they are used, and who performs them. Additionally, investigators who investigate infant deaths should have knowledge about specific aspects of infant forensic autopsies and should know their roles and responsibilities before, during, and after the autopsy is complete.

9.2 WHY SHOULD MEDICOLEGAL DEATH INVESTIGATORS (MDIs) BE INFORMED?

During infant death investigations, MDIs are the eyes and ears for the forensic pathologist. The MDI investigates the death scene, conducts the initial postmortem infant assessment, interviews caregivers, and conducts the doll reenactment with primary witnesses. Their investigation provides clues as to the cause and manner of the infant's death and, as a result of their investigative insight and intuition, may have an opinion or theory about the cause of death. MDIs who are knowledgeable about the autopsy protocol will know which tests and procedures are considered routine and which tests must be requested if a specific question or concern was raised during the investigation. In jurisdictions that do not utilize the expertise of a forensic pathologist, MDIs should have knowledge regarding the minimum forensic infant autopsy recommendations that have or are being developed and proposed and ensure that those tests or procedures are being conducted.

The investigator is often the individual who explains procedures to and answers questions from the family and next of kin. Surviving family members may have questions or concerns regarding the autopsy and are likely to ask questions while or after being interviewed by the investigator. The MDI should, therefore, have knowledge of the autopsy procedure to accurately answer questions and provide information. The next of kin may inquire how the autopsy will affect the family's funeral arrangements or when the family can expect to be notified of the autopsy results. The MDI, who often has an established rapport with the family, may be the professional who will relay autopsy findings to them. The family may then have additional questions that the investigator should be prepared to answer.

The MDI is often the liaison between the forensic pathologist and law enforcement personnel; therefore, the MDI will be the individual to relay information and explain procedures and results to them. The MDI may be the individual who will explain the forensic pathologist's findings to other involved professionals to ensure that all investigative personnel have a clear picture of the findings and what those findings represent. MDIs are the hub of an infant death investigation as they are often the go-betweens and the go-to persons for all investigative agencies and surviving family members. An understanding of autopsy protocol and procedure ensures a thorough and complete investigation as this primary investigator is knowledgeable of the minimum investigative requirements and the minimum autopsy recommendations. The MDI also has the ability to communicate that information to the appropriate individuals and assist in determining what additional case-specific procedures and tests should be requested and completed.

9.3 AUTOPSY BASICS

MDIs should have knowledge of a variety of aspects related to autopsy protocol. These aspects include the two types of autopsies, medical and forensic; when each type is used; who conducts autopsy; and when each may be utilized during an infant death investigation. This general knowledge can then be built upon as investigators become aware of the specific investigative needs of the forensic pathologist, law enforcement personnel, and next of kin before, during, and after an infant autopsy.

9.3.1 The Medical Autopsy

A *medical autopsy,* also referred to as a clinical or academic autopsy, is a postmortem examination performed in hospitals to identify the extent of a decedent's medical condition that is suspected to have caused the person's death. This type of autopsy is often utilized for research and study purposes to identify disease processes and to evaluate the effect of medical treatment. Medical autopsies may or may not include an examination of all organ systems, as the focus area may only include the area of the body known to have medical complications. As an example, a medical autopsy conducted on an individual with a known heart condition may only be completed on the cardiovascular system. The extent to which the autopsy is conducted is at the discretion of the individual performing or requesting the autopsy.

A clinical or academic autopsy may be performed on infants and young children who died in a hospital setting after a lengthy medical illness, or if they died at home from a known terminal medical condition. Medical autopsies are not recommended for infants who die suddenly or unexpectedly. This will usually only occur if the child is diagnosed with a terminal condition and in which a prearranged plan is in place between the family and the primary physician to conduct a medical autopsy after the child's death. In those rare cases, the MDI should communicate with the infant's primary physician to determine the best course of action for the case.

Medical autopsies may be performed at the request of the family and the next of kin must provide consent for one to be conducted. A *medical doctor* (MD), who completed 4 years of medical school and a 4-year residency program, or a *pathologist,* an MD who specializes in pathology, most often performs medical autopsies.

9.3.2 The Forensic Autopsy

A forensic autopsy is a postmortem examination that is conducted by a forensic pathologist pursuant to state statutes. Under the direction and order of a medical examiner (ME) or coroner, this autopsy is conducted for medicolegal purposes to identify the cause and manner of an individual's death. In most jurisdictions, it is not necessary to seek the permission of the next of kin prior to conducting a forensic autopsy. A designated representative, usually the ME or coroner, is authorized to direct the completion of a forensic autopsy without the consent of the next of kin.

All infant death investigations in which the death was sudden and unexpected should include a forensic autopsy as it is an all-inclusive postmortem examination. The external body is examined from head to toe; full-body x-rays are taken; organ systems are examined grossly and microscopically; toxicology analysis is completed; and additional case-specific tests and screenings are completed in order for the forensic pathologist to identify the COD and MOD. It is recommended that the individual conducting an infant forensic autopsy be a *board certified forensic pathologist,* an MD who is certified in forensic pathology by the American Board of Pathology.

9.4 COMMUNICATION

The communication between the MDI and the forensic pathologist is paramount to the investigation of the death of any infant or young child. If either professional does not communicate with the other, it will be difficult for each to do their respectful jobs and it will make it more difficult to determine the COD and MOD. Thorough and complete investigations must include open communication between all investigative personnel; however, the communication between the forensic pathologist and the MDI is vital. Their communication must be *mutual* and *horizontal:* the MDI must provide the forensic pathologist with all investigative information needed to conduct the autopsy, and the forensic pathologist must communicate with the MDI findings to include those that are consistent with the investigator's findings and those that are not. A breakdown in communication, in either direction, may be detrimental to the case.

The type and organizational structure of the death investigation system that is in place in each state will influence the way the forensic pathologist and the MDI communicate. In some jurisdictions, the forensic pathologist and the MDI are housed in the same office. In other jurisdictions, they may be located in different offices, different municipalities, or different counties. Regardless of the circumstances and distance between the two, communication must occur either in written form or verbally. Some investigative agencies may choose to e-mail or fax a completed narrative report, investigative checklist, or form, such as the Sudden Unexplained Infant Death Scene Investigation Report Form, to the forensic pathologist. It is recommended, however, that they communicate verbally to be able to ensure accurate understanding of all information submitted and to ensure that the communication needs of both are met.

9.5 THE INFANT FORENSIC AUTOPSY: BEFORE, DURING, AND AFTER

Infant death investigations are unique. The type of information that should be obtained during the investigation as well as specific information that should be provided to the forensic pathologist will affect the outcome of the case and the COD and MOD determinations. MDIs should have an understanding of their roles and responsibilities before the autopsy as well as the specific needs of the next of kin, law enforcement, and the forensic pathologist. It is beneficial for MDIs to also have basic knowledge of the autopsy procedure with a general understanding of what will occur during the autopsy and the reasons for those procedures. This knowledge prepares them to answer questions and provide information to the family and law enforcement personnel as needed. Finally, investigators should be aware of their roles and responsibilities after the autopsy is complete. Communication with the forensic pathologist, law enforcement, and the family; the release of the body to a funeral home; and preparations for investigative follow-up should occur after the autopsy is complete. Investigators must realize that an autopsy is not the investigation nor does it complete the investigation. The autopsy may be the beginning if inconsistencies are found between the forensic pathologist's findings and other investigative aspects of the case.

9.5.1 Before the Infant Autopsy

Before the forensic autopsy begins, investigators should communicate with the infant's family, law enforcement personnel, and the forensic pathologist to be certain that all important information is communicated and questions regarding the case are answered. Neglecting to identify and respond to the needs of the family, law enforcement, and the forensic pathologist prior to the start of the autopsy places the investigation and the relationship between those parties at risk.

9.5.1.1 Next of Kin Considerations and Needs

Although it may not be necessary to obtain permission from the next of kin before authorizing a forensic autopsy, investigators should work closely with them to answer their questions. Families may initially reject the idea of an autopsy being performed on their children. Prior to the autopsy being conducted, investigators should address the family's objections, their fears, and their lack of knowledge about autopsy procedure. It will be easier to work with the family in the future if their fears are addressed, their questions are answered, and they are provided information about the autopsy before it begins. Investigators should provide the next of kin with information regarding the autopsy schedule, the amount of time it will take to complete the autopsy, when the body may be released to the funeral home following the autopsy, and when the family can expect to be notified of the results. A family's fear of an autopsy may be lessened if their questions are answered and they are provided information about the procedure and what to expect.

9.5.1.1.1 Religious Concerns

Special accommodations may need to be considered and addressed if the family objects to an autopsy due to religious reasons. To understand the specifics of the objection, investigators should discuss with the family their specific religious objections to determine if it is possible to accommodate the family's needs and concerns. After discussing with the family their concerns, investigators may be able to work with the forensic pathologist to meet the religious needs of the family while at the same time meet the investigative needs of the case. Although investigators may, depending on their jurisdiction, have the authority to override religious requests and complete the autopsy without the family's permission, everyone is best served if the objections are understood and if the investigator tries, in good faith, to make special accommodations possible.

> *Case Example 9.1* A Jewish family initially objected to an autopsy being conducted on their child. The investigator worked with the family and their rabbi to identify the specific concerns that each had in regard to the autopsy. The family stated that they would agree to the autopsy if their rabbi could be present to ensure that their child's body was handled appropriately and according to custom. The investigator communicated the needs of the family to the forensic pathologist and accommodations were made to meet their needs. The autopsy met investigational needs; the family's rabbi was present, which met their religious and personal needs; and the relationship between the investigator and the family was maintained in the event additional information must be obtained from them in the future.

9.5.1.1.2 Organ Donation

Organ donation requests should be addressed prior to autopsy to ensure the requests of the family are known and to provide organ procurement agencies an opportunity to speak with the family. In most jurisdictions, an organ procurement agency is notified of all deaths to determine if the deceased is a suitable organ donor. In cases in which the infant died at the hospital, a hospital representative will notify the appropriate agency that the death has occurred. The procurement agency, based on the information received, may attempt to contact the family to determine if they are interested in organ donation. Based on information provided by the hospital representative, the procurement agency may elect to decline the case and choose not to contact the next of kin.

Depending on the jurisdiction, it may be the responsibility of the MDI to notify the procurement agency if the infant died outside of a hospital. When notified, the procurement agency will request the name and age of the deceased, the name and contact information for the next of kin, the cause of death if known, as well as any known medical conditions. The procurement agency, based on the information provided by the MDI, may elect against contacting the family, which is frequently the case with infant deaths that occur outside a hospital.

The organ procurement agency should be notified, however, if the family is requesting organ donation or if they would like to speak with someone regarding the donation process. Ultimately, the decision to authorize an organ donation will be at the discretion of the ME or coroner who has jurisdiction over the case; however, it is recommended that the forensic pathologist be advised that the family is considering organ donation. Open communication between the investigator, the family, the forensic pathologist, and the organ procurement agency may provide a solution to meet the needs of all involved. It may be possible for accommodations to be made that do not interfere with investigative proceedings yet meet the needs of the family.

9.5.1.2 Law Enforcement Personnel's Considerations or Needs

MDIs should communicate openly with the law enforcement personnel who are involved in the investigation surrounding the death of the infant. Depending on the agency's policy and the policy at the autopsy facility, a detective or crime scene technician may want to be present during the autopsy to photograph injuries, take custody of evidence, or to be able to ask questions of the forensic pathologist. Law enforcement personnel should be provided the date, time, and location for the autopsy in the event that a representative from their agency needs to be present.

9.5.1.3 Forensic Pathologist's Consideration and Needs

Prior to beginning the autopsy of an infant, the forensic pathologist should be provided all demographic and pertinent information regarding the infant and the circumstances of the death. This will include information regarding the infant's health, the family's history, scene information, the MDI's findings during the initial postmortem assessment, and other investigational concerns including inconsistencies that have been noted between each of those components. There are many critical details that should be communicated with the forensic pathologist prior to the forensic autopsy being conducted as listed in Table 9.1.

9.5.2 During Autopsy: Recommendations

The Committee on Child Abuse and Neglect recommended in 2001 that postmortem examinations for infants be completed within 24 hours of the death and include a complete radiographic survey, toxicology testing, and metabolic screening.[1] More recently, the National Association of Medical Examiners (NAME) Ad Hoc Committee on Sudden Unexplained Infant Deaths has proposed recommendations for infant death investigations with the goal of identifying the "bare minimum" recommendations that would constitute a complete investigation.[2] Investigators

TABLE 9.1
Forensic Pathologist's Needs Prior to Autopsy

	Information to Provide Forensic Pathologist Prior to Autopsy
Demographics	• Infant's name • Infant's age, date of birth, and race • Date, time, and location infant was pronounced dead • Date, time, and location infant was found unresponsive • Name and title of MDI, agency affiliation, and case number • Name of law enforcement agency
Infant Health	• Birth history (i.e., gestation, mode, anomalies, injuries) • Diagnosed medical conditions • Prior hospitalizations • Current medications (i.e., prescription, over-the-counter, herbal) • History of accidents, injuries, or falls • Behavioral changes during last 48 hours of infant's life (i.e., inconsolable, fussy, sleepy, loss of appetite, dietary changes, alteration in bowel or bladder habits) • Signs and symptoms of illness during last 48 hours of infant's life (i.e., fever, cough, colic, diarrhea, runny nose, vomiting, seizure) • Vaccinations received within 48 hours of death
Family History	• Prior infant or child deaths • History of family genetic disorders • Prior history with law enforcement or social service agencies
Scene Information	• Environmental hazards (i.e., hypo- or hyperthermia, carbon monoxide, smoking, drugs, alcohol, contaminants) • Unsafe sleep location or condition (i.e., adult-sized bed, couch, excessive pillows, soft bedding, soft toys, bed sharing, cosleeping, sharing sleep surface with others) • Asphyxia concerns (i.e., choking, wedging, overlying, suffocation) • Infant's location and position when last seen alive and when found by caregivers
MDI's Postmortem Assessment	• Initial abnormal findings • Resuscitative efforts
Investigational Concerns	• Other suspicious or concerning circumstances • Inconsistencies between scene investigation, report by witnesses or caregivers, and the initial postmortem assessment • Requests for organ donation • Autopsy objections • Name of the funeral home family wishes to use

should be aware of these recommendations to be able to provide accurate information to law enforcement and the next of kin as necessary.

Depending on the jurisdiction, MDIs may want or need to be present during the forensic autopsy. Their presence at the autopsy allows them the opportunity to obtain additional photographs, reassess and compare injuries noted during the investigation, and to be able to communicate directly with and ask questions of the forensic pathologists. Their presence may also be beneficial to the forensic pathologists who may have additional questions for the investigators. In addition, the investigator's presence at autopsy may benefit the family, as the MDI will be better equipped to answer their questions following the autopsy.

The forensic autopsy is a comprehensive examination and evaluation of the decedent's body to identify disease or injury that may have caused or contributed to the individual's death. During the autopsy, it is important that the procedure and the findings be as thoroughly documented as judicial proceedings may follow. Forensic autopsies of infants may include photodocumentation of the decedent and any evidentiary items that are present for the forensic pathologist to review: radiographs (x-rays); body measurements; documentation of external findings on a body diagram; collection of blood, urine, vitreous, and deoxyribonucleic acid (DNA) samples; the inspection and dissection of organ systems; microscopic evaluation of organ tissue; as well as other tests and screenings as dictated by the case.

Photodocumentation of the decedent, including a mug shot, and other close-up photographs of significant external marks or injuries will occur at the beginning of the autopsy. Additional photographs may also be taken of significant internal findings as noted during the course of the autopsy. The personal effects and evidentiary items may also be photographed by the forensic pathologist to document the items that accompanied the remains to their facility. Items that may have caused an injury to the infant or left a pattern injury on the infant should be present during the autopsy for evaluation and comparison. For example, if the pattern injury of a shoe print was noted on an infant's abdomen, the shoe, if recovered, should be present for evaluation and comparison to the pattern injury on the infant to identify if the shoe and the pattern injury match.

X-rays should be taken during all infant autopsies. NAME recommends that at a minimum, a single view radiograph, referred to as a *babygram* be taken.[2] This x-ray may reveal the presence of old or new traumatic injuries as well as skeletal abnormalities that may be due to natural causes. A complete skeletal series of x-rays, however, is highly desirable in cases that involve suspicious circumstances or in which inconsistencies are found during the investigation.

During the forensic autopsy, the infant's body measurements will be obtained including weight, length, and head circumference, all of which may be compared to growth charts. These measurements along with any external findings on the body will be documented on an infant body diagram. Each external finding on the body will be measured, described, and documented on the diagram as well as in the final autopsy report.

Samples of blood, urine, and vitreous fluid should also be collected during all infant autopsies. Toxicology tests may be performed on the blood and urine samples to evaluate them for the presence of medications (i.e., prescribed and over-the-counter) as well as for alcohol and illicit drugs that the infant may have been exposed to. Substances that are identified at the scene, such as contaminants and specific medications or herbal remedies, should be communicated to the forensic pathologist to determine if additional toxicology tests need to be conducted. *Vitreous fluid,* which is the substance located in the orbit of the eye, is often used to evaluate the infant's hydration status. This fluid may also be used for metabolic and additional toxicology testing as indicated. NAME also recommends that during infant death investigations, a DNA sample and a blood spot card should be collected and archived for future genetic testing and metabolic screenings.[2]

The internal examination of the decedent's remains includes the inspection, removal, and dissection of organ systems. The organs are weighed, measured, and evaluated grossly and then microscopically. The Ad Hoc Committee for Sudden Unexplained Infant Death[2] has proposed recommendations regarding which organs should be weighed, removed, dissected, and microscopically examined. Investigators should keep abreast of the proposed recommendations to ensure that their cases are investigated per recommendations and guidelines.

9.5.3 After the Infant Autopsy

Upon the completion of the autopsy, the forensic pathologist should communicate the findings to the investigator. The findings should then be provided to and shared with the appropriate individuals and agencies. The next of kin should be notified when the autopsy is complete and when the infant's body will be released from the custody of the ME's or coroner's office. The completion of the autopsy does not complete the investigation, as investigators should follow up on concerns or questions that may have been raised during the autopsy, continue to obtain and review records, and make preparations for the investigative child death review.

9.5.3.1 Communicate with the Forensic Pathologist

Just as the forensic pathologist needs to know the findings during the medicolegal death investigation, so does the MDI need to know the autopsy findings. Once the autopsy is complete, the forensic pathologist may have been able to determine a COD; however, a COD may not be fully identified until laboratory, toxicology, microscopic evaluations, as well as other additional tests or screenings have been complete. The forensic pathologist should communicate with the MDI findings that were noted during the autopsy, in particular those findings that were consistent or inconsistent with the information obtained from the scene, interviews, records reviews, and doll reenactments. Questions, concerns, and inconsistencies raised by the forensic pathologist during the autopsy should be shared with the investigator so that the investigator can follow up on those concerns either by reinterviewing witnesses, reviewing scene photographs, or other investigative actions.

9.5.3.2 Communicate Findings with Law Enforcement

Communication with law enforcement personnel is crucial and should not be omitted. After obtaining the autopsy information from the forensic pathologist, the investigator should notify the law enforcement contact and provide that individual with the autopsy findings to develop an investigative plan. Depending on the information provided by the forensic pathologist, investigators may decide to immediately reinterview witnesses or may decide to wait until all results from tests and screenings are available. Law enforcement personnel should be kept informed about the autopsy findings and what those findings may represent.

9.5.3.3 Communicate Findings with the Next of Kin

After communicating with the forensic pathologist, someone should contact the family to provide them with the results of the autopsy. In some jurisdictions, the forensic pathologist may communicate directly with the next of kin; in other jurisdictions, it may be the investigator. The way in which the information is provided to them may also vary from jurisdiction to jurisdiction. Some agencies provide the information over the phone, while others prefer to meet the next of kin in person. The method may also be determined by the autopsy results, and if they are or are not consistent with other aspects of the investigation. It findings are inconsistent, it may be beneficial to meet with the next of kin in person. Regardless of the method, the findings of the autopsy should be relayed to the family, and the family should be given an opportunity to ask questions regarding those findings. The next of kin should be reminded that they may obtain a copy of the autopsy report when it is completed. The family should also be notified that the infant's body is ready to be released to their funeral home of choice. There will be cases in which investigators may decide not to immediately reveal all abnormal autopsy findings to the next of kin. This will most often be the situation if it is suspected that someone intentionally harmed the infant.

9.5.3.4 Investigative Child Death Review and Follow-Up

Following the autopsy, the investigator should prepare for the investigative child death review; continue to obtain medical, social service, and criminal history records; and conduct follow-up interviews with caregivers, witnesses and next of kin as may be indicated by the case. Investigators may also be awaiting laboratory, toxicology, or microscopic results that may then indicate that further investigation should ensue.

9.6 SUMMARY

The investigator's role before, during, and after the investigation is vital to ensuring that all pertinent information is provided to and shared with the appropriate individuals. Communication before the autopsy may relieve some of the family's fears and may assist in accommodating their religious and personal requests. Communication with the forensic pathologists before the autopsies provides them with pertinent information that may guide them in evaluating the cases and in making decisions regarding the need for additional tests. Investigators should be aware of the procedures that occur during a forensic autopsy to relay accurate information to the next of kin and law enforcement and then must follow through after the autopsy to ensure that accurate information is provided to all involved parties.

REFERENCES

1. American Academy of Pediatrics Committee on Child Abuse and Neglect, Distinguishing sudden infant death syndrome from child abuse fatalities, *Pediatrics,* 107 (2), 437–441, 2001.

2. Corey, T.S., Hanzlick, R., Howard, J., Nelson, C., and Krous, H., A Functional Approach to Sudden Unexplained Infant Deaths. Prepared by the NAME Ad Hoc Committee on Sudden Unexplained Infant Death. Approved by the NAME Board of Directors on October 14, 2005. http://www.thename.org.

RESOURCES

American Board of Pathology, https://www.abpath.org/Default.aspx.

National Association of Medical Examiners, Forensic Autopsy Performance Standards, report, October 2005.

10 Records Review: Let the Records Speak

10.1 INTRODUCTION

A thorough infant death investigation does not end at the scene or with the autopsy. Both of those pieces are crucial to the investigation, but just as crucial and often missed, is an in-depth review of records related to the infant and the infant's caregivers. A review of the infant's and family's medical and social histories as well as the criminal history of caregivers or witnesses who have had recent contact with the infant may provide information that redirects the investigation, provides insight into motive, corroborates witness statements, or provides new leads for investigators.

It is useful to provide this information to the forensic pathologist prior to the autopsy, however, due to time restraints and logistics it may be difficult to do so. It is crucial, however, to have all of the information available at the investigative child death review, which will be discussed in Chapter 11. The investigator should not close or consider the case complete until all applicable records have been reviewed and considered.

10.2 THE HEALTH INSURANCE PORTABILITY AND ACCOUNTABILITY ACT OF 1996 (HIPAA)

These five letters have affected the ability of some medicolegal death investigators (MDIs) to review medical records when investigating infant deaths. HIPAA established new regulations designed to protect the privacy of certain individually identifiable health information and data often referred to as *protected health information* (PHI). As a result, many health care institutions have established additional policies regarding the release of medical records. These policies, in some jurisdictions, have become roadblocks to investigation and investigators need to have an understanding of the law and how HIPAA affects their investigations.

The HIPAA privacy rule, which creates national standards to protect an individual's medical records and other personal health information, expressly permits health care information disclosure to public health authorities and law enforcement authorities without an individual's authorization in certain situations. In the public health arena, information can be released, without an individual's permission or authorization, to prevent or control disease, injury or disability, for the purpose of public health surveillance, investigation and intervention.[1]

The privacy rule also permits disclosure of PHI to law enforcement officials, coroners, and medical examiners (MEs) without the individual's written authorization. According to the Office of Civil Rights, protected health information may be disclosed "to law enforcement officials for law enforcement purposes" such as "to alert law enforcement of a person's death," may be disclosed "to coroners or MEs to identify a deceased person, determine the cause of death or to perform other functions authorized by law" and protected health information may be disclosed to "facilitate the donation and transplantation of cadaveric organs, eyes, and tissue."[2–4] There are other purposes by which PHI is permitted to be disclosed to law enforcement authorities that may be helpful during an infant death investigation. A comprehensive review of the HIPAA privacy rule can be found at the Office for Civil Rights HIPAA Web site at http://www.hhs.gov/ocr/hipaa/.

In order for the above PHI to be released to law enforcement, MEs, or coroners, a court order or court-ordered warrant, a subpoena or summons by a judicial officer, a grand jury subpoena or a written administrative request must be provided to the agency or facility in which the PHI is located. The agency or facility may then rely upon the public official as to what information is considered the minimum amount of information needed to meet the needs of the investigation. The privacy rule also states that the agency or facility disclosing the PHI must verify the identity and authority of the person to which information is being disclosed, prior to releasing that information.

10.3 INFANT'S MEDICAL RECORD REVIEW

The investigator should seek out any and all medical records that pertain to the deceased infant, even those records that are considered well-baby check-ups in which no medical problems were noted. This medical record review should include a review of the infant's birth record; all emergency room (ER) and hospital admissions; as well as pediatrician, family practice, and health clinic records, if applicable.

The investigator should first review the infant's birth record including the biological mother's prenatal and delivery record. These records can be obtained by contacting the medical records department at the hospital where the infant was born. Depending on the jurisdiction and state statutes, the hospital may require a subpoena or an authorization to release medical records, signed by the birth mother, before releasing that information to the investigator. Regardless of the steps needed to obtain a copy of the birth record, it should not be omitted from the records review. Some of the information included in the medical record may have already been, or will be obtained, during interviews with family members. It is still important to review the medical records and all professional documentation to verify and corroborate the information that was or will be provided by caregivers or witnesses during interviews. Important aspects of the birth record that investigators should review and communicate to the forensic pathologist are listed in Table 10.1.

The infant's medical record review should include any records from ER visits and hospital admissions, if applicable. The infant's caregivers should be able to provide information regarding hospital and ER visits including the name of the facility in which the infant was seen. In some cases, it may be necessary to call the hospitals in the area and determine if the infant was ever seen in those facilities. This may be the case if investigators suspect that caregivers are withholding medical information regarding the infant. If the infant was pronounced dead in an ER, a copy of that emergency record should be reviewed and kept in the infant's death investigation file.

TABLE 10.1
Birth Records Review

Birth Records Review: Items of Interest

- Prenatal care — Document the month of gestation in which the biological mother sought prenatal care (e.g., 8th week of gestation vs. 8th month of gestation).
- Pregnancy complications — Health and environmental concerns (e.g., high blood pressure, diabetes, tobacco, alcohol, as well as prescription and street drug usage).
- Gestation at delivery — Preterm, full-term or postterm.
- Mode of delivery — Vaginal or C-section.
- Assistive devices used during delivery (i.e., forceps or vacuum extraction).
- Complications during delivery (e.g., breech position, cord around the infant's neck).
- Initial physical exams — APGAR score and birth weight.
- Abnormal physical findings at birth (e.g., retinal hemorrhages, fractured clavicle).
- Initial feeding method — Breast fed, bottle fed, or combination.
- Length of infant's hospital stay after delivery and reasons for a delayed discharge if applicable.

Investigators should obtain all infant medical records from physician offices or health clinics that examined the infant. Again, caregivers should be able to provide the names of pediatricians or other physicians who treated the infant and where those offices are located. The birth record may provide the name of the pediatrician who examined the infant in the hospital immediately after delivery. This may be the same pediatrician that followed the infant after being discharged from the hospital. Medical records from health clinics and physician offices provide information regarding the follow-up care the infant received or the lack of medical care the infant received after delivery. Table 10.2 provides a sample list of health care information that should be reviewed during the infant death investigation and communicated to the forensic pathologist.

> *Case Example 10.1* A forensic autopsy revealed that a 1-month-old baby died from pneumonia. The mother stated that she called the pediatrician's office multiple times to report the infant's condition. Documentation in the infant's medical record at the pediatrician's office indicated that the mother called the office one time to report that the infant had "a low grade fever of 100 degrees." According to the record, the mother was instructed to bring the infant to the pediatrician's office the next morning if the fever continued. The infant was never brought to the pediatrician's office and died 3 days later. During the initial interview with investigators, the mother reported that the infant's fever was continuously 101 degrees or higher.

Investigators should keep in mind that caregivers may have taken the infant to many different physicians, clinics, or ERs. During interviews, caregivers should be asked to provide the names of all physicians and facilities to which the infant was taken for treatment. Documentation in medical records may provide information about physician consults or additional examinations by other physicians or clinics. In some cases, it may be helpful to develop a time line for the infant's medical appointments, injuries, and illnesses, especially if the infant has been taken to multiple medical providers.

TABLE 10.2
Medical Records Review: Items of Interest

Medical Records Review: Items of Interest
• Normal physical findings.
• Abnormal physical findings.
• Amount of weight gain or loss at each appointment.
• Infant growth charts — Note the percentile in which the infant was located to determine if the infant's growth was below average, average, or above average.
• Medical problems or health concerns noted by the health care providers or reported by caregivers (e.g., colic, fevers, rashes, difficulty feeding, teething pain, gastrointestinal problems, vomiting, diarrhea, coughing, respiratory complications, and apnea).
• Immunization history — Document the vaccines the infant received, the date they were administered, and any known complications related to the vaccines. The immunization history should be compared to the recommended immunization schedule. It may be necessary to determine the reason the infant did not receive vaccines as per the recommended schedule.
• Documentation of scheduled appointments and phone calls to the health care provider's office. Physician offices maintain appointment records that document whether the patient attended scheduled appointments or if they were a no-show. The patient's record should also reflect any calls made to the office by caregivers who may have had questions or concerns in regard to the infant.
• Documentation of instructions given to caregivers at appointments or via phone. This information may be valuable if the caregiver did not follow instructions or the recommendations of health care providers.

10.4 PHARMACY RECORDS

Investigators should obtain pharmacy records if the infant was prescribed any medications that were not available for purchase over the counter. Health care facilities and physicians document in the patient's medical records if a prescription is called to a pharmacy or if a paper prescription is given to the family. During caregiver interviews or the medical records review, investigators should determine which pharmacy filled the infant's prescriptions and then obtain a copy of the infant's medication records from that pharmacy. The pharmacy records will list all prescriptions that were filled for a particular patient at that location as well as the name of the physician who wrote or called in the prescription. If the family used multiple physicians, the investigator may be able to identify those physicians through the pharmacy records and vice versa as the physician's records may provide information about multiple pharmacies used by the caregivers. Pharmacy records when used in conjunction with medical records may prove to be extremely helpful in establishing time lines.

> *Case Example 10.2* An infant was examined by health care providers for a fever and subsequently diagnosed with an infection. According to the medical records, an antibiotic prescription was written and given to the family with instructions to fill the prescription, start the medication immediately, and continue giving the medication to the infant until it was gone. The infant died 5 days later and the medication bottle was not available for review. The investigator obtained the pharmacy records and learned that the prescription was filled the same day the infant died.

10.5 STATE HEALTH AND HOME HEALTH AGENCIES

In many state and local jurisdictions, newborns that are considered at risk may be referred to a state health agency that provides at home visits with the infant and family following discharge from the hospital. Nursing personnel from these visiting home health or state agencies often can provide valuable information regarding the living conditions at the infant's residence while the infant was alive, the appropriateness of care given by family members, any health and safety concerns that may have been recognized, and what steps were taken to address those concerns. These agencies will have a case file for each client visited and those records should be reviewed. Investigators may also want to consider inviting the visiting nurse or caseworker to participate in the investigative child death review.

Case Example 10.3 A referral was made to a state health agency for home visits with a newborn and the family following the infant's birth and recent discharge from the hospital. During a home visit, the nurse or caseworker noted the family did not have a separate sleeping area for the newborn. The family reported they could not afford a crib, bassinet, or playpen and were therefore placing the baby on the same sleep surface with the parents. The nurse educated the family about the risks of bed sharing and gave the family a bassinet to use. The infant was found unresponsive a few weeks later while sleeping on an adult bed with the parents. During the initial interview, the parents denied they were bed sharing or that they ever had.

10.6 FAMILY MEDICAL RECORDS REVIEW

During the course of an investigation, it may be necessary to review not only the infant's medical records, but also the medical records of caregivers, in particular, the biological parents, primary witnesses, or siblings. An authorization to release medical records will need to be signed by the person whose records investigators want to review. In cases of suspected criminal negligence or foul play, investigators may need to issue a subpoena or court order. Sibling medical records may be most important if there is concern that the siblings may have sustained prior injuries or illnesses that coincide with the infant's injuries or illnesses. A review of the sibling's medical records may indicate a pattern of behavior that may have contributed to the infant's death.

10.7 SOCIAL SERVICE RECORDS REVIEW

Following the death of any child, including infants, investigators should contact the local governmental agency that is charged with the responsibility of protecting children. The agency may be referred to by many names such as child protective services, department of social services, or department of children and family services. Investigators should determine if the social service agency has an open case with this infant or the family or has ever had a case involving either of them.

The MDI should review all relevant file information from this agency and interview caseworkers that are familiar with the family situation. Investigators should identify the reason that the social service agency became involved with the family, the number of visits made to the home, and the final outcome and disposition of the case. Some agencies are able to provide information regarding any and all complaints that may have been founded or unfounded regarding the child or family. The investigator should also request that the caseworker and the file be present at the upcoming investigative child death review.

Reports of abuse or neglect may be important to the investigation as well as other information about services that were or are being provided. Programs that the family is or was enrolled in, such as the Women, Infants, and Children program, the food stamp program, and other services provided to the family, give insight into the family's day-to-day life. This agency may also be able to provide employment and financial information that may be pertinent in some cases.

10.8 BIRTH CERTIFICATES

The infant's birth certificate may provide valuable information to investigators if there are questions related to paternity; as a result, it may be necessary to obtain a copy of the infant's birth certificate from the vital records department. This certificate may provide the name of the infant's biological father, or more importantly, the person presumed to be the biological father. Paternal information may be blank on the birth certificate for a number of reasons. The father may be unknown or unidentified if the mother chose not to disclose the pregnancy or birth to him. The presumed father may have been aware of the pregnancy and birth, however, refused to be listed on the birth certificate without paternity confirmation.

A paternity test may be requested after an infant's death. In most jurisdictions, paternity testing is not provided by the ME's or coroner's office, and the requesting individual must arrange paternity testing with a private laboratory. A blood sample, obtained from the infant at autopsy, will be released to the private laboratory that is under contract to perform the test after a release is signed by the next of kin, or once the ME or coroner, who has jurisdiction over the case, has authorized the blood sample to be released.

Investigators can request the vital records department in their jurisdiction to query all birth certificates for children born to a particular person. It may be important to query all birth records listing the biological mother or father if the investigator suspects that there may be other deceased children that the family or caregivers are not reporting. This will only provide records for births that occurred in the state queried. If the mother or father have been transient, it is possible that they may have given birth to other children in other states, and as a result, the investigator would have to query additional states to search for birth certificates in those states.

10.9 SCHOOL RECORDS

School records for surviving siblings may be beneficial if there are concerns regarding frequent relocations of the family or if it is suspected that a young sibling may have information about the infant's death. Families that move frequently and children who are transferred in and out of schools frequently may not be stable, and there may be a greater risk for violent behavior. Frequent moving prevents children from becoming comfortable with other people to whom they may disclose information such as abuse, domestic violence, or what they may have observed when the infant died.

Teachers or guidance counselors may document in the school records, behaviors exhibited or comments made by these children. School records prior to the death may provide insight into conditions at the time of the infant's death; however, investigators should not overlook the importance of reviewing school records weeks and even months after the infant's death. Surviving children may be vocal at school with teachers or counselors in regard to the circumstances before, during, and after the death. This information may be vital in complicated investigations in which foul play may be suspected.

10.10 CRIMINAL RECORDS REVIEW

The National Crime Information Center (NCIC) is a comprehensive computerized database of criminal justice information that is managed by the Criminal Justice Investigative Services Division of the Federal Bureau of Investigation (FBI). The database, which is operational 24 hours a day, 365 days a year, provides criminal justice agencies with prompt information, upon request, in regard to individual criminal record histories, stolen properties, missing persons, and fugitives.

MDIs should request that a law enforcement official run a NCIC criminal background check on all primary witnesses to include the parents, caregivers, and other persons who may have had direct contact with the infant shortly prior to the infant's death. Prior criminal domestic violence charges or prior drug charges provide information to investigators that may help identify a pattern of behavior that may have contributed to the death. The criminal history of primary witnesses provides insight into the family and relational dynamics that may have existed around the infant. It is equally important to note that a primary witness or caregiver does not have a criminal history.

10.11 PREVIOUS INFANT DEATHS

When investigating infants' and children's deaths, it is important to determine if there are any previous unexplained infant or child deaths in the family. This information, according to the NAME recommendations, should be provided to the forensic pathologist.[5] If it is found that other children have died in the custody of the caregivers that are being investigated or in the deceased infant's immediate family, then the MDI should acquire copies of those children's death investigative reports, copies of the autopsy reports, and copies of the death certificates. If a previous death occurred in another jurisdiction, investigators should speak with the lead investigating officer for the other case. Information should be obtained regarding the specifics of the case to determine if there are similarities between the two. It may be necessary to obtain a copy of the other deceased child's medical records and social service records, if they have not already been obtained, to determine if the cases may be related and have similar circumstances or findings.

10.12 SUMMARY

An infant death investigation is not complete until all applicable medical records, social service records, and criminal histories are obtained. The information provided in these records may either corroborate witness statements or provide documentation that there are inconsistencies between reports made by caregivers and professional persons who interacted with the infant and family prior to the infant's death. Investigators cannot rely on these records alone to determine the cause or manner of the infant's death. However, they are tools that when reviewed and considered in conjunction with the autopsy, death scene investigation, and witness interview, can help ensure that the investigation was complete and thorough, which increases the likelihood that an accurate determination of the cause and manner of death is made.

REFERENCES

1. Centers for Disease Control and Prevention, HIPAA privacy rule and public health. Guidance from CDC and the U.S. Department of Health and Human Services, *Morbid. Mortal. Wkly. Rep.*, 52, Suppl. 1–17, 19–20, 2003.
2. U.S. Department of Health and Human Services, Privacy of Health Information/HIPAA: Disclosures for Law Enforcement Purposes, fact sheet, available at the HIPAA Web site of the Office of Civil Rights http://www.hhs.gov/ocr/hipaa/ (accessed July 8, 2006).
3. U.S. Department of Health and Human Services, Office for Civil Rights Privacy Brief: Summary of the HIPAA Privacy Rule, report, available at http://www.hhs.gov/ocr/privacysummary.pdf (accessed August 15, 2006).
4. U.S. Department of Health and Human Services, HIPAA Administrative Simplification: Regulation Text, 45 CFR Parts 160,162, and 164 (Unofficial Version, as amended through February 16, 2006), report, available at http://www.hhs.gov/ocr/AdminSimpRegText.pdf (accessed August 15, 2006).
5. Corey, T.S., Hanzlick, R., Howard, J., Nelson, C., and Krous, H., A Functional Approach to Sudden Unexplained Infant Deaths. Prepared by the NAME Ad Hoc Committee on Sudden Unexplained Infant Death. Approved by the NAME Board of Directors on October 14, 2005. http://www.thename.org.

11 Child Death Review: It Brings It All Together

11.1 INTRODUCTION

Child death reviews (CDRs) are vital to ensuring a thorough and complete investigation. These reviews may be organized at the local, regional, or state level and may be either investigative or retrospective in nature. The objectives and organizational structure of each are different; however, both are extremely valuable and effective for a variety of different reasons. Investigators should be aware of the benefits that each may provide and should implement them in their local jurisdiction if they are not currently a part of their investigative process.

11.2 HISTORY

CDR and child fatality review teams (CFRTs) have been a hot topic in the area of death investigation for many years. The first documented CDR team was organized in Los Angeles, California in 1978, under the direction of Dr. Michael Durfee and the Los Angeles County Interagency Council on Child Abuse and Neglect. At that time, the public and policymakers were becoming more aware of child abuse and other violence against children that was occurring in the United States. As a result, agencies began exploring ways to share information to analyze suspicious and preventable child deaths. The approach of this team was to implement a multiagency process to "coordinate and integrate data and resources from coroners, law enforcement, courts, child protective services and health care providers"[1] to identify child death trends, evaluate investigation systems, and to develop prevention programs based on the deaths reviewed.

After the implementation of CDRs in California, other states and local jurisdictions followed suit and began organizing CFRTs in their jurisdictions. According to the U.S. Department of Justice, by 1990, 12 states had established CFRTs and within a few years, all 50 states and many foreign countries had active teams.[2] The trend continues as many states report active child fatality teams at the state level as well as a growing number of local, county, and municipal review teams.

11.3 TYPES OF CHILD DEATH REVIEWS (CDRs)

For the purpose of this book, there are two identifiable approaches to CDR that medicolegal death investigators (MDIs) should have knowledge of as well as be aware of the impact the review may or may not have on their investigation. The most common type is a retrospective review conducted by CFRTs, whose members are often appointed or selected to represent a specific agency or aspect of the review. They meet periodically to retrospectively review child deaths that occurred in a designated jurisdiction. These teams may review all child deaths or only those child deaths that meet specific criteria, and they may be organized at the local, regional, or state level. In a survey of CDR teams across the country, Webster et al. found that 45% of CDR teams reviewed deaths from all causes while approximately 12% reviewed only deaths due to child maltreatment.[3]

Reviews conducted by CFRTs are usually retrospective in nature and, as a result, are effective in providing statistical data, making recommendations for system improvements that affect the method by which child deaths are investigated, and in developing recommendations for the implementation of prevention initiatives. They may be less effective, however, in helping investigators investigate specific cases as the time frame in which reviews occur may be months or years after a death occurred. Team members may have the ability and resources to make recommendations to implement policy changes; however, they may not have the ability, authority, or experience to engage in the actual investigation into the death of a child.

An investigative CDR, which is less common, is organized at the local level and is extremely effective to the death investigation process. According to Webster et al.'s survey, which was published in 2003, only seven states reported that the CDR contributed to the death investigation as "the majority of reviews were retrospective occurring months to years after the child's death."[3] The time frame by which an investigative review occurs and the individuals that participate in the review provide an effective and timely investigative tool that has the ability to impact the individual case being investigated and those persons with the legal responsibility to investigate the death. The American Academy of Pediatrics recommended in 2001 that "locally based infant death investigation" should "review collected data with participation of the medical examiner or coroner in the review."[4]

11.3.1 Investigative vs. Retrospective: The Primary Differences

The primary objective of each type of review will determine the persons participating in the review, the time frame in which the review occurs, and the organization and structure of the review as well as the potential outcomes. An *investigative review,* which has a narrower scope, has the greatest ability to impact investigators and their active investigation into the death of a child. A *retrospective child fatality review* has a broader scope and may be less effective in impacting the investigation or case management of a specific death, yet may have a greater impact on child death prevention initiatives, policy changes, and legislative issues. A closer look at each will follow, beginning with the investigative review, which should occur early in the investigation of a child's death, followed by a closer look at retrospective reviews, which often meet months or years after a death has occurred.[3]

11.4 INVESTIGATIVE CHILD DEATH REVIEW (ICDR)

An ICDR is an investigative tool implemented to facilitate communication and information sharing among emergency response, investigative, and social service agencies that are or were involved in the response, investigation, and follow-up of child deaths in their local jurisdiction. The goal of an ICDR is to ensure a thorough and complete investigation to accurately identify the cause, manner, and circumstances surrounding a child's death. This is accomplished through the active participation of professionals who have immediate and personal knowledge of, or have had interaction with, the child, the family, or the scene prior to, during, or after the death of the child. Prosecutorial agencies responsible for further investigation and prosecution of suspects should also be present.

There is significant potential for underreporting of child deaths and mismanagement of child death investigations. Miscommunication among the agencies involved in investigations compounds the problem. An ICDR is a tool by which the case can be reviewed at the local level by the persons and agencies responsible for investigating the specific circumstances surrounding the child's death. An ICDR is a crucial component and investigative tool that agencies should consider incorporating into their infant death investigation protocols as an adjunct to scene investigations, records reviews, and doll reenactments.

11.4.1 Primary Objective

The primary objective of an ICDR is to ensure that all information, relative to a case, is obtained and reviewed to determine the cause of death (COD) and manner of death (MOD). This is important not only for parental grieving, data collection, prevention efforts, and such, but also to bring to justice those individuals who may have contributed to the death. In the survey conducted by Webster et al., only 13 states stated that assistance with the prosecution of a child's death was one of their goals or objectives.[3]

Participants working together ensure that all investigative aspects of the case are reviewed. Additional tasks that should be completed will be identified and then assigned to an agency or individual for completion, ensuring that all aspects of the case are considered prior to making any final decisions about COD or MOD. The organizational structure of this investigative review, including those who should participate, the period in which the review should take place, and the format of the review, which are all important factors, will impact the success and effectiveness of the review. These factors, critical to an ICDR, will be discussed in great detail later in the text. An example of the implementation and development of an ICDR is located in Box 11.1.

11.4.2 Secondary Objectives

There are a number of secondary objectives that may be met during ICDRs; these may benefit the family, the community, and the agencies that participate in the review process. Professional first responders (PFRs) and investigators are in a unique position when responding to a child's death, and their assessments and observations may be critical not only to the death investigation but also to the safety and welfare of survivors and the community at large. A few of the most common and effective objectives are described below.

BOX 11.1
Example of a Local ICDR

Death investigators in Charleston County, South Carolina in 1992, recognized that one of the greatest problems in investigating child deaths was a lack of communication among the agencies involved. Law enforcement, the forensic pathologist, MDIs, emergency services personnel, child protective service representatives, and the solicitor's office, which is the prosecutorial agency, all worked independently. It was apparent that each agency had some information; however, each only had a partial picture of the case being investigated.

The coroner's office recognized this problem, organized an ICDR to facilitate information sharing among agencies, ensuring that agency representatives had a complete picture of the child's death being investigated. The investigative reviews were held within 7 days of the child's death and all involved professionals were asked to attend in person. Initially the investigative review was organized to determine if a local ICDR would affect the immediate investigation of the death or the outcomes; it did both.

The review, organized to ensure that all investigative personnel had the same information, required that the actual individuals who were involved in the response, investigation, or management of the case, be present for the review. Initially agencies and individual agency representatives were reluctant and felt that the review would be a waste of time. Every effort was made to ensure that the case review was timely, organized, and limited to 1 hour. Their succinct and systematic approach kept all participants on track and promoted a productive and organized review. After many reviews, it became apparent to all agencies that the ICDR was one of the most useful and valuable tools available to ensure that each child's death was thoroughly and completely investigated. The information gained during the review has the ability to affect the outcome of the case including the COD and MOD determinations, whether charges are brought against suspects, and the type of services that need to be provided by the child protective agency. It also became apparent that the ICDR was a time saver.

While investigating and reviewing a child's death, it may become evident that the family or caregivers should be referred to local social service agencies for assistance following the death of a child. Referrals for support services are most effective when handled at the local level soon after a death has occurred. The local review may identify immediate needs, facilitate referrals, and follow up to ensure delivery of those services. For example, during the scene investigation, it may be noted that the residence did not have electricity or water service, or that there was a lack of food or other basic necessities in the home. During the ICDR, the appropriate agencies are made aware of observations and concerns and representatives can initiate appropriate referrals. For example, a representative from the child protective services agency that is present should be designated to ensure that appropriate referrals are made to immediately assist and intervene on the family's behalf. During the investigative review, concerns may be raised regarding the family's response to the death, and as a result, referrals may be made to a chaplain, counselor, support group, or local mental health agency to ensure proper follow-up care for those individuals.

ICDRs provide a mechanism to ensure timely notification and intervention for the welfare and protection of other children who may be in an unsafe situation. In most states, professionals such as emergency medical services (EMS) and law enforcement personnel are mandatory reporters if there is a concern regarding the abuse, neglect, or welfare of a child, and the ICDR facilitates reporting. This review will provide child protective services with insight into the living conditions at the residence, safety concerns about individuals who may have access to the children, and other details about the family and children at risk. This review should help social service caseworkers put in motion services that are needed to ensure the care and safety of surviving children in the same family or at the same incident location, such as a day-care center.

Trends in child death may become apparent during an ICDR, giving rise to prevention programs to be developed and implemented by local agencies in their own jurisdictions. Statistics and prevention programs are effective when implemented at the state level; however, prevention programs may be equally or more effective when developed and implemented by community representatives at the local level. This will be discussed in detail in Chapter 13.

Finally investigative reviews provide an avenue for agencies to evaluate their responses to infant death investigations and, as a result, may provide teaching opportunities within their agency. During the review process, agency representatives may identify areas where their agency performs well and areas that may need improvement. This review promotes interagency coordination as participants evaluate their agency's role and determine how they can improve their investigation of infant deaths. The review is a great catalyst for individual and agency education, as each will learn how they can improve in their role and work cooperatively with other agencies; this will ultimately improve the way all deaths are investigated.

11.4.3 Preparation Considerations

An investigative review can be organized and managed by any interested agency that is involved in investigating the death of a child. However, since the primary objective of the ICDR is to ensure that all information relevant to the case is obtained and reviewed for the purpose of determining the COD and MOD, it is logical that the agency with the primary responsibility for determining the COD and MOD would be the agency that organizes this investigative review. In most jurisdictions, that agency will either be a medical examiner's (ME) office or a coroner's office. Most importantly, the agency that assumes the organizational responsibility should take the initiative to ensure that the objectives are met.

The agency responsible for the organization of the ICDR should designate an individual to coordinate and facilitate the review. The coordinator should set up the review to include the date, time, and location. This individual should also notify all participants of the review and ensure that each participant is aware of the items they should bring to the review to ensure its success.

It is recommended that an ICDR be scheduled within 1 week of a child's death and efforts should be taken to limit each review to 1 hour. Very complicated cases may require more time; however, 1 hour is sufficient for most reviews. The review should take place in a conference room that allows all participants to sit around one table; this facilitates communication and sharing among participants who will feel that they are an active part of a multidisciplinary review.

The coordinator should advise all participants of the logistics of the review and should schedule a transcriber or court reporter to formally document the investigative review. Formal documentation and recording of the investigative elements of the case are recommended, and it is desirable to have this done by a court reporter. A formal transcript of the review is most helpful if new information should become available or if the death will be prosecuted and is in trial preparation. It is often months or years before cases make it through the court system and go to trial. Memories fade over time; however, this formal documentation provides a means by which information is preserved and can be reviewed in the future. This review gives all parties an opportunity to document what is known about the case, have an official transcript of the review and then be able to refer back to it months and years later if and when the case moves forward in the court system. This official transcript should be filed in the ME's or coroner's office, and a copy may be provided to the prosecuting agency per its request.

Some agencies may seek funding for the ICDR process and there may be funding sources available. Webster et al. stated that 59% of CDR programs surveyed reported that they have inadequate or no funding.[3] Agencies that are committed to thoroughly investigating child deaths will find ways to implement a review with or without additional funding, as an investigative review is an extension of the investigation and should become a routine investigative tool similar to the scene investigation and doll reenactment.

11.4.3.1 Time Frame

Effective investigative reviews should be conducted soon after an infant's or child's death to promote communication among agencies. This communication may affect how each agency proceeds. It is recommended that children's deaths be reviewed within 7 days of the death. A delay of 1 week gives all agencies and investigators adequate time to request and acquire the necessary reports and records that should be discussed during the review. The time frame also provides investigators the opportunity to have photographs developed, to obtain a copy of the 9-1-1 recordings, and any other items that may be helpful during the review. Although the complete autopsy report will not be available as laboratory tests will often be pending, the forensic pathologist should participate in the review to provide investigators with the initial autopsy findings. The period for the review is early enough to be helpful to investigators as they continue investigating the death prior to the autopsy results becoming available.

Most investigations cannot and will not be completed in 1 week. It may be necessary for some cases to be reviewed again as test results are received or as new information is available. For example, the forensic pathologist may report there were no physical findings at autopsy that explained the death, and that the cause of death is pending until toxicology and laboratory studies are complete. Initially, investigators may suspect that an unidentified natural cause or an accidental death due to overlying may be responsible for the death. If toxicology results reveal that the infant died from an overdose, the investigative review team may need to meet again to review new information and develop a revised plan of action regarding the investigation of this death.

11.4.3.2 Participants

One significant difference between a retrospective review and an investigative review are those persons who should be present and participate. Both use a multidisciplinary team approach with representatives from multiple agencies and disciplines. The investigative review, however, is most effective if the individuals who responded to the death are present as opposed to a representative from their agency who did not respond to the death. This is an inherent difference between the two types of reviews.

It is appropriate for an agency representative to participate in a retrospective review; however, for an investigative review to be most effective, the actual responding individuals should be present. For example, it is common for both investigative and retrospective CDRs to have a representative from EMS participate in the review process. The EMS representative, for both types of reviews, may attend to provide information regarding EMS policies and may provide a copy of and interpret what is documented in the EMS report. The EMS personnel who participate in the investigative review, however, will be the emergency medical technicians (EMTs) and paramedics who were working the night of the child's death and responded to the scene. These individuals will not only be able to provide general information obtained from a report but will be able to provide specific subjective information that may not be documented. Other participants of the investigative review will have the opportunity to ask the responding EMTs and paramedics questions regarding their observations, impressions, and concerns that may not be documented in their report. The EMS representative who is appointed to participate in a retrospective CDR will not be able to provide specific details about the case other than what is documented in the report, as the representative may not have personal knowledge of circumstances surrounding the death.

As a second example, both types of review usually have a representative from a ME's or coroner's office participate in the review. This individual is able to provide general information to the team based on that office's review and interpretation of the autopsy report. Unless this individual, however, is the actual investigator or examiner for the death, he or she will not be familiar with the small nuances of the investigation and will not be able to make changes to the case should new information become available. During an ICDR, the forensic pathologist responsible for the case will be present at the review to both gain information from the other participants and provide information to investigators.

Each professional will be able to provide insight, expertise, and suggestions that may affect the outcome of the case. Law enforcement investigators need information from EMS, death investigators, pathologists, social services agencies, and the prosecuting attorney. In the same regard, the forensic pathologist, death investigators, social service agencies, and prosecuting attorney need information from law enforcement. Each agency depends on other agencies if the investigation is going to be complete and thorough. One agency is no more important than another and each person and the agency that person represents are significant to the investigation of infant deaths. It is only through working together, investigatively, that a complete and thorough investigation can actually occur.

11.4.3.3 Who Should Be Present for an Investigative Review?

The general makeup of persons present for each investigative review will be the same; however, the individuals will be different depending on the jurisdiction in which the incident occurred and the individuals who personally responded to the death. In general, the following individuals should be present for an ICDR:

- All PFRs who arrived on scene. This may include:
  - Fire department personnel.
  - Ambulance personnel, including EMTs and paramedics.
  - Police officers who may have arrived on scene prior to fire or EMS personnel.
- Law enforcement officers including:
  - The first law enforcement officer to arrive on scene.
  - The detective assigned to the case.
  - Any law enforcement officer who responded to the scene and had significant interaction with either the infant, caregivers, or witnesses.
- ME or coroner's office representatives including:
  - The MDI who was the infant investigator.
  - The MDI who was the scene investigator.
  - The forensic pathologist who performed the autopsy.
  - Any other professional person from either of these offices who has significant interaction with the case.
- District attorney, solicitor, or prosecutor:
  - The participation of the prosecutor is vital as they are able to educate investigators regarding criminal law as it pertains to the case under investigation. In many jurisdictions, prosecutors may be assigned to specific types of cases. As a result, the same prosecutor may be present for all of the reviews.
  - The prosecutor's assistant or investigator if needed.
- Child protective service representatives:
  - Only one representative from this agency may be present for the review if the deceased infant or the family has never had prior contact with this agency.
  - Caseworkers and supervisors should attend the investigative review if the agency had an open case involving the child or family.
- Court reporter:
  - The use of a court reporter helps keep the review on target and provides formal documentation of the review that may be used in the future to clarify information or be used as a guide for trial preparation.

- Any other agency or professional who has significant information regarding the case and in which there is no or limited written documentation. These individuals may be requested to be present at reviews if the information is believed to have significance to the case.
  - Primary physicians, obstetricians, and pediatricians with knowledge of the infant and family.
  - Home health care personnel who visited the infant and family in the residence or incident location.
  - Psychiatrist, psychologist, or mental health worker who may have knowledge of the family.
  - Parole officers that may have knowledge of the family or witnesses.
  - Additional hospital personnel who may have knowledge of the case being investigated; this may include nurses, social workers, clerks, and others.
  - School, preschool, or day-care providers
  - Forensic toxicologist
- Review facilitator — This individual's role is to ensure that the review starts on time, proceeds in a goal-directed manner to meet the review objectives, and flows from one witness to the next. The facilitator ensures that the review pertains to the facts of the case and does not stray as the result of emotion or opinion.

11.4.3.4 What Items Should Be Obtained and Present for the Review

The review will be most successful if all records regarding the case are retrieved and available for reference if necessary. This also ensures that all information is collected in one location for ease of organization and retrieval in the future. Items that should be present at all investigative reviews include:

- Copy of 9-1-1 recordings—There may be one or more recordings depending on how the emergency dispatch center is organized in the jurisdiction of the death. There may be only one 9-1-1 recording in some jurisdictions while others may have two: one recorded by an EMS communication system and another from law enforcement. How the calls were received and dispatched will determine if one or more recordings are available.
- Copy of the EMS run sheet or call sheet.
- Copy of fire department response form if applicable.
- Copy of all photographs taken by law enforcement, death investigators, and forensic pathologists.
- Copy of emergency room record where infant was transported and pronounced dead.
- Copy of infant's entire medical record including birth record.
- Copy of the mother's prenatal and obstetric history.
- Copy of all police reports and witness statements.
- Copy of criminal history reports from the National Crime Identification Center (NCIC).
- Copy of autopsy report and toxicology report if available.

BOX 11.2
Sample ICDR Introduction

"This is the ICDR for Joshua Lee Campbell a 3-month-old infant with a date of birth, 2/6/2006, and a date of death, 5/15/2006. This review will consist of three parts. We will begin with the play-by-play of events, which is a chronological review of events beginning with the 9-1-1 recording, followed by PFRs, law enforcement, death investigators, and the forensic pathologist's report. Following the play-by-play there will be a history review in which we will discuss the medical, social, and criminal histories of involved persons. The third part of the review, which will be off the record, is a working and planning session. This is a factual review. Please do not interject your opinions and please be advised that much of the information discussed today is confidential in nature. After each of you provides information regarding your involvement, observations, and actions, any participant may ask questions to ensure understanding of the circumstances. This review is not designed to evaluate individual or agency performance but rather to gather all investigative information regarding the death to accurately determine the cause, manner, and circumstances surrounding the death."

- Copy of any other records that may be important to the case.
- Copy of child protective services case file if applicable.

11.4.4 Three-Part Organization

The organizational structure of an ICDR is critical to the success of the review and the outcomes that follow. An ICDR has three main components; all three parts are extremely valuable and should be completed in the following order. The review cannot and will not be thorough or accurate without all three parts. The three parts of the review are:

1. Play-by-play review
2. History review
3. Off-the-record review (working session for discussion and planning)

Prior to the start of the review, all persons present should be introduced and their roles explained. The goals and format for the review should also be explained. This will provide information to those persons who have not participated in an investigative review before. This will provide introductory information so they will know what to expect and what is expected of them. An example of an ICDR introduction is in Box 11.2.

11.4.4.1 Play-by-Play Review

The *play-by-play review* is a chronological review of events surrounding an infant's death that begins when witnesses or caregivers first contact emergency personnel for help. Usually this first contact will be the 9-1-1 call; however, it may be contact with hospital personnel if the caregivers transported the infant to the emergency room in their private vehicle. The play-by-play review is a factual account of events as reported by professionals who responded to the incident. Information reported will include who responded, what they observed during the incident, and their actions in regard to the infant, witnesses, and the scene. The purpose of the play-by-play segment of the review is to ensure that there is a chronological documentation of the known facts and circumstances surrounding the infant's death. The objective is to clearly understand the events and identify the roles, actions, and observations of those who responded to the death. This part of the review is not for the purpose of evaluating or assessing how each individual or agency performed or to put blame on professionals for their actions but rather to thoroughly document the events.

The play-by play segment will most often begin with the review of the 9-1-1 recording. The 9-1-1 call is usually the reason emergency personnel become involved in the case. It may be necessary to listen to the 9-1-1 recording more than one time if the voices or information on the tape are hard to hear or understand. Participants should listen closely for the caller's identity and specific information and details provided. Emergency dispatch personnel will often try to gather information from the caller and provide first aid or cardiopulmonary resuscitation (CPR) instruction as needed. A partial example of a transcribed 9-1-1 recording from an ICDR is in Box 11.3.

PFRs who arrived at the incident location will report what they saw, heard, and did on arrival as well as what they did while on scene and once they departed the scene. These individuals, fire department personnel, ambulance crew, or law enforcement personnel, should speak in the order in which they became involved in the case. After each person provides information regarding their role and observations, other review participants may ask questions to ensure clear understanding of events and to elicit more information. It is not necessary or time efficient for participants, such as EMS and law enforcement, to read verbatim their entire reports. Participants will have access to copies of those reports if needed. The important investigative information may not be documented in their formal reports but rather in other subtle and subjective observations and descriptions that they may recall during the review. A partial example of a transcribed first responder account is located in Box 11.4.

Following the reports of professional responders, investigative personnel, including law enforcement and the MDIs, will discuss the information obtained from hospital personnel, the initial postmortem assessment findings, the death scene findings, as well as witness reports that were obtained during primary witness interviews. Photographs taken of the postmortem infant assessment and of the scene should be available for participants to review. A partial example of an infant investigator's report is in Box 11.5, and a partial example of a scene investigator's report is located in Box 11.6.

The forensic pathologist will complete the play-by-play section by providing information regarding the autopsy findings and the possible causes for those findings. Photographs of significant physical findings should be available for review. Participants may then have questions regarding the forensic pathologist's findings and pending tests. A partial example of a forensic pathologist's account during an ICDR is provided in Box 11.7.

BOX 11.3
Sample Transcript: 9-1-1 Recording

Operator:	This is 9-1-1. What is your emergency?
Caller:	My baby, my baby, isn't breathing and (*inaudible*). Send someone quickly.
Operator:	Ma'am where are you located?
Caller:	316 46th Street. I … I … don't know what happened. (*Screams*)
Operator:	Where is the baby now?
Caller:	He's right here on the couch, hurry, I … he's blue … I … I (*inaudible*).
Operator:	Ma'am, what is your name?
Caller:	Shelly. Hurry, hurry.
Operator:	Ma'am, how old is the baby?
Caller:	He's 3 months, only 3 months, he's … (*screams*).
Operator:	Is the baby breathing? Ma'am? Ma'am, listen to me. Is the baby breathing?
Caller:	No, he's … (*inaudible*) (*Male voice in the background*)
Operator:	Ma'am, ma'am we need to start CPR, do you know CPR? Ma'am?
Caller:	I don't know what to do, he's … he's … hurry, hurry.
Operator:	Ma'am, the paramedics are on the way; they will be there in a few minutes. Is someone there with you that can go outside and flag them down? Ma'am?
Caller:	Go outside. Go outside. Hurry and look for the ambulance.
Operator:	Ma'am we need to start CPR. Ma'am, are you listening? Ma'am?
Caller:	Yes, yes. Go outside and look for the ambulance. Yes, yes, I'm listening. Tell them to hurry, please hurry.

11.4.4.2 History Review

After completion of the play-by-play segment, the facilitator should direct the participants to turn their attention to the history review section of the ICDR. The history review segment is a comprehensive review of the infant's and family's medical, social, and criminal histories as well as any involvement the infant or family has had with child protective services. The purpose of the history review is for all participants to get to know the infant and family. This segment of the review should begin with a description of the infant's known medical history; followed by the family's significant medical and social histories including physical and mental health histories; smoking, alcohol, and drug usage; work history; and the family structure. A partial example of a history review transcript is provided in Box 11.8.

Law enforcement personnel should be prepared to discuss the criminal histories of all persons of interest that were present on scene when the infant was found

BOX 11.4
Sample Transcript: First Responders

Fireman:	I'm Tom Walker with the Mason City Fire Department. We received notification from dispatch of a baby in full arrest at 314 46th street. Myself and Kevin McAdams arrived on scene at 0754. When we arrived there was a white male on the sidewalk waving us to the location. I entered the scene and saw the mother, I guess it was the mother, on the phone. The baby was lying on the couch next to her. I went over and looked at the baby who wasn't moving. I immediately tried to see if the baby was breathing or if there was a pulse when the paramedic came though the door. The paramedics checked him out and then moved him to the ambulance. I offered to drive the ambulance for them while they worked on the baby in the back.
Investigator:	Did you observe anyone else at the location other than the woman on the phone and the male outside waving you in?
Fireman:	No.
Investigator:	Was anyone performing CPR when you arrived?
Fireman:	No.
Prosecutor:	Do you remember what the baby was wearing when you arrived?
Fireman:	Uhm, I think a zip-up sleeper kind of thing.
Prosecutor:	Would you describe the residence: what type is it and describe what it looked like?
Fireman:	Ya, this is a single-wide mobile home that seemed to be in pretty good shape. The inside was pretty clean other than a bunch of beer bottles that were around the living room. I didn't go into any of the other rooms of the house. Once the paramedics came, I left and went to get into the ambulance to help them drive.
Investigator:	Will you describe how the baby appeared and felt?
Fireman:	I just remember he was cold; I didn't notice any bleeding or anything. He was just pale and cold.
Facilitator:	Mr. Walker, is there anything else you think would be important for investigators to know or are there any additional questions for Mr. Walker? (*pause*) If not, let's move on to Paramedic Lewis.
Paramedic:	I'm Paramedic Lewis with the County Emergency Medical Services. We were dispatched at 0748 to 314 46th Street for an unresponsive infant. We arrived on scene at 0756. When we arrived, the fire department was already on scene. I went in the house and saw Fireman Walker assessing the infant. When he saw me, he stepped aside, and I quickly realized that the baby was not breathing. There was a man and a woman in the room, and I asked them how old the baby was and if he had any medical problems. They stated the baby was 3 months old and was healthy. I carried

continued

BOX 11.4 (continued)
Sample Transcript: First Responders

Paramedic: (continued)	the baby out to the truck and began CPR while my partner Medic Williams got supplies ready to intubate and start lines. Fireman Walker offered to drive the ambulance to the hospital. While en route to Memorial Hospital, we inserted an IV in the left AC, intubated, and continued CPR until we arrived at the emergency room, and they took over.
Investigator:	Will you describe the baby's appearance, including what the baby was wearing when you arrived?
Paramedic:	Sure. The baby was dressed in a pajama-type sleeper that zipped up and had feet in it. We removed the sleeper when we got into the truck so we could assess him further. He was cool to the touch and was really pale. I didn't notice any trauma to the baby other than a small cut on the baby's lip.
Investigator:	Did you notice the cut on the lip before or after you attempted to intubate the baby?
Paramedic:	Before.
Investigator:	Did you notice anyone in the home other than the man and woman who were in the living room?
Paramedic:	No.
Investigator:	What did you do with the clothes that were removed from the baby?
Paramedic:	I gave them to a nurse at Memorial Hospital.
Prosecutor:	Sir, would you describe the residence?
Paramedic:	Sure. It was mobile home, and it appeared to be fairly clean. I did notice that there were a lot of beer cans in the living room, and I thought I smelled marijuana.
Prosecutor:	Did you see any drug paraphernalia?
Paramedic:	No, I just thought I smelled it.
Investigator:	Did either the man or woman at the residence tell you what happened?
Paramedic:	Not really, I don't remember the man saying anything, the lady said that he was 3 months old and that he was healthy. All I remember her saying was that she just found him that way.
Investigator:	Did either of them ride with you to the hospital?
Paramedic:	No, but we left really quick and really didn't give them a chance to. I told them we were going to Memorial and the lady said okay. We had been at the hospital about 15 minutes when she arrived.
Investigator:	You said, "When she arrived." Did the man go to the hospital as well?
Paramedic:	If he did, I didn't see him. I only saw her.

BOX 11.5
Sample Transcript: Infant Investigator

Infant investigator:	This is Mary Nelson with the coroner's office. I was notified by EMS at 0802 that they were en route to Memorial Hospital with a 3-month-old that was in full arrest. I contacted Henry Stevens from our office to assist me with the case. I responded to the hospital to find that the baby had been pronounced dead by Dr. Randalls at 0827. I spoke with the paramedics and the fireman who transported the baby and then I interviewed hospital personnel. It was reported by hospital staff that there were no signs of trauma and that the infant appeared to be healthy and well nourished. The ER physician noted a small cut on the lip but stated it probably occurred when the baby was intubated. The hospital staff stated that the mother was at the hospital, and that she was very upset. No other person was with her at that time. I proceeded to assess the infant. I noticed the cut on the lip but no other physical findings and the baby appeared to be well cared for and well nourished. He was only wearing a diaper when I assessed him. The charge nurse gave me the clothing EMS took off during transport. While at the hospital, I, along with Detective Mitchell of the City Police Department, interviewed the mother, Shelly Campbell. The mother stated that she fed the baby a bottle around 2200 and laid him on his back in a playpen that is in the living room. She covered him with a light blanket and then left to go to work. She stated she was a nurse's aid at the nursing home and worked from 2300 to 0700. She stated that her boyfriend, Marcus Lloyd, stayed with the baby when she worked. She arrived home from work around 0745 and went to check on the baby, who she says was on his stomach in the playpen. She bent down to pat his back and noticed he didn't look right. She stated he was very pale and when she touched him he felt cold. She picked him up and started screaming. She placed him on the couch and called 9-1-1. I asked Ms. Campbell if it would be all right if the officer and death investigator on scene could enter her residence to see if they could determine what may have caused her son's death. She agreed and I notified Henry Stevens that permission had been granted to enter the residence. I asked Ms. Campbell if her baby had any medical conditions or had suffered any injuries that she knew of and she stated that he did not have any medical problems and was not taking any medications. She did not mention the cut on the lip and at this point in the investigation I did not ask her about it.

continued

BOX 11.5 (continued)
Sample Transcript: Infant Investigator

Prosecutor:	Did she say where her boyfriend was when she got home?
Investigator:	She stated that she did not see him when she got home and assumed that he was asleep in her bed. After she started screaming, he came into the living room to see what was wrong.
Prosecutor:	Did she say what the baby was wearing when she left to go to work?
Investigator:	Yes, she described the same clothing: a footed zip-up sleeper that the charge gave me at the hospital.
DCFS representative:	Is the boyfriend the father of the baby?
Investigator:	I asked her that question, and she stated that she wasn't sure; she thought he probably was, but there was a chance that he was not.
DCFS:	Is the boyfriend aware that he may not be the father?
Investigator:	I don't know. I didn't interview the boyfriend, and I did not ask the mother that question.
Prosecutor:	Did anyone check to see if the mother was actually at work?
L.E. officer:	Yes, we did obtain her work record. Ms. Campbell clocked in to work at 2302 and clocked out at 0726.

unresponsive as well as the primary caregivers or others as they relate to the infant's death. The criminal histories of the persons present may provide insight into the dynamics that may have been at work at the time of the infant's death. Drug abuse, domestic violence, or child endangerment charges should always be reviewed to determine if there may be a relationship between prior charges and the infant's death.

A representative from child protective services should provide information to the participants regarding any open or closed cases related to the infant or the infant's family. Important to the death investigation would be a description of the complaints for which a referral was made to the agency. Case information related to either the infant or the family, the current state of the case, and any additional information that may assist investigators while investigating the death of the child should be reviewed.

11.4.4.3 Off-the-Record Review: Working and Planning Session

After the play-by-play and history reviews are completed, the facilitator should ask all participants if there is anything else that they would like to discuss on the record before stopping transcription. The *off-the-record review* is a working session in which participants discuss the factual information provided during the review and develop a plan to continue investigating the circumstances surrounding the death if that is determined to be necessary. This segment is not recorded as the information

BOX 11.6
Sample Transcript: Scene Investigator

Scene investigator: I'm Henry Stevens with the coroner's office. I received a page from Mary Nelson at 0805 stating that there was an infant in full arrest being transported to Memorial Hospital. Mary stated that she would respond to the hospital and asked me to respond to the incident location at 314 46th Street. En route, I contacted the City Police Department to make sure they were aware of the situation and asked that an officer respond or remain on scene. I arrived on scene at 0835 and met with Officer Mallory who was already there.

When I arrived, a young white male was sitting on the steps of the mobile home. He identified himself as Marcus Lloyd, the boyfriend of the baby's mother. I asked Mr. Lloyd if he resided here, and he said that this was his residence. I asked permission to enter the residence to take a look at the baby's sleep area to try to determine what may have happened to the baby. He granted permission.

The mobile home was in good condition and was neat. I did not see any beer cans or bottles in the living room, as you may note in my photographs. There was a playpen in the living room, and there were two thin blankets in the bottom. I didn't see any purge pattern on the blankets or in the playpen. There were a couple of bed pillows on the couch along with a blanket. On the coffee table were two baby bottles, one was empty and one was half-full. Both were taken into evidence by the police department. There were a couple of prescription bottles on an end table, both prescribed to the mother. They were Darvocet and Ambien. There was no crib in the home and the playpen was the only appropriate sleeping area for the baby. There were a number of beer cans and bottles in the trash behind the house.

After walking through the scene, I, along with Officer Mallory, interviewed Mr. Lloyd. Mr. Lloyd stated that his girlfriend left the house at 2245 to go to work and before she left, she fed the baby and placed him in the playpen. He stated that a friend, Richard Martin, stopped by the house around 2330 for a couple of drinks and they talked for a while. The baby woke up around 0300 and was really fussy. He tried to give it a bottle but nothing he did consoled the baby, so Mr. Lloyd put him back in the playpen on his stomach and hoped he would fall asleep. His friend got tired of the baby's crying and left the residence around 0400. Mr. Lloyd stated he went into the bedroom, shut the door, and went to sleep. The baby stopped crying, so he thought that the baby fell asleep also. He awoke that morning when his girlfriend started screaming.

continued

BOX 11.6 (continued)
Sample Transcript: Scene Investigator

Scene investigator: (continued)	I asked Mr. Lloyd if he was aware of any medical problems that the baby may have had. He stated he didn't think there were any problems but wasn't really sure. I asked if he was aware of any recent injuries and he stated "no."
Prosecutor:	Did Mr. Lloyd state how much he had to drink?
Investigator:	He estimated that he had two beers, and that his friend may have had more than that.
Prosecutor:	How many beer cans and bottles would you estimate were in the trash?
Investigator:	They were not counted, but I would estimate a case.
Prosecutor:	Has his friend, Richard Martin, been interviewed?
Investigator:	Yes, we interviewed him the following day. Mr. Martin stated that he did stop by the house around 2330 to have a few drinks since the girlfriend was at work. He stated he brought a case of beer with him and that Mr. Lloyd had bottles of beer in the refrigerator. He stated that they each drank 6 or 7 beers. He was there when the baby woke up around 0330 or so and said that Mr. Lloyd tried to feed the baby but that he was really fussy. Mr. Martin said he got tired of the crying and left about 0400 and went home.

discussed may not be factual and some of the discussion may include opinions, theories, hunches, and intuitions. This working session provides an opportunity for participants to brainstorm possible scenarios, identify any aspects of the investigation that should be reinvestigated, decide whether or not primary witnesses should be reinterviewed, and identify additional witnesses.

11.4.5 Additional Concerns and Issues

The investigative review may trigger emotional responses such as anger, frustration, grief, and disappointment from the participants. The review, occurring so quickly after the infant's death, may in some ways be a debriefing for some of the participants. Although this is not designed to be a debriefing exercise, some of the aspects of the review have debriefing qualities.

The general purpose of a psychological debriefing is to allow individuals who have gone through or witnessed a traumatic event an opportunity to review their response and reactions to that event. In essence, an ICDR may be the only emotional outlet some professionals have following their involvement with a child's death. The deaths of infants and children can be emotionally difficult for all persons, including emergency response personnel, law enforcement, and death investigators who "have seen it all."

Listening to the 9-1-1 recording and reviewing the circumstances surrounding the infant's death may be difficult, and the facilitator should be aware that participants

BOX 11.7
Sample Transcript: Forensic Pathologist

Pathologist: This is Dr. Brent Hiller. I examined the remains of baby Joshua Campbell. The autopsy was started at 1030 the day of the death. This 3-month male appeared to be age appropriate in regard to growth and development and was well nourished. A complete skeletal x-ray was completed with no abnormalities or fractures noted. The external exam was benign other than the superficial cut on the bottom lip. Internally there were no significant findings. At this time, we are pending the cause and manner of death awaiting toxicology and laboratory studies and hope to have those results in a few weeks.

Prosecutor: Did the baby have teeth?

Pathologist: No, this baby is too young to have teeth.

Prosecutor: Are there any thoughts as to what might have caused the cut to the lip?

Pathologist: Well, at this age, it is hard to say. If the baby had teeth it might be from biting the lip. The other thought would be that it occurred when the baby was resuscitated; however, the paramedic stated it was there before they attempted to intubate. It may be that the baby hit his mouth on something.

Prosecutor: Is it possible to tell if the cut was fresh or old?

Pathologist: The cut appeared to be fairly fresh as there was no evidence of healing.

may show outward signs of emotion during the review. Participants may have feelings of anger toward witnesses who they perceive to be unremorseful or noncaring; they may be disappointed in themselves for having not been able to save the child; and they may have feelings of grief after seeing the child and witnessing the reaction of the family and caregivers. Regardless of their emotions, the off-the-record segment is an appropriate setting for participants to express their feeling and concerns regarding the case.

Case Example 11.1 A 9-1-1 call was made reporting an unresponsive infant. The first person on scene was a young police officer. When the officer arrived on scene, the mother handed her the phone. When the officer got on the phone, the dispatcher instructed the officer to begin CPR. The officer hesitated and told the dispatcher that she did know how to perform CPR. The dispatcher tried to give the officer instructions over the phone and it was apparent on the 9-1-1 recording that the officer was shaken by the realization that she was the only emergency response person on scene, and that she did not know how to perform CPR on an infant. The officer was present for the investigative review and became upset when the 9-1-1 recording was played. The traumatic event and the fact that she felt helpless during that event sparked emotions in her during the review. A positive outcome, however, occurred as a result of this review. The police agency, recognizing that many of their officers were not trained in CPR, began offering courses to their officers to include adult, child, and infant CPR.

BOX 11.8
Sample Transcript: History Review

Facilitator: At this time, the play-by play segment has been completed. Let's move on to the history review, beginning with the known medical history.

Infant Investigator: During my interview with the mother and through the records review, I learned that Baby Campbell was born on 2/6/2006 at Mercy Hospital. He was a full-term baby born at 39 weeks. He was born via vaginal delivery with no assistive devices being used. His Apgar scores were 8 and 9. He remained in the hospital for 2 days and was discharged home without any complications. He was breast-fed while in the hospital; however, the mother stopped breast-feeding a few days later and started feeding the baby Enfamil®* with iron.

The mother stated that he was followed by Midtown Pediatrics, and that he has not had any medical problems and has only been seen for regular well-baby appointments. She stated he has not been on any medications and is up-to-date on his immunizations.

The mother stated that she does not have any significant medical history. She reported that this was her first pregnancy, and that she did not have any medical problems during her pregnancy or delivery. She denied being on any medications, but stated that she did have a couple of prescriptions that she received after she delivered. She could not recall the names of the medications but stated that one was for pain and the other for sleep.

The mother denied any known family medical history or any knowledge of other child deaths in her family. She stated she didn't think that the two potential fathers had any medical conditions but did not know about their family histories. The records I reviewed confirmed the mother's report.

L.E. Officer: This is Detective Mitchell. I ran an NCIC criminal history on all three persons: the mother, Shelly Campbell; the boyfriend, Marcus Lloyd; and the friend, Richard Martin. Ms. Campbell came out clean, she did not have any type of record. Mr. Lloyd has a few charges including two DUIs, possession of marijuana, and public intox. Mr. Martin also had a few charges including trespassing and a possession of marijuana charge.

DCFS Representative: This is Ms. Maynard with the Department of Child and Family Services. We do not have an open case with this infant or the mother and have not received any complaints about this family. The mother did apply for the WIC program to get formula, but that is all we know about them.

BOX 11.8 (continued)
Sample Transcript: History Review

Facilitator:	Are there any questions regarding the medical, criminal, or social service histories of this family or the persons involved before we go off the record?

* Registered trademark of Mead Johnson Nutritionals, Evansville, IN.

11.5 RETROSPECTIVE CDRs

11.5.1 Primary Objective

Retrospective reviews are those that take place after the investigation of an infant's or child's death is complete. The majority of CDRs fall into this category, as most reviews occur months to years following a child's death.[3] CDR teams may be organized at the local, regional, or state level and may have a variety of goals and objectives depending on the jurisdiction, the population, and the mission of the team. The majority of CDR teams state that preventing premature child deaths as is the primary purpose for the review.[3] The National Maternal and Child Health (MCH) Center for Child Death Review states that the purpose of CDRs is "to conduct a comprehensive, multidisciplinary review of child deaths, to better understand how and why children die, and use the findings to take action that can prevent other deaths and improve the health and safety of children."[5]

These goals are met through retrospective reviews of child deaths that occur in specific jurisdictions. During the review process, teams are able to generate and review statistics for child deaths that occurred in their areas. Teams may then be able to identify risk factors for child deaths and recognize child death trends. The teams can then use that information to develop and implement public awareness campaigns and prevention programs. Strategies to address these needs may include community education programs to promote child health and safety or policy and legislative changes. Teams often are charged with advising the governor and legislative representatives of statutory changes that should be made to state policy and practices that may prevent child deaths.

11.5.2 Secondary Objectives

As with investigative reviews, there are a number of secondary objectives that may be identified. These objectives will vary from team to team based on the jurisdiction, the population, and the mission of the team. Secondary objectives may fall into a number of categories including investigational and case management objectives, systems and quality improvement objectives, advocacy and legislative objectives, as well as public awareness and additional prevention initiates, as discussed earlier.

One secondary objective for some retrospective reviews is to evaluate the investigational and case management processes that local jurisdictions use to investigate child deaths. The team may assess the completeness and thoroughness of investigations and, as a result, may provide investigational recommendations to those local jurisdictions. Teams may evaluate whether or not deaths are investigated similarly in various regions in their jurisdiction and subsequently identify the types of training needed and to whom it should be directed. Teams may be able to identify investigative system problems with regard to child death investigations and make recommendations as to how to change those systems.

Teams may also establish objectives to evaluate and identify inconsistent reporting or classification of child deaths. Teams often recognize that for the primary objective of the review to be met, deaths not only have to be thoroughly investigated, but the classification of those deaths must also be consistent, based on state and national guidelines. Inconsistent reporting and classification results in inaccurate statistics that will ultimately result in ineffective prevention programs. In order for teams to focus their attention in the right areas, they must rely on statistics that are accurate and uniformly reported across the region.

Systems and quality improvement may be a secondary objective for some teams. Teams may try to improve the ways in which all agencies respond to child deaths. During reviews, teams may recognize opportunities for training and identify areas in which systems changes should be made. *Systems changes* may improve the response and quality of care agencies provide to victims, witnesses, and survivors. For example, during a review process, the South Carolina State Child Fatality Review Team learned that some EMS providers were using inappropriately sized intubation tubes with pediatric patients. The tubes were noted to be too small; therefore, the pediatric patients were not receiving adequate ventilation. As a result of their findings, the CFRT made EMS training recommendations to address the systems and quality issues that were identified during reviews.[6]

Advocacy is another important objective for many CDR teams. During reviews, the team or individual members of the team may advocate on behalf of the deceased child or the surviving family members. Advocacy for the deceased child may include recommending further investigation or criminal prosecution of suspects. Team members may also advocate for surviving children in the home if safety or welfare concerns are raised. This may be addressed by ensuring that child protective agencies assess the living condition of surviving children. The team may also advocate for the surviving family members by evaluating whether or not appropriate services were provided to them. If survivors were not provided needed services, the team may try to identify what systems changes should be made to improve service access to these persons. CDR teams may have the ability to recommend that needed services be provided to families.

Following the review process, another secondary objective may be identified that leads to teams working closely with the media or other agencies to increase public awareness regarding child health and safety issues. Public awareness campaigns frequently grow out of the identification of child death trends, and as a result, possible preventative measures to decrease the risk of injury or death to other children are set forth. Public awareness campaigns provide the community with information and education regarding a recognized health issue. The public is then empowered to make necessary changes in their lives that may impact their children.

In many states, legislation mandates the implementation and management of CDR teams. As a result of that legislation, some teams have the ability to recommend to public officials the need for public policy or legislative changes that should be made. These changes may include suggestions that may reduce future child deaths, such as car seat legislation; other changes may impact child death investigation by requiring a minimum number of training hours for law enforcement and death investigators.

11.5.3 Child Fatality or Death Review Team Members: Who Are They?

The makeup of child fatality or death review teams is similar to that of investigative reviews. Teams are made up of representatives from the following agencies who are appointed or selected by an oversight committee, organization, or agency to manage the review process. Teams are often made up of core members with occasional ad hoc or guest members as may be needed to accurately review some deaths. The core team usually includes a representative from each of the following disciplines:

- EMS
- Law enforcement
- ME's or coroner's office
- Child protective services
- Prosecutor
- Public health
- Family practice physician or pediatrician

The members of child fatality or death review teams are charged with the responsibility to actively participate in the review of child deaths as dictated by either legislative mandates or the team mission. Each individual on the team represents a specialized disciple and should then work within their discipline to educate and promote child health and safety initiatives to their peers. CDRs are only effective if the team members take an active role to ensure that the objectives are met. Teams that review deaths, gather information, and then do nothing with that information are ineffective and do nothing to improve the investigation or prevention of children's death. Teams that are active and make it a priority to work together to meet the review's objectives have the ability to change the way child deaths are investigated and may possibly save the lives of many children.

11.5.4 Where to Begin?

MDIs are in a unique position to be able to initiate an investigative or retrospective CDR team or to become actively involved in an existing team. Investigators should become familiar with the objectives of CDR teams in their jurisdictions and actively seek to establish investigative and retrospective reviews if they are not already in place. There are a number of resources available to teach professionals how to set up and manage a CDR team. Training resources are also available to help individuals and teams best meet their primary objectives. Two excellent resources available to professionals are The National Center on Child Fatality Review and the National MCH Center for Child Death Review.

The National Center on Child Fatality Review (NCFR) whose mission is "to develop and promote a nationwide system of Child Fatality Review Teams to improve the health, safety and well being of children and reduce preventable child fatalities and severe injuries ... through the establishment, support and expansion of a national network of multiagency, multidisciplinary, local, regional and state Child Fatality Review Teams" has a number of educational and training resources available to professionals. Training materials include published manuals regarding the development and management of CDR teams as well as videos and online Web-based educational programs. The NCFR also maintains two Listservs, the NCFR-L and the Child-Fatal-L, in which professions associated with CFRTs can learn more about CDR and connect with other teams and team members across the country.[7]

The National MCH Center for Child Death Review is "a resource center for state and local CDR programs which promotes, supports and enhances CDR methodology and activities at the state, community and national levels." This organization has available both print- and Web-based training materials and is able to provide technical assistance, strategic planning, and consultation services to CDR programs.[8]

11.6 SUMMARY

CDRs play an important role in the investigation and prevention of infants' and children's deaths. Investigative reviews are conducted early during the investigation of a child's death and participants are those individuals who responded to or are responsible for the investigation of the death or the administration of services following the death. The investigative review has the ability to have the greatest impact on the MDI and the investigation that is under their direction. Retrospective reviews are those that occur after the investigation is complete. They provide information regarding child death statistics and death investigation systems and are effective in the development and promotion of child injury and death prevention initiatives. All individuals involved in the investigation of infants' or children's deaths should be familiar with both types of reviews and should actively participate in the review process. In this way, they may improve the manner by which infants' and children's deaths are investigated and impact the community, as lives are saved through prevention programs and initiatives.

REFERENCES

1. Durfee, M., Gellert, G., and Tilton-Durfee, D., Origins and clinical relevance of child death review teams, *Child. Today,* 21 (2), 29–33, 1992.
2. U.S. Department of Justice, The National Center of Child Fatality Review, *OJJDP Fact Sheet,* 12, April 2001.
3. Webster, R.A., Schnitzer, P.G., Jenny, C., and Ewigman, B.G., Child death review: The state of the nation, *Am. J. Prev. Med.,* 25 (1), 58–64, 2003.
4. American Academy of Pediatrics Committee on Child Abuse and Neglect, Distinguishing sudden infant death syndrome from child abuse fatalities, *Pediatrics,* 107 (2), 437–441, 2001.

5. National MCH Center for Child Death Review, Child Death Review Process, available at http://www.childdeathreview.org (accessed August 3, 2006).
6. South Carolina Department of Health and Environmental Control, EMS Memo, October 2005.
7. National Center for Child Fatality Review, Listservs available at www.ican-ncfr.org (accessed August 3, 2006).
8. National MCH Center of Child Death Review, Web site http://www.childdeath-review.org (accessed August 3, 2006).

RESOURCES

Durfee, M., Grief and mourning for the child death review team, available at www.ican-ncfr.org (accessed August 3, 2006).

Durfee, M., Gellert, G., and Tilton-Durfee, D., Origins and clinical relevance of child death review teams, *J. Am. Med. Assoc.*, 267, 3172–3175, 1992.

Durfee, M. and Tilton-Durfee, D., Multiagency child death review teams: Experience in the United States, *Child Abuse Rev.*, 4, 377–381, 1995.

Durfee, M., Tilton-Durfee, D., and West, M., Child fatality review: An international movement, *Child Abuse Negl.*, 6, 619–636, 2002.

National Center for Child Death Review, www.childdeathreview.org.

The National Center on Child Fatality Review, www.ican-ncfr.org.

12 Family or Caregiver Follow-Up and Referral

12.1 INTRODUCTION

The completion of an infant death investigation does not mean that the case is closed. Much can be accomplished after the completion of any death investigation that may impact the surviving family members and the public at large. Through family follow-up and referral, and prevention and proactive public education campaigns, medicolegal death investigators (MDIs) may possibly help decrease the number of unexpected infant deaths that occur each year.

MDIs can have a positive effect on their community by taking the knowledge that they gain from death investigations to not only provide comfort, support, and referral to families, but also to educate the public regarding risk factors, health and safety issues, and potential causes of injury, thus decreasing the morbidity and mortality rates in their communities. By initiating prevention and education programs directed toward the surviving family and the community, MDIs become professionals who not only react to incidents, but are also proactive in preventing others. This chapter will address family follow-up and referral needs that impact the family directly. The following chapter will address ways investigators can impact their community.

12.2 FAMILY FOLLOW-UP

Just as it is important for the MDI to understand what occurs during the forensic autopsy of an infant, it is important for the MDI to understand what the findings were and what the autopsy report states. The MDI is often the individual that has developed a rapport with the family and as a result may be the person best suited to review the results with them. The American Academy of Pediatrics recommends that family members obtain reliable information after the completion of the autopsy.[1] It may be necessary to explain and answer questions regarding its content, if the forensic pathologist is not available.

The MDI should offer to meet with the next of kin to go over the autopsy report with them and explain the forensic pathologist's findings and answer questions. It is important that the MDIs be truthful about the cause of death (COD) and manner of death (MOD) when explaining autopsy findings and answering questions for the surviving next of kin. Some immediate next of kin may request a copy of the autopsy report, and it should be provided to them, in keeping with each agency's policy. If the next of kin does not want a copy of the autopsy report immediately following the death, assure them that if they change their mind in the future, they can request a copy when they are ready. The grief process will be different for each family and some may not be emotionally ready to receive a copy of the autopsy report immediately.

Regardless of the final determination regarding the COD and MOD, MDIs should follow up with surviving family members to provide information and answer questions. Follow-up meetings are beneficial to the family or caregivers and to those persons who are and will provide emotional support for the family. MDIs should be truthful with the family, even if the death was not from natural causes. When the MDI is open and honest regarding the COD and MOD, the family is then better able to move through the grief process with correct information as opposed to rumors or suspicions.

It is extremely important for the MDI to follow up with families in cases in which the COD is not natural, where the manner is accidental in nature or in which the COD or MOD is undetermined. These may be the most difficult cases to follow up with, however, as they have the potential to have the most impact on the family. After a thorough and complete investigation, investigators may still have suspicions about the COD or MOD, even if there were no physical findings and the COD or MOD is left as *undetermined*. In infant deaths, this may be especially true if the scene or environment in which the infant was located placed the infant at risk for injury or death. During a follow-up meeting, it may be appropriate to discuss the concerns the investigator may have had during the investigation.

This dialogue, between the MDI and family members, provides an opportunity for the family to learn environmental conditions or other circumstances that may have placed the infant at a greater risk for injury and death. The information provided by the MDI enables the caregivers to make educated decisions and changes in their environment and lifestyle decisions that may decrease the risk of injury or death to other infants or young children in the care of the caregiver or family. This open dialogue is especially important in those cases in which there are concerns with regard to the possibility of suffocation due to bed sharing or cosleeping. Some investigators are reluctant to tell family members that they have suspicions that their child may have died accidentally while bed sharing or cosleeping. Some investigators feel they are causing additional pain to the family by suggesting that their actions may have contributed to the death. While that is a valid concern, there are two reasons why MDIs should be honest with the caregivers and family regarding their concerns.

First, family members who were cosleeping with an infant that died may have concerns, whether they verbalize them or not, that their actions may have contributed to the infant's death. Bringing the topic to the forefront for discussion may allow those family members to begin healing. Burying their concerns or denying that those actions may have unintentionally contributed to the death forces them to live with guilt, doubt, and questions that may complicate their grief and slow down their healing process. These caregivers may try to hide their concerns and suspicions from those persons that could be emotional support for them.

Second, by discussing the risk factors and educating the family, the MDI provides the family with information and knowledge that may affect the lives of other infants and children in the family. If the family does not understand what the risk factors are or what behaviors can place an infant at increased risk for injury or death, they are not likely to change their behavior. However, if the MDI discusses the risk factors associated with cosleeping, then the family has information that empowers them to make decisions that may affect the lives of other infants that may be in their care.

12.3 FAMILY REFERRALS

A follow-up meeting with family members after the investigation is complete provides an opportunity for the MDI to assess how the family is coping following the death and whether or not it might be helpful to refer them to other agencies and community resources for assistance. Although some MDIs believe their job is finished when the death investigation is complete, it is not. If the MDI has developed a rapport with family members, they may feel comfortable speaking with the MDI about family circumstances and dynamics since the death. Family members may then be open to suggestions by the MDI regarding community assistance and referrals. The MDI is in a unique position to identify needed resources having been at the incident location and their residence, if different.

There are a number of referrals that may be helpful. Referrals for support groups, grief groups, mental health, spiritual or genetic counseling, and social service agencies for food stamps or other financial assistance are a few of the possibilities. Each community will have different agencies that may assist families and it may be helpful for MDIs to develop a list of community resources that are available to families following the death of an infant or young child.

12.3.1 Support Groups

> Children are not suppose to die.... Parents expect to see their children grow and mature. Ultimately, parents expect to die and leave their children behind.... This is the natural course of life events, the life cycle continuing as it should. The loss of a child is the loss of innocence, the death of the most vulnerable and dependent. The death of a child signifies the loss of the future, of hopes and dreams, of new strength, and of perfection.[2]

There are a number of infant death support groups available to assist families after a child's death; however, it may be many months before some families are ready to join a support group to help them deal with the death of an infant or child. Infant death or infant loss support groups may be local, state, national, or international organizations that may be managed by either counseling professionals or by parents or family members who have also experienced the loss of a child. These support groups provide emotional and peer support to family members after an infant or child death. Many of the infant death support groups provide places where surviving family members can receive encouragement, emotional support, and empathy from individuals who have also lost a child and understand what they are going through. Parents and other surviving family members need to be made aware of the great benefits other parents have gained from attending infant death support groups. Support groups are often available through area hospitals, churches, funeral homes, and hospice agencies.

National and international organizations that provide support following a child's death may have local chapters of the organization in a number of areas of the country. Some of the local chapters provide face-to-face support group meetings while other organizations offer Web-based support via e-mail or online bulletin boards. A few organizations that offer local, state, or national support are listed below.

Compassionate Friends is a national nonprofit self-help support organization whose mission is to "assist families toward the positive resolution of grief following the death of a child of any age and to provide information to help others be supportive."[3] Compassionate Friends has local chapters available in all 50 states and Puerto Rico with regularly scheduled support group meetings where those who have lost a child can receive support from others who have also lost a child. The goal of local chapters is to provide a caring environment "in which bereaved parents, grandparents and siblings can work through their grief with the help of others who have 'been there.'"[3]

BPUSA or *Bereaved Parents of the USA* is "a national nonprofit self-help group that offers support, understanding, compassion and hope to bereaved parents, grandparents and siblings who are struggling to rebuild their lives after the death of their children, grandchildren or siblings."[4] With a strong desire to help other families survive after the death of their child, volunteer bereaved parents offer support in local chapter support groups to others just as they were helped and supported following the death of their own child. There are currently 22 states that have local chapters of BPUSA, who meet regularly to provide support to bereaved parents and families.

The *M.I.S.S. Foundation* (*Mothers in Sympathy and Support*) is an international organization that "provides immediate and ongoing support to grieving families."[5] This volunteer-based organization is committed to providing crisis support and long-term aid to families after the death of a child. Local M.I.S.S. Foundation support groups are currently available in 25 states as well as England, Ireland, and Mexico. The foundation also offers online discussion forums that are available to provide support and sharing for grieving families.

Share: Pregnant and Infant Loss Support, Inc. is another national organization that provides information and support free of charge for bereaved parents. Their mission "is to serve those whose lives are touched by the tragic death of a baby through early pregnancy loss, stillbirth, or in the first few months of life."[6] This organization has been dedicated to supporting bereaved parents and families since 1977. There are local Share support groups all across the United States and as well as in Canada and England.

12.3.2 Grief Counseling

In 1976, Neugeboren wrote,

> A wife who loses a husband is called a widow. A husband who loses a wife is called a widower. A child who loses his parents is called an orphan. But … there is no word for a parent who loses a child, that's how awful the loss is![7]

After the death of a child, parents and other surviving family members may need professional grief counseling. Grief counseling may be offered at the local level by many organizations and professionals. MDIs may refer family members to grief counseling services in their community. Grief counseling may be available through the private or public sector from psychologists, clergy, counselors, or other persons with skills in grief counseling. Many spiritual leaders including chaplains, pastors, rabbis, or other clergy will often provide grief counseling to members and non-members of their congregations. Many hospice agencies provide grief services to persons who have lost a loved one to terminal medical conditions as well as to those who lost a loved one unexpectedly. Over the past few years, some funeral homes have begun employing social workers or counselors who are able to offer grief-counseling services to their clients and to other members of the community. There are national organizations that focus on grief counseling and one organization that specializes in grief after the death of a child is listed below.

First Candle/SIDS Alliance is a national not-for-profit organization whose goal is "to ensure that compassionate and comprehensive grief services are brought to the family's doorstep"[8] after the death of an infant or child. This organization provides a state-by-state list of grief and support group resources available to those who have been affected by an infant death and provides 24-hour bilingual crisis counseling via phone. This organization also provides resources to professionals including guidelines that were created by the Bereavement Support Work Team of the National SIDS and Infant Death Program Support Center (NSIDPSC). These guidelines are available on its Web site and provide information regarding the grief support needs of families after the loss of an infant and how clergy, funeral home directors, and medical professionals can offer the best support to them.

12.3.3 Mental Health Counseling

After an intense investigation and having had many opportunities to interact with family members and caregivers of the deceased, the MDI is in a unique position to have witnessed and possibly recognized signs of mental illness in surviving family members. If a MDI observes behaviors or actions that are believed to be signs of mental illness, the investigator should take the time to make a proper referral to those agencies that are equipped to assess and assist those persons. In an individual who has a history of mental illness, the death of an infant or child may trigger an exacerbation of their mental illness. For some, the death may impact their ability to care for themselves appropriately: they may intentionally or unintentionally stop taking their medications or the stress associated with the circumstances surrounding the death may precipitate new symptoms. In extreme circumstances, a family member or caregiver may exhibit signs that they may harm themselves or another person. In cases where there is concern that family members or caregivers are experiencing suicidal or homicidal ideations, investigators should and must refer them to the proper mental health agency for assistance.

Agencies that provide mental health services will vary depending on the jurisdiction; however, a state agency, such as the department of mental health, will be able to provide assistance and direction. In some jurisdictions, there are mental health counselors and emergency crisis counselors who may be able to respond immediately to the scene or other location if a referral is made for immediate mental health assistance.

For example, the South Carolina Department of Mental Health in Charleston and Dorchester counties formed the Assessment and Mobile Crisis Unit, which is a team of psychologists and counselors who function under the direction of a psychiatrist. When a referral is made to this team by law enforcement or other emergency health care providers, mental health professionals will immediately respond to locations within their jurisdiction to assist with psychiatric and mental health emergencies.

12.3.4 Spiritual or Emotional Counseling

> Parental grief is overwhelming; there is nothing that can prepare a parent for its enormity or devastation; parental grief never ends but only changes in intensity and manner of expression; parental grief affects the head, the heart, and the spirit.[9]

The spiritual and emotional needs of those persons who have suffered the loss of an infant or young child is another area that should not be overlooked by MDIs as they work closely with families, caregivers, witnesses, and even other professionals.

When called to investigate an infant's or child's death, it may be appropriate when speaking to family or witnesses, to ask them if they would like someone to notify their minister, rabbi, or other spiritual leader of the death and request that they respond to the person's location for support. It may be that the family has a spiritual leader that they would like notified of the death or who has already been notified. In other cases, the family may not want any spiritual leader notified or called. There may be cases in which the family would like a spiritual leader called, yet they do not have a relationship with one to call. Some agencies, including hospitals and law enforcement agencies, have developed relationships with local clergy who volunteer their time to assist during emergency and crisis situations; they can either provide the spiritual care that the person needs or refer them to another spiritual leader that may be more appropriate for the family, depending on their needs, their religious affiliation, and their location. For example, the mission of the Coastal Crisis Chaplaincy program in Charleston, South Carolina is to "provide pastoral care and counseling for employees and families of law enforcement and emergency service agencies, as well as the general public. This ministry offers comfort and counsel to the survivors of crime whose lives have changed suddenly and forever due to a violent act or unexpected tragedy. The Chaplaincy Ministry is for all emergency personnel and their families in their time of need. In addition, the chaplains are available to minister to the citizens in their time of unexpected need."[10]

12.3.5 Genetic Counseling

After the forensic autopsy and all ancillary tests are complete, the forensic pathologist or other medical personnel may either confirm or suspect that there may be a genetic disorder that may have caused the death of the infant. In those cases, it would be appropriate for the family to be referred for genetic counseling. In cases where there is either confirmation or concern that a genetic disorder is completely or partially responsible for the death, the family should be given a copy of the autopsy results and referred to their primary health care provider. The MDI or pathologist may want to contact the family's primary health care provider to discuss the results of the autopsy and concerns regarding a genetic cause. At that time, either the primary health care provider or the MDI, if the family does not have a primary care provider, may want to suggest that the family seek and complete genetic counseling to determine the possibility of their having the genetic condition or other family members having the same genetic condition.

Genetic counselors can help family members assess their risk for certain hereditary diseases, offer guidance, provide information regarding support groups, and assist the family in making decisions with regard to the counselor's findings. Genetic counseling is often sought by families who have a known history of genetic disorders, infertility, miscarriages, still births, or infant deaths.

12.3.6 Social Service Referrals

Social service referrals for those persons who have lost an infant or young child may assist the family in receiving goods and services for which they were qualified prior to the death or for services needed after the death. During the investigation, MDIs may determine that the family needs resources that may be provided by local and state social service agencies. The local departments of social services or children and family services are able to provide public assistance to families, including access to health care, services to the elderly, food stamps, child support enforcement assistance, and other specialized services as indicated.

Another program to which MDIs may refer families is the Women, Infants, and Children (WIC) program. This "Special Supplemental Nutrition Program for Women, Infants, and Children—better known as the WIC Program—serves to safeguard the health of low-income women, infants, and children up to age 5 who are at nutritional risk by providing nutritious foods to supplement diets, information on healthy eating, and referrals to health care."[11] Families who have other children under the age of 5 that are not able to provide nutritious foods should be referred to the agency that administers the WIC program in the jurisdiction in which the family resides. This federal program is administered by the U.S. Department of Agriculture at the national and regional levels. In most states, the agency that administers the program at the state and local levels is the Department of Health.

During the death investigation, concerns regarding the living conditions of family members or caregivers of the deceased infant or other surviving family members may come to light. If the living conditions of the survivors are deplorable and they reside in Section 8 or subsidized housing, the MDI or other investigator should initiate a referral to the housing authority that manages the property in question. Some families do not have electricity or water as a result of the structural conditions of the residence. Those cases should be reported to the agency that oversees subsidized housing, which is the U.S. Department of Housing and Urban Development (HUD). Their mission is to provide decent, safe, sanitary, and affordable housing to low- and moderate-income families.[12] HUD also oversees the maintenance of public housing projects and inspects and oversees Section 8 housing.

12.4 SUMMARY

MDIs are in a unique position to provide follow-up care and referrals to families and caregivers of infants who die suddenly and unexpectedly. The care and compassion that can be shown to these survivors has the ability to positively affect the rest of their lives. As stated in a publication by the National SIDS Resource Center, "Children are valuable and precious symbols of what lies ahead. Children are considered the hope of the future. When a child dies, that hope is lost."[9] Professional death investigators are not able to bring back these children; however, the way in which these investigators interact with the survivors, with empathy and desire to assist them begin the healing process, may dramatically impact their lives and provide some hope that with time they will heal.

REFERENCES

1. American Academy of Pediatrics Committee on Child Abuse and Neglect, Distinguishing sudden infant death syndrome from child abuse fatalities, *Pediatrics,* 107 (2), 347–441, 2001.
2. Arnold, J.H. and Gemma, P.B., *A Child Dies: A Portrait of Family Grief,* 2nd ed., The Charles Press Publishers, Philadelphia, 1994, p. 39.
3. Compassionate Friends, http://www.compassionatefriends.org (accessed July 4, 2006).
4. Bereaved Parents of the USA, http://www.bereavedparentsusa.org (accessed July 4, 2006).
5. M.I.S.S. Foundation, http://www.misschildren.org (accessed July 4, 2006).
6. Share: Pregnancy and Infant Loss Support, Inc., www.nationalshareoffice.com (accessed July 4, 2006).
7. Neugeboren, J., *An Orphan's Tale.*, Holt, Rinehart & Winston, New York, 1976, p. 154.
8. First Candle/SIDS Alliance, http://www.firstcandle.org (accessed July 4, 2006).
9. National SIDS Resource Center, *The Death of a Child—The Grief of the Parents: A Lifetime Journey,* Circle Solutions Inc., Vienna, VA, 1997, pp. 33, 45, available at http://www.ican-ncfr.org (accessed July 4, 2006).
10. Coastal Crisis Chaplaincy, http://www.coastalcrisischaplain.org (accessed July 4, 2006).
11. Women, Infants, and Children Program, http://www.fns.usda.gov/wic/ (accessed July 4, 2006).
12. U.S Department of Housing and Urban Development, http://www.hud.gov/ (accessed July 4, 2006).

RESOURCES

Assessment/Mobile Crisis (A/MC), 2100 Charlie Hall Boulevard, Charleston, SC 29414.
BPUSA—Bereaved Parents of the U.S.A., P.O. Box 95, Park Forest, IL 60466.
Coastal Crisis Chaplaincy, P.O. Box 21833, Charleston, SC 29413.
Compassionate Friends, Inc., P.O. Box 3696, Oak Brook, IL 60522-3696.
First Candle/SIDS Alliance, 1314 Bedford Ave., Suite 210, Baltimore, MD 21208.
M.I.S.S. Foundation (Mothers in Sympathy and Support), P.O. Box 5333, Peoria, AZ 85385-5333, http://www.misschildren.org/.

National SIDS & Infant Death Program Support Center (NSIDPSC), 8280 Greensboro Drive, Suite 300, McLean, VA 22102, www.sidscenter.org.

National Society of Genetic Counselors, http://www.nsgc.org.

Share: Pregnancy and Infant Loss Support, Inc., National Share Office, St. Joseph Health Care, 300 First Capitol Drive, St. Charles, MO 63301-2893.

ADDITIONAL READING

Bramblete, J., *When Good-Bye Is Forever: Learning to Live Again after the Loss of a Child*, Ballantine Books, New York, 1991.

DeFrain, J., Ernst, L., Jakub, D., and Taylor, J., *Sudden Infant Death Syndrome: Enduring the Loss,* Lexington Books, Lexington, KY, 1991.

Durfee, M., Grief and mourning, article available at www.ican-ncfr.org (accessed July 4, 2006).

Fleming, P., Blair, P., Sidebotham, P., and Hayler, T., Investigating sudden and unexplained infant deaths in infancy and childhood and caring for bereaved families: An integrated multiagency approach, *Br. Med. J.*, 328, 331–334, 2004.

13 Where Do We Go from Here?

In order to answer the question, "Where do we go from here?" ... we must first honestly recognize where we are now.[1]

Martin Luther King, 1967

13.1 INTRODUCTION

Infant deaths are difficult to investigate. Due to infant vulnerabilities, investigators must rely on their observation, assessment, and interview skills to conduct a comprehensive investigation. The emotions that are exhibited after an infant's death may impact the investigator's ability to effectively interact with the infant's family, caregivers, and other witnesses, including professional responders. Investigator bias can impact the investigation if decisions regarding the case are not in accordance with agency policy, national guidelines, or professional standards of practice and conduct.

Across the country, infant deaths are investigated differently. Not all investigators or agencies recognize the complex nature of infant deaths: some may not be equipped with necessary knowledge to thoroughly conduct them or deny the possibility that a family member could unintentionally or would intentionally cause the death of an infant. Investigators may be uncomfortable acknowledging that a family member may have placed an infant in an unsafe situation, resulting in an incomplete investigation in which the death may then be classified inaccurately.

Organizations, agencies, medicolegal death investigators (MDIs), and law enforcement personnel must evaluate the methods they use to investigate infant deaths for changes and improvements to be made. Over the past few years, the standards by which all deaths are investigated has risen. Investigators and agencies should be aware of and make it a priority to follow recommended state and national death investigation guidelines. They should also strive to meet or exceed the professional standards of practice including establishing agency policies, based on current guidelines, jurisdictional laws, and statutes. Professionals should also seek to validate their practices and strive to obtain national certifications in their specialty.

It is through consistent professional practice that, as a profession, MDIs can be certain that all infant deaths are investigated thoroughly and completely in all jurisdictions. Only after a comprehensive investigation can the cause and manner of death be accurately identified and classified on the death certificate. This accurate classification can then be used to develop and implement proactive prevention programs to educate the lay public regarding factors or hazards that may increase an infant's risk of injury or death. Individual agencies that conduct thorough investigations will be able to implement prevention programs in their jurisdictions sooner, thus decreasing the number of infant deaths that occur in their community.

13.2 DEATH INVESTIGATION GUIDELINES

In 1996, the Centers for Disease Control and Prevention (CDC) published guidelines for the investigation of sudden, unexplained infant death and the Sudden, Unexplained Infant Death Investigation Report Form (SUIDIRF).[2] These national guidelines were recommended by the Interagency Panel on Sudden Infant Death Syndrome, a group of professionals brought together to collectively develop the guidelines. The guidelines were widely accepted and endorsed by professional organizations such as the National Association of Medical Examiners (NAME). The 1996 SUIDIRF was used voluntarily by some states and local jurisdictions. It was felt that the form was cumbersome and not user friendly, and as a result, it was revised and released nationally in 2006. Along with the revision, the CDC, under the direction of Occupational Research and Assessment, Inc., developed infant death investigation training materials to train investigators how to use the form to consistently gather data and conduct an infant death investigation. In 2006, the CDC began hosting national training academies. Five members from each state participate in a training academy and then return to their respective states prepared to train additional personnel and investigators.

Also in 1996, the National Institute of Justice convened a work group, the National Medicolegal Review Panel, to develop guidelines for investigating all types of deaths. In 1998, they published the "National Guidelines for Death Investigation" report that was later renamed, in 1999, as "Death Investigation: A Guide for the Scene Investigator."[3] This widely accepted manual recommended skills and tasks that should be completed when investigating any death. These death investigation guidelines were, and still are, widely accepted and endorsed by organizations such as NAME and the American Board of Medicolegal Death Investigators, Inc.℠ (ABMDI). Following the development of the guidelines and their endorsement by professional organizations, state and local agencies began to develop death investigation policies to be followed in their jurisdictions that were consistent with the national guidelines as well as state and local laws.

To promote professional conduct and high investigational standards, organizations such as ABMDI developed standards of practice that must be adhered to by all members of the organization. *Standards of practice* are those characteristics and competencies that professionals, in a given specialty, are expected to meet during professional practice. A code of ethics and training requirements have been developed by ABMDI; however, these standards are not currently mandatory for all employed death investigators in all jurisdictions. Individuals who investigate deaths, however, should be aware of the national and state guidelines and the standards of practice that professional organizations endorse.

13.3 AGENCY POLICIES AND PROTOCOLS

Local jurisdictions should establish agency policies and protocols that are consistent with national and state guidelines as well as local and state laws. *State and national guidelines* often provide information regarding the minimum requirements to safely and professionally practice in a specialty. They are general and basic and usually do not contradict state or local laws. *Standards of practice and codes of conduct* developed by organizations are often those items that are considered the minimal requirements to meet professional practice. Local agencies should then, at a minimum, develop operational policies consistent with the minimum standard of practice guidelines; however, it is beneficial to the community in which the agency has jurisdiction if the standards of practice and local investigative guidelines are set higher than the minimum recommendations.

13.4 PROFESSIONAL CERTIFICATION

Professional certification is available to MDIs. The certifications are administered by ABMDI, and currently, there are two levels of certification. The first level is the registry certification. According to the ABMDI, this entry-level certification "provides official recognition that an individual has acquired basic knowledge and demonstrated proficiency in the standards of practice necessary to properly conduct a competent, thorough medicolegal death investigation."[4] The second level of recognition is the advanced board certification, which is "available to experienced registered MDIs who prove their mastery of all aspects of medicolegal death investigation."[5] MDIs should strive to be leaders in their professional specialty and validate their skill sets to ensure that they are equipped with the knowledge and skills necessary to conduct thorough and complete infant death investigations.

Currently, there is not a certification available in which MDIs can become certified in infant or child death investigations. That may change in the future, however, as infant death investigations pose unique challenges that may best be served by individuals with specialized training and certification in the area. Some agencies that have investigators with exceptional experience in the area of infant or child death investigation or have an individual designated to the investigation and follow-up of all infant and child deaths in their jurisdiction may use the title of infant death or child death investigation specialist.

13.5 DEATH CERTIFICATE COMPLETION

Regulations have been developed to ensure that death certificates are certified consistently. Generally, death certificates are able to be certified by a medical examiner (ME), physician, or coroner. Regardless of the individual's title, all persons who are legally able to sign death certificates should be aware of the guidelines and regulations for doing so. The system by which deaths and diseases are classified is established by the World Health Organization and is referred to as the international classification of diseases (ICD). The tenth and most recent edition *(International Statistical Classification of Diseases and Related Health Problems)*, referred to as the ICD-10, was published in 1992.[6]

In 2003, the CDC published *Medical Examiners' and Coroners' Handbook on Death Registration and Fetal Death Reporting* to provide information to MEs and coroners regarding the proper way to complete and file death certificates and to ensure that medical information related to the death was properly documented on the certificate.[7] The information that is reported on a death certificate may have many uses. First, the information is considered evidence and may be introduced in court. Second, personal information regarding the decedent and the circumstances of the death may be used to settle estates. Third, death certificates are a source for state and national mortality statistics, which may be used to determine which diseases or injuries are studied and receive research funds or funds to establish prevention initiatives. Fourth, the death certificate is a document that may provide closure for the family who is seeking information regarding the cause for their loved one's death.

Individuals who have the responsibility of certifying death certificates should take that responsibility very seriously to ensure that they are certifying infant deaths properly. Even though a forensic pathologist may perform the autopsy, another individual may investigate the death, and yet another individual may complete the death certificate. The information documented on the death certificate may impact the family, criminal and civil litigation, the state in which the death occurred, as well as national statistics and funding. Persons who certify infant deaths must ensure that they are doing so in accordance with state and national regulations.

13.6 PROACTIVE PREVENTION INITIATIVES

Prevention initiatives are often developed and promoted by public health agencies, social service organizations, and advocacy groups. Due to their professional positions, however, MDIs are in a unique position to take the knowledge they gained while investigating deaths and implement educational prevention programs that may result in a decrease in the number of premature infant deaths in their community.

Some death investigators may not consider it their job to engage in educational and prevention initiatives. Those who recognize preventable injury and death risk factors, however, are obligated professionally and ethically to act on that knowledge. Investigators may choose to provide information to other individuals or organizations that have the ability to engage in prevention campaigns, or the investigators, and the agencies they represent, may take an active role in educating the lay public about risk factors that were identified by death investigators during the course of their work. MEs, coroners, and MDIs can significantly impact and influence the public. The lay public is intrigued and fascinated by crime scene and death investigation, as a result, prevention and educational initiatives organized by representatives from a ME's or coroner's office will garner the attention of the lay public, the media, and other professionals.

Case Example 13.1 In an initiative to educate the public regarding the risks associated with cosleeping and unsafe sleep environments, the Charleston County Coroner's Office participated in Expectant Parent and Baby Health Fairs that were sponsored by local hospitals in their community. A booth was set up to provide statistical information and educational material to families; however, the investigators took their prevention initiative to another level as they demonstrated those risk factors with full-size cribs, bassinets, and demonstration dolls. Many expectant parents visited the booth to learn ways in which they may decrease their infant's risk of injury or death. Investigators stated to fair attendees, "You don't want to meet me while I am working. Let me show you what risk factors we have identified that are associated with infant deaths in our county." The coroner's office staff immediately had the attention of the expectant parents who were then provided information that allowed them to then make informed decisions regarding child care practices. Numerous parents returned to the booth more than one time and commented during evaluations that the booth, set up and managed by the coroner's office, was most informative and the only booth that provided information that may save the life of their child.

Through active community involvement, MDIs are able to provide the lay public as well as other professionals and institutions information that may result in systems changes. During prevention and education initiatives, investigators should seek to develop working relationships with other agencies in their community that may benefit from the information provided by death investigators. Those agencies can educate persons within their agency, develop or change their agency's policies, and can then promote the prevention initiative to their clients.

Case Example 13.2 The Charleston County Coroner's Office initiated a Back-to-Sleep campaign in their community. One of the objectives of the campaign was to ensure that key representatives from hospital obstetric units, in the Charleston County area, were aware of the American Academy of Pediatrics's recommendations that infants be placed on their backs to sleep. During the campaign, each facility reviewed their hospital policies to ensure that staff was modeling this behavior and placing infants on their backs while in the hospital. Facilities developed educational material to be distributed to all new parents prior to being discharged from the hospital. Some facilities even established policies directing staff to document, in the medical records, that new parents received educational material about safe sleep environments before being discharged from the hospital.

13.7 SUMMARY

So where should professional MDIs go from here? Investigators first must recognize their important role. To conduct a thorough and complete infant death investigation, investigators should follow established guidelines and protocols. Investigators should then meet and exceed professional standards of practice and think outside the box to incorporate advanced investigative techniques and approaches into their investigations. Finally, after conducting thorough investigations and certifying the infant's death according to national regulations, death investigators should take a proactive approach to decrease the number of infant deaths in their communities.

MDIs who recognize a death trend should take a proactive approach to do something about it. They are, in this author's opinion, morally, ethically, and professionally obligated to act on that knowledge to prevent additional premature deaths. Providing information to the lay public may change a tragic course of events for a family who may be unknowingly placing their infant at great risk for injury or death. Death investigators are public servants who have the ability to positively impact individuals and families in their jurisdictions, not only in the professional manner by which deaths are investigated, but by also attempting to prevent premature deaths from occurring. MDIs will never know which premature deaths were prevented, which lives were saved, which families received prevention information that resulted in a change from an unsafe sleep environment to a safe environment, or which infants benefited from medical breakthroughs that prevented their death. Just knowing that lives may be saved and that families may not have to suffer the tragic loss of an infant is reward enough.

REFERENCES

1. King, M.L., Where Do We Go from Here?, Annual Report delivered at the 11th Convention of the Southern Christian Leadership Conference, Atlanta, GA, August 16, 1967.
2. Centers for Disease Control and Prevention, Guidelines for death scene investigation of sudden, unexplained infant deaths: Recommendations of the Interagency Panel on Sudden Infant Death Syndrome, *Morbid. Mortal. Wkly. Rep.,* 45, RR-10, 1996.
3. National Medical Review Panel, Death Investigation: A Guide for the Scene Investigator, report, National Institute of Justice, Washington, D.C., 1999.
4. American Board of Medicolegal Death Investigators, Inc., Registry Certification, article available at http://www.slu.edu/organizations/abmdi/index.phtml?page=certification (accessed August 12, 2006).
5. American Board of Medicolegal Death Investigators, Inc., Board Certified Fellows, article available at http://www.slu.edu/organizations/abmdi/index.phtml?page=board-certification (accessed August 12, 2006).
6. World Health Organization, *International Statistical Classification of Diseases and Related Health Problems,* 10th rev., World Health Organization, Geneva, 1992.
7. Centers for Disease Control and Prevention, *Medical Examiners' and Coroners' Handbook on Death Registration and Fetal Death Reporting 2003 Revision,* Department of Health and Human Services, Hyattsville, MD, 2003.

RESOURCES

American Board of Medicolegal Death Investigators, Inc. (ABMDI), http://www.slu.edu/organizations/abmdi/.

National Association of Medical Examiners (NAME), http://www.thename.org.

Index

Page references given in **boldface** type refer to tables. Page references in *italics* refer to illustrations.

F

G

H

I

Q

R

S

T

U

V

W

X

www.ingramcontent.com/pod-product-compliance
Lightning Source LLC
LaVergne TN
LVHW011125300926
849160LV00008B/517
* 9 7 8 1 0 3 2 9 2 5 1 4 1 *